Chilton

CHILTON'S Repair and Tune-Up Guide:

Mazda Pick-Ups

ILLUSTRATED

Prepared by the
Automotive Editorial Department

Chilton Book Company
Chilton Way
Radnor, Pa. 19089
215—687-8200

president and chief executive officer **WILLIAM A. BARBOUR;** executive vice president **K. ROBERT BRINK;** vice president and general manager **WILLIAM D. BYRNE;** editor-in-chief **JOHN D. KELLY;** managing editor **JOHN H. WEISE, S.A.E.;** assistant managing editor **PETER J. MEYER;** senior editor **KERRY A. FREEMAN;** editor **KERRY A. FREEMAN**

CHILTON BOOK COMPANY   RADNOR, PENNSYLVANIA

Copyright © 1975 by Chilton Book Company
First Edition
All Rights Reserved
Published in Radnor, Pa. by Chilton Book Company
and simultaneously in Ontario, Canada
by Thomas Nelson & Sons, Ltd.
Manufactured in the United States of America

Library of Congress Cataloging in Publication Data

Chilton Book Company. Automotive Editorial Dept.
   Chilton's repair and tune-up guide: Mazda pick-ups.
  1. Mazda trucks.   I. Title.   II. Title: Mazda pick-ups.
TL230.5.M3C47   1975   629.28'7'3   75-4537
ISBN 0-8019-6273-0
ISBN 0-8019-6274-9 pbk.

ACKNOWLEDGMENTS

Chilton Book Company expresses appreciation to the following for their cooperation and technical assistance:

Mazda Motors of America
3040 E. Ana Street
Compton, California 90221

Toyo Kogyo Co., Ltd.
6047 Fuchu-machi, Aki-gun
Hiroshima, Japan

YBH MAZDA, Inc.
West Chester Pike
Edgemont, Pennsylvania 19028

CLOSED CASE

629.287
C439 mab
Copy 1

Although the information in this guide is based on industry sources and is as complete as possible at the time of publication, the possibility exists that the manufacturer made later changes which could not be included here. While striving for total accuracy, Chilton Book Company cannot assume responsibility for any errors, changes, or omissions that may occur in the compilation of this data.

Contents

Chapter 1 General Information and Maintenance 1

How To Use This Book, 1
Tools and Equipment, 1
History, 2
Serial Number Identification, 3
Routine Maintenance, 4
Tire Inflation Pressure, 16

Capacities Chart, 17
Lubrication, 18
Lubricant Recommendations, 18
Pushing, Towing and Jump Starting, 21
Hoisting and Jacking, 22

Chapter 2 Tune-Up and Troubleshooting 24

Tune-Up Procedures, 24
Rotary Pick-Up Tune-Up Specifications, 24
B-1600 Tune-Up Specifications, 25
  Spark Plugs, 26

Breaker Points and Condenser, 28
Dwell Angle, 28
Ignition Timing, 30
Valve Lash, 32
Carburetor, 33

Chapter 3 Engine and Engine Rebuilding—B-1600 only . . 35

Engine Electrical, 35
  Distributor, 35
  Firing Order, 35
  Alternator, 36
  Regulator, 37
  Starter, 38
Engine Mechanical, 40
  Battery and Starter Specifications, 40
  General Engine Specifications, 40
  Valve Specifications, 41
  Crankshaft and Connecting Rod Specifications, 41
  Piston Clearance Specifications, 41
  Ring Gap Specifications, 41
  Ring Side Clearance Specifications, 41
  B-1600 Torque Specifications, 42
  Engine Removal and Installation, 42
  Cylinder Head, 43
  Cylinder Head Torque Sequence, 44

Rocker Shafts, 45
Intake Manifold, 46
Exhaust Manifold, 46
Cylinder Front Cover, 46
Front Cover Oil Seal, 47
Timing Chain and Tensioner, 47
Timing Chain Tensioner, 49
Camshaft, 49
Pistons and Connecting Rods, 50
Engine Lubrication, 52
  Oil Pan, 52
  Rear Main Oil Seal, 52
  Oil Pump, 52
Engine Cooling, 53
  Radiator, 53
  Water Pump, 54
  Thermostat, 54
Engine Rebuilding, 55

Chapter 4 Engine and Engine Rebuilding—Rotary Pick-Up only . 77

Engine Electrical, 77
  Distributor, 77
  Firing Order, 78
  Alternator, 78
  Regulator, 78
  Starter, 79
  Battery, 79
  Battery and Starter Specifications, 80
Engine Mechanical, 80
  Design, 80
  General Engine Specifications, 81
  Eccentric Shaft Specifications, 81

Rotor and Housings Specifications, 82
Seal Clearances, 82
Seal Specifications, 82
Torque Specifications, 82
Engine Removal and Installation, 83
Engine Disassembly, 83
Engine Assembly, 95
Intake Manifold, 101
Thermal Reactor, 101
Engine Lubrication, 101
  Oil Pan, 102
  Oil Pump, 102

iii

CONTENTS

Metering Oil Pump, 102
Oil Cooler, 103
Engine Cooling, 104
Radiator, 104
Water Pump, 104
Thermostat, 105

Chapter 5 Emission Controls and Fuel System 106

Emission Controls—B-1600, 106
Emission Controls—Rotary Pick-Up, 109
   Air Injection System Diagnosis Chart, 110
Fuel System, 117
Electric Fuel Pump, 117
Carburetor, 118
Carburetor Adjustments, 123
Carburetor Specifications, 125

Chapter 6 Clutch and Transmission 126

Manual Transmission, 126
   Removal and Installation, 126
Clutch, 127
   Adjustments, 127
   Removal and Installation, 128
   Master Cylinder, 128
   Slave Cylinder, 130
Automatic Transmission, 132

Chapter 7 Drive Train 134

Driveshaft and U-Joints, 134
   Removal and Installation, 134
   U-Joint Overhaul, 134
Rear Axle, 136
   Axle Shaft, 136
Differential, 137
Bearing Failure Chart, 141
General Drive Axle Diagnosis, 146
Noise Diagnosis Chart, 147

Chapter 8 Suspension and Steering 148

Front Suspension, 148
   Shock Absorber, 148
   Upper Control Arm, 150
   Lower Control Arm, 150
   Ball Joints, 151
   Front End Alignment, 151
Rear Suspension, 152
Springs, 152
Wheel Alignment Specifications, 152
Shock Absorber, 154
Steering, 154
   Steering Wheel, 154
   Ignition Switch, 155
   Steering Linkage, 156

Chapter 9 Brakes 158

Adjustment, 158
Brake Specifications, 159
Hydraulic System, 160
   Master Cylinder, 160
   Pressure Differential Valve, 162
   Brake Bleeding, 163
Front Drum Brakes, 163
   Brake Drum, 163
   Brake Shoes, 164
   Wheel Cylinder, 165
   Front Wheel Bearings, 166
Front Disc Brakes, 167
   Disc Brake Pad, 167
   Disc Brake Caliper, 168
   Brake Disc, 170
   Front Wheel Bearings, 171
Rear Drum Brakes, 171
   Brake Drums, 171
   Brake Shoes, 172
   Wheel Cylinder, 173
Parking Brake, 174

Chapter 10 Body 176

Doors, 176
Hood, 179
Tailgate, 180
Fuel Tank, 180
Wiring Diagrams, 181

Appendix 186

Chapter One
General Information and Maintenance

How To Use This Book

This book is intended to serve as a guide to the maintenance, repair and tune-up of all Mazda pickup trucks from 1972–75.

To use it properly, each operation must be approached logically and the recommended procedures read and thoroughly understood before attempting any work. Naturally, the required tools and a clean, uncluttered place to work must be available. Cleanliness especially in brake system work, cannot be overemphasized.

Each chapter is constructed so that descriptions, procedures and specifications can be easily located, allowing experienced mechanics to isolate only the information they find useful, and yet provide the inexperienced mechanic with background information to further expand his understanding of his truck.

Wherever possible, detailed operational descriptions are included. Factory tools have also been virtually eliminated, except where absolutely necessary, with the substitution of more readily available tools.

Tools And Equipment

It would be impossible to catalog each tool that you would need to perform each or any operation in this book. It would also not be wise for the amateur to rush out and buy an expensive set of tools on the theory that he may need one of them at some time. The best approach is to proceed slowly, gathering together a good quality set of those tools that are used most frequently. Don't be misled by the low cost of bargain tools. It is far better to spend a little more for better quality. Forged wrenches, 10 or 12 point sockets and fine tooth ratchets are by far preferable to their less expensive counterparts. As any good mechanic can tell you, there are few worse experiences than trying to work on a car or truck with bad tools. Your monetary savings will be far outweighed by frustration and mangled knuckles.

Begin accumulating those tools which are used most frequently; those associated with routine maintenance and tune-up.

You will find that almost every nut and bolt on your Mazda is metric. In addition

1

GENERAL INFORMATION AND MAINTENANCE

to the normal assortment of screwdrivers and pliers and the tool kit that comes with your truck, you should have the following tools for routine maintenance jobs.
1. Metric wrenches—sockets and combination open-end/box wrenches to at least 18 mm.
2. Jackstands—for support.
3. Band wrench—for oil filters.
4. Oil filler spout—for pouring oil.
5. Grease gun—for chassis lubrication.
6. Hydrometer—for checking the battery.
7. A container for draining oil.
8. Many rags for wiping up the inevitable mess.

In addition to the above items there are several others that are not absolutely necessary, but handy to have around. These include oil dry, a transmission funnel and the usual supply of lubricants, antifreeze, and fluids, although these can be purchased as needed. This is a basic list for routine maintenance, but only your personal needs and desire can accurately determine your list of tools.

The second list of tools is for tune-ups. While the tools involved here are slightly more sophisticated, they need not be outrageously expensive. There are several inexpensive tach/dwell meters on the market that are every bit as good for the average mechanic as a $100.00 professional model. Just be sure that it goes to at least 1,200–1,500 rpm on the tach scale and that it works on 4, 6 or 8 cylinder engines. A basic list of tune-up equipment could include:
1. Tach/dwell meter;
2. Spark plug wrench;
3. Timing light (A DC light that works off the car's battery is best, although an AC light that plugs into 110 V house current will suffice at some sacrifice in brightness);
4. Wire spark plug gauge;
5. Set of feeler blades.

Here again, be guided by your own needs. A feeler blade will set the point gap as easily as a dwell meter will read dwell, but slightly less accurately. And since you will need a tachometer anyway . . . well, make your own decision.

History

Toyo Kogyo Co., Ltd., Mazda's parent company, began manufacturing cork products over fifty years ago. In 1927, the company expanded into the machinery and tool business; by 1930 they were producing motorcycles under the Mazda name.

The first three-wheeled trucks appeared in 1931. The first automobile prototype was built in 1940, but it was not until twenty years later that a production car, the Mazda R-360 coupe, was sold.

In the interim, Toyo Kogyo produced light three-wheeled trucks, reaching, in 1957, a peak annual production of 20,000 units.

Shortly after automobile production began in 1960, Toyo Kogyo obtained a license from NSU-Wankel to develop and produce the rotary engine.

The first prototype car powered by this engine was the Mazda 110S, a two passenger sports car which appeared in August 1963. The car did not go on sale until it had been thoroughly tested. The first units were offered for sale in May 1967. The 110S was soon joined by a smaller, cheaper model which put the rotary engine within the reach of the average consumer. Various models powered by the rotary engine were produced for the Japanese home market.

In 1970, Toyo Kogyo began importing Mazda cars (both rotary engined and conventional) into the United States. At first they were available only in the Pacific Northwest, but they have rapidly expanded their market to include almost all of the U.S.

Inspired by the success of the rotary-engined cars in this country, Mazda was moved to expand their horizons into the light truck market. The first Mazda pickups arrived in the United States in December of 1972. These were titled as 1972 vehicles and approximately 4,800 were sold. The following year, which was the first full model year for the truck, approximately 14,000 B-1600 piston-engined trucks were sold.

Currently, there are two models being sold; the B-1600 with a conventional pis-

GENERAL INFORMATION AND MAINTENANCE

ton engine and the slightly larger rotary-engined version.

Serial Number Identification

CHASSIS NUMBER

The chassis number is stamped on the front of the left frame member, visible from the engine compartment.

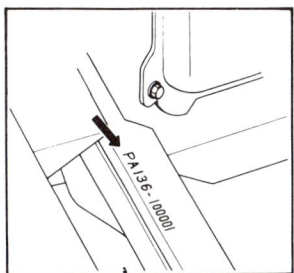

Chassis number location (© Toyo Kogyo Co., Ltd.)

ENGINE NUMBER

The engine number of the B-1600 is stamped on a machined pad on the right, front side of the engine block. On the Rotary Pick-up Truck, the engine number is located on a pad at the front of the engine housing, behind the distributor.

MODEL PLATE

The model plate, containing the truck model, engine model, engine displacement and chassis number is riveted to the right rear corner of the engine compartment on the firewall.

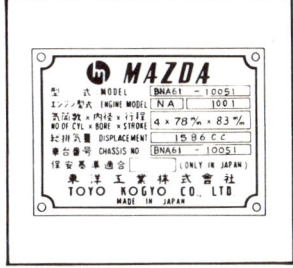

Model plate (© Toyo Kogyo Co., Ltd.)

MOTOR VEHICLE SAFETY CERTIFICATION LABEL

This label is attached to the left door lock pillar and proclaims the fact that the truck conforms to all necessary safety regulations in effect at the time of manufacture.

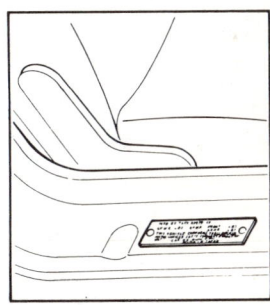

Motor vehicle safety certification label (© Toyo Kogyo Co., Ltd.)

Rotary Pick-Up engine number location (© Toyo Kogyo Co., Ltd.)

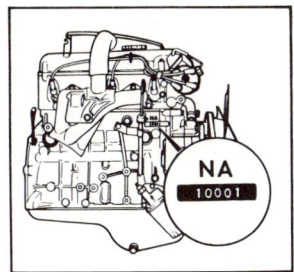

B-1600 engine number location (© Toyo Kogyo Co., Ltd.)

Emission control certification label (© Toyo Kogyo Co., Ltd.)

GENERAL INFORMATION AND MAINTENANCE

EMISSION CONTROL CERTIFICATION LABEL

This label is found attached to the right-hand panel of the engine compartment, and states that the truck conforms to the emission regulations for the country of destination.

Routine Maintenance

Routine, or preventive maintenance is exactly as it implies; maintenance that is performed at suggested intervals that keeps small problems from becoming large ones. For example, it is much easier (and cheaper in the long run) to check the engine oil regularly than to have the engine run low on oil and damage the bearings (a major overhaul job). Read this chapter carefully and follow its recommendations closely for as close to optimum performance as possible.

MAINTENANCE INTERVALS

The following charts give the maintenance intervals suggested by the factory. Follow these recommendations using the procedures in this chapter to perform services.

Routine Maintenance Intervals

Rotary Pick-Up

Emissions Control Systems: Required Maintenance Services	\multicolumn{13}{c}{Service Intervals—number of months or thousands of miles, whichever comes first}
	2	6	10	14	18	22	26	30	34	38	42	46	50
Engine													
Engine oil	R	R	R	R	R	R	R	R	R	R	R	R	R
Engine oil filter		R		R		R		R		R		R	
Engine and accessory drive belts	I	I	I	I	I	I	I	I	I	I	I	I	I
Metering oil pump	I	I	I	I	I	I	I	I	I	I	I	I	I
Engine compression pressure				I			I			I		I	
Starting assist system	\multicolumn{13}{l}{Sub-zero weather use only. Inspect seasonally.}
Fuel and Evaporative Emissions Control Systems													
Idle speed	I	I	I	I	I	I	I	I	I	I	I	I	I
Idle mixture		I		I		I		I		I			I
Fuel filter			R			R			R			R	
Air cleaner element		I	I	I	I	I	R	I	I	I	I	R	I
Carburetor float level		I		I		I		I		I			I
Carburetor linkage and choke mechanism			I			I			I			I	

GENERAL INFORMATION AND MAINTENANCE

Routine Maintenance Intervals (cont.)

Rotary Pick-Up

Emissions Control Systems: Required Maintenance Services	2	6	10	14	18	22	26	30	34	38	42	46	50
Fuel and Evaporative Emissions Control Systems													
Fuel line and connections	I	I	I	I	I	I	I	I	I	I	I	I	I
Canister						I						I	
Evaporative emission control system, fuel tank and vapor lines			I			I			I			I	
Check valve						I						I	
Ignition System													
Ignition timing and advance systems	I	I	I	I	I	I	I	I	I	I	I	I	I
Distributor breaker points	I	I	I	I	I	I	I	I	I	I	I	I	I
Distributor cap, rotor and condensers			I			I			I			I	
Ignition coils			I			I			I			I	
Spark plugs	I	I	I	I	I	I	I	I	I	I	I	I	I
Spark plug wires			I			I			I			I	
Distributor cam			I			I			I			I	
Ventilation System													
Ventilation valve						I						I	
Ventilation hoses			I			I			I			I	
Exhaust Emissions Control System													
Air pump			I			I			I			I	
Air hoses and vacuum sensing tubes			I			I			I			I	
Idle switch	I	I	I	I	I	I	I	I	I	I	I	I	I
Air control valve			I			I			I			I	
Check valve			I			I			I			I	
Control unit	I		I			I			I			I	

6 GENERAL INFORMATION AND MAINTENANCE

Routine Maintenance Intervals (cont.)

Rotary Pick-Up

Emissions Control Systems: Required Maintenance Services	2	6	10	14	18	22	26	30	34	38	42	46	50
Exhaust Emissions Control System													
Deceleration control valve			I			I			I			I	
Thermosensor and thermo detector			I			I			I			I	
Thermal reactor			I			I			I			I	
Exhaust pipe flange bolts			T			T			T			T	
Choke switch, choke relay and carburetor heater			I			I			I			I	
Automatic throttle release system			I			I			I			I	
Water temperature switch			I			I			I			I	
Heat hazard warning system			I			I			I			I	
Downshift solenoid (automatic transmission)			I			I			I			I	
Altitude compensator						I						I	

Regular Systems: Required Maintenance Services	2	6	10	14	18	22	26	30	34	38	42	46	50
Cooling System													
Cooling system hoses			I			I			I			I	
Electrical System													
Battery electrolyte level and specific gravity	I	I	I	I	I	I	I	I	I	I	I	I	I
Operation of lights and instruments	I	I	I	I	I	I	I	I	I	I	I	I	I
Chassis and Body													
Clutch pedal	I	I	I	I	I	I	I	I	I	I	I	I	I
Clutch fluid	I	I	I	I	I	I	I	I	I	I	I	I	I
Manual transmission oil	R			R			R			R			R
Automatic transmission fluid	I	I	I	I	I	I	I	I	I	I	I	I	I
Rear axle oil	R			R			R			R			R

GENERAL INFORMATION AND MAINTENANCE

Routine Maintenance Intervals (cont.)

Rotary Pick-Up

Regular Systems: Required Maintenance Services	Service Intervals—number of months or thousands of miles, whichever comes first												
	2	6	10	14	18	22	26	30	34	38	42	46	50
Chassis and Body													
Steering gear oil			I		I			I			I		
Steering wheel play	I	I	I	I	I	I	I	I	I	I	I	I	I
Brake pedal	I	I	I	I	I	I	I	I	I	I	I	I	I
Brake fluid	I	I	I	I	I	I	I	I	I	I	I	I	I
Parking brake	I	I	I	I	I	I	I	I	I	I	I	I	I
Drum brake lining			I			I			I			I	
Disc brake pad		I		I		I		I		I		I	
Hoses (automatic transmission)	Replace every four years												
Piston cups of master cylinders and wheel cylinders	Replace every two years												
Brake hoses (vacuum hoses of power brake)	Replace every four years												
Front wheel bearings	Lubricate or replace every 30,000 miles or two years												
Front suspension ball joints													
Steering ball joints and idler arm													
Upper arm shafts													

R—Replace or change
I —Inspect, correct, and replace, if necessary
T—Tighten

Routine Maintenance Intervals

B-1600

Emissions Control Systems: Required Maintenance Services	Service Intervals—number of months or thousands of miles, whichever comes first												
	2	6	10	14	18	22	26	30	34	38	42	46	50
Engine													
Engine oil	R	R	R	R	R	R	R	R	R	R	R	R	R
Engine oil filter		R		R		R		R		R		R	
Engine drive belt		I	I	I	I	I	I	I	I	I	I	I	I

GENERAL INFORMATION AND MAINTENANCE

Routine Maintenance Intervals (cont.)

B-1600

Emissions Control Systems: Required Maintenance Services	\multicolumn{13}{c}{Service Intervals—number of months or thousands of miles, whichever comes first}
	2	6	10	14	18	22	26	30	34	38	42	46	50
Engine													
Engine valve clearance	I	I	I	I	I	I	I	I	I	I	I	I	I
Intake and exhaust manifolds and cylinder head bolts	T		T		T		T		T		T		T
Engine compression pressure						I						I	
Fuel and Evaporative Emissions Control Systems													
Idle speed and idle speed mixture (CO)	I	I	I	I	I	I	I	I	I	I	I	I	I
Fuel filter			R			R			R			R	
Air cleaner element	I	I	I	I	I	R	I	I	I	I	I	R	I
Carburetor float level	I			I			I			I			I
Carburetor linkage and choke mechanism				I			I			I		I	
Fuel line and connections	I	I	I	I	I	I	I	I	I	I	I	I	I
Fuel cut valve (throttle solenoid)				I			I			I		I	
Canister						R						R	
Evaporative emission control system, fuel tank and vapor lines				I			I			I		I	
Check valve						I						I	
Ignition System													
Ignition timing and advance system	I	I	I	I	I	I	I	I	I	I	I	I	I
Distributor breaker points	I	I	I	I	I	I	I	I	I	I	I	I	I
Distributor cap, rotor and condenser			I			I			I			I	
Ignition coil			I			I			I			I	
Spark plugs	I	I	I	I	I	I	I	I	I	I	I	I	I
Spark plug wires			I			I			I			I	

GENERAL INFORMATION AND MAINTENANCE

Routine Maintenance Intervals (cont.)

B-1600

Emissions Control Systems: Required Maintenance Services	\multicolumn{12}{c}{Service Intervals—number of months or thousands of miles, whichever comes first}
	2	6	10	14	18	22	26	30	34	38	42	46	50

Crankcase Ventilation System

| PCV valve | | | I | | | R | | I | | | R | | |
| Ventilation hoses | | | I | | | I | | | I | | | I | |

Exhaust Emissions Control Systems

| Servo diaphragm and control valve | I | I | I | I | I | I | I | I | I | I | I | I | I |
| Vacuum sensing hoses | | | I | | | I | | | I | | | I | |

Regular Systems: Required Maintenance Services	\multicolumn{12}{c}{Service Intervals—number of months or thousands of miles, whichever comes first}
	2	6	10	14	18	22	26	30	34	38	42	46	50

Cooling System

| Cooling system hoses | | | I | | | I | | | I | | | I | |

Electrical System

| Battery electrolyte level and specific gravity | I | I | I | I | I | I | I | I | I | I | I | I | I |
| Operation of lights and instruments | I | I | I | I | I | I | I | I | I | I | I | I | I |

Chassis and Body

Clutch pedal	I	I	I	I	I	I	I	I	I	I	I	I	I
Clutch fluid	I	I	I	I	I	I	I	I	I	I	I	I	I
Manual transmission oil	R			R			R			R			R
Rear axle oil	R			R			R			R			R
Steering gear oil			I			I			I			I	
Steering wheel play	I	I	I	I	I	I	I	I	I	I	I	I	I
Brake pedal	I	I	I	I	I	I	I	I	I	I	I	I	I
Brake fluid	I	I	I	I	I	I	I	I	I	I	I	I	I
Parking brake	I	I	I	I	I	I	I	I	I	I	I	I	I

GENERAL INFORMATION AND MAINTENANCE

Routine Maintenance Intervals (cont.)

B-1600

Regular Systems: Required Maintenance Services	Service Intervals—number of months or thousands of miles, whichever comes first
	2 6 10 14 18 22 26 30 34 38 42 46 50

Chassis and Body

Brake lining	I I I I
Piston cups of master cylinder and wheel cylinders	Replace every two years
Brake hoses (vacuum hoses of power brake)	Replace every four years
Front wheel bearings	
Front suspension ball joints	Lubricate or replace every 30,000 miles or two years
Upper arm shafts (Pick Up only)	
Steering ball joints and idler arm	

R—Replace or change
I —Inspect, correct, and replace, if necessary
T—Tighten

AIR CLEANER

The air cleaner should be serviced at the recommended interval. The air cleaner uses a disposable paper element located in a housing on top of the engine. To remove the element, simply unscrew the wing nut on the top of the housing and lift off the cover plate. Lift out the element. The element can be cleaned with compressed air (if it is available) by blowing through the air

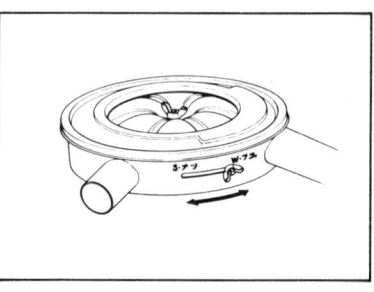

Air cleaner housing—B-1600. To prevent icing, move the lever to "S" below 50°–60°F; above 50°–60°F, move the lever to "W." (© Toyo Kogyo Co., Ltd.)

cleaner from the inside out. If compressed air is not available, tap the air cleaner element lightly on a hard surface to dislodge the dirt. If a used air cleaner is reinstalled, rotate it 180° from its previous position.

NOTE: *In severe service, such as off-road use or in extremely dusty areas, the maintenance interval should be cut in half.*

PCV VALVE

The Positive Crankcase Ventilation (PCV) valve should be inspected for

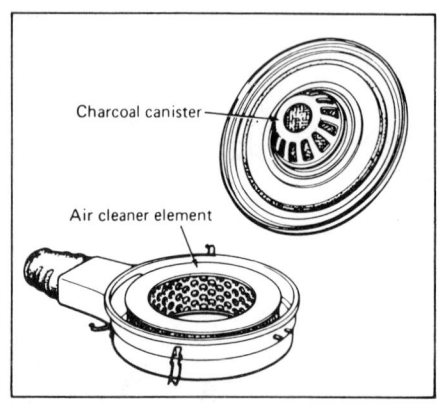

Air cleaner and charcoal canister—Rotary Pick-Up (© Toyo Kogyo Co., Ltd.)

GENERAL INFORMATION AND MAINTENANCE

blockage periodically. It is located in a special fitting in the intake manifold, just below the carburetor.

Testing the PCV VALVE

The simplest test for the PCV valve is to remove it from its fitting and shake it. A distinct rattle should be heard; if not, replace the valve.

The other way to test it involves removing the hose from the PCV valve and running the engine at idle or slightly above. Hold your finger over the end of the valve. A distinct vacuum should be felt. Suddenly release the accelerator pedal. Little or no vacuum (or at least a distinct drop in vacuum) should be felt. If not replace the valve.

Removal and Installation

1. Remove the air cleaner.
2. Disconnect the hose from the PCV valve.
3. Remove the valve from the special fitting in the intake manifold.
4. Install the valve in the intake manifold fitting and connect the hose to the valve.
5. Connect the hose to the air cleaner and install the air filter.
6. Check for loose clamps or cracks in the PCV lines and replace the hoses if cracked.

NOTE: *If your engine exhibits lower than normal gas mileage and poor idle characteristics for no apparent reason, suspect the PCV valve. It is probably blocked and should be replaced.*

EVAPORATIVE CANISTER

Rotary Pick-Up

The charcoal filter for the evaporative emission control (EEC) system is located in the top of the air cleaner case. It should be checked as indicated.

1. Unfasten the clips and remove the top of the air cleaner case.
2. Inspect the air cleaner element and clean it as necessary.
3. Check the condition of the charcoal filter. If it is saturated with fuel and oil, replace it by unscrewing it from the case. Screw the replacement filter in place.
4. Check the condition of the PCV valve as outlined above.

Evaporative canister—B-1600 (© Toyo Kogyo Co., Ltd.)

B-1600

The evaporative canister is located under the hood in the engine compartment and is designed to store fuel vapors and prevent their escaping into the atmosphere. When the engine is not running, fuel that has evaporated into the condenser tank is returned to the fuel tank as the ambient temperatures rise and the vapors are condensed. During periods when the engine is running, fuel vapor that has not condensed in the condenser tank moves to the carbon canister. The stored vapors are removed by fresh air through the bottom of the inlet hole and passed through the air cleaner to the combustion chamber. Because of the design of the system, the only maintenance associated with the canister is to replace it periodically as indicated in the "Maintenance Interval" charts.

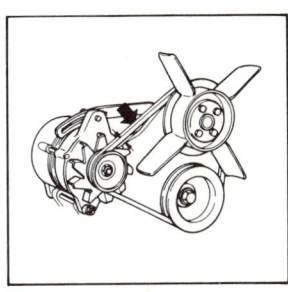

Checking belt tension—B-1600 (© Toyo Kogyo Co., Ltd.)

DRIVE BELTS

Tension Checking and Adjusting

FAN BELT—B-1600

The fan belt should be checked for wear and tension as indicated in the

GENERAL INFORMATION AND MAINTENANCE

"Maintenance Interval" charts. If the belt is worn, cracked or frayed, replace it with a new one. To check the belt tension:

1. Apply thumb pressure (about 22 lbs) to the fan belt midway between the pulleys and check the deflection. It should be approximately 3/8 in. for new belts and 1/2 in. for used belts.
2. To adjust the tension, loosen the alternator mounting bolt and adjusting bolt.
3. Move the alternator in the direction necessary to loosen or tighten the tension.
4. Tighten the mounting and adjusting bolts and recheck the tension.

FAN BELT & AIR PUMP BELT— ROTARY PICK-UP

Both belts should be checked for tension and wear according to the "Maintenance Interval" charts. If either belt is worn, frayed, or cracked, replace it with a new belt.

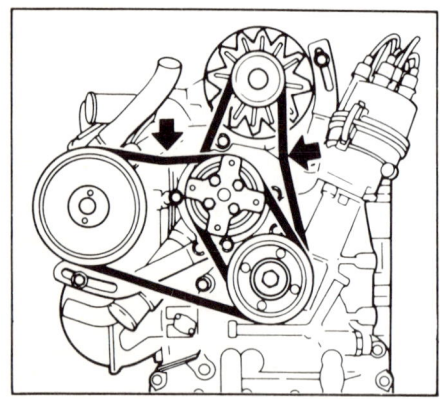

Checking fan belt and air pump belt tension—Rotary Pick-Up (© Toyo Kogyo Co., Ltd.)

To check and adjust the belt tension:
1. Apply thumb pressure (about 22 lbs) to the belt midway between the pulleys and check the deflection. The deflection should be:

	New (in.)	Used (in.)
Fan Belt	0.4–0.5	0.5–0.6
Air Pump Belt	0.3	0.3–0.4

2. To adjust the tension on the fan belt, loosen the alternator mounting and adjusting bolts. Move the alternator until the proper tension is obtained and tighten the mounting and adjusting bolts. Recheck the tension.
3. To adjust the air pump drive belt, loosen the air pump mounting and adjusting bolts. Move the air pump until the proper tension is obtained. Tighten the mounting and adjusting bolts and recheck the tension.

FLUID LEVEL CHECKS

Engine Oil

Under normal operating conditions, the Mazda rotary engine burns about one quart of oil every 1,000–1,400 miles as part of its combustion process. Therefore, the oil level should be checked frequently.

The engine oil should be checked on a regular basis, ideally at each fuel stop. If the truck is used for trailer towing or, for heavy-duty use, it would be wise to check it more often.

When checking the oil level, it is best that the oil be at operating temperature, although checking the level immediately after stopping will give a false reading because all of the oil will not have drained back into the crankcase. Be sure that the truck is on a level surface, allowing time for all of the oil to drain back into the crankcase.

1. Open the hood and locate the dipstick. It is located on the right-hand (passenger's side) of the engine just behind the alternator.
2. Remove the dipstick and wipe it clean with a rag.
3. Insert the dipstick fully into the tube and remove it again. Hold the dipstick horizontal and read the level on the dipstick. The level should be between the "F" (Full) and "L" (Low) marks. If

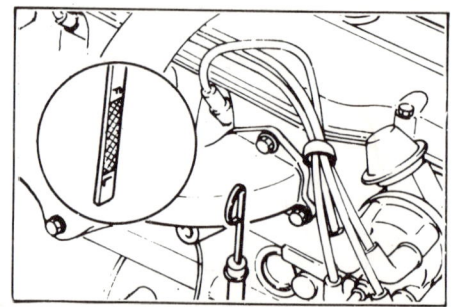

Engine oil dipstick—B-1600 (© Toyo Kogyo Co., Ltd.)

GENERAL INFORMATION AND MAINTENANCE

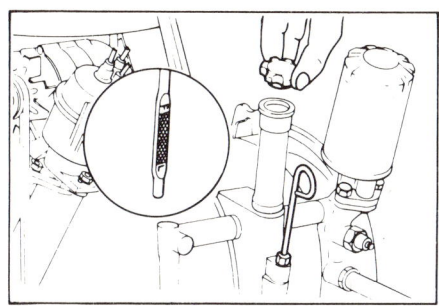

Engine oil dipstick—Rotary Pick-Up (© Toyo Kogyo Co., Ltd.)

the oil level is at or below the "L" mark, sufficient oil should be added to restore the level to the proper place. Oil is added through the capped opening in the top of the valve cover. See the section on "Oil and Fuel Recommendations" for the proper viscosity and oil to use.

4. Replace the dipstick and check the level after adding oil. Be careful not to overfill the crankcase.

Transmission

MANUAL

1. Clean the dirt away from the area of the filler plug.
2. Jack the truck if necessary and support it on jackstands.

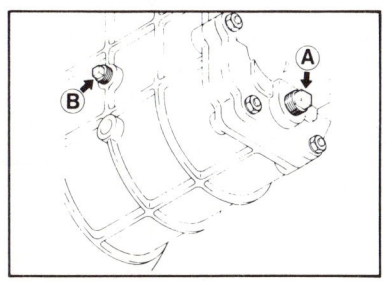

B-1600 manual transmission drain plug (A) and fill plug (B) (© Toyo Kogyo Co., Ltd.)

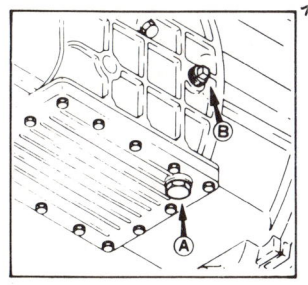

Rotary Pick-Up manual transmission drain plug (A) and fill plug (B) (© Toyo Kogyo Co., Ltd.)

3. Remove the filler plug from the case. The filler plug is the one on the side of the case. Do not remove the plug from the bottom of the case unless you wish to drain the transmission.
4. If lubricant flows from the area of the filler plug as it is removed, the level is satisfactory. If lubricant does not flow from the filler hole when the plug is removed, add enough of the specified lubricant to bring the level to the bottom of the filler hole with the truck in a level position.

AUTOMATIC

1. Drive the vehicle for several miles to bring the fluid level to operating temperature.
2. Park the truck on a level surface.
3. Put the automatic transmission in PARK. Leave the engine running.
4. Remove the dipstick from the tube and wipe it clean.
5. Reinsert the dipstick so that it is fully seated.

Automatic transmission dipstick (© Toyo Kogyo Co., Ltd.)

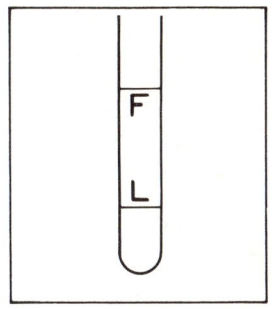

Automatic transmission dipstick markings (© Toyo Kogyo Co., Ltd.)

6. Remove the dipstick and note the reading. If the fluid is at or below the "Add" mark, add sufficient fluid to bring the level to the "Full" mark. Do not

GENERAL INFORMATION AND MAINTENANCE

overfill the transmission. Overfilling will lead to fluid aeration.

7. Replace the dipstick in the tube.

Brake Master Cylinder

Check the level of the fluid in the brake master cylinder at the specified interval or more often. The brake master cylinder is located at the left rear corner of the engine compartment.

1. Park the truck on a level surface.
2. Clean all dirt from the area of the master cylinder cover.

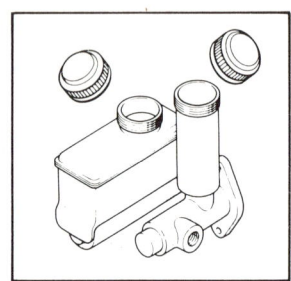

Brake master cylinder (left) and clutch master cylinder (right) (© Toyo Kogyo Co., Ltd.)

3. Remove the top from the master cylinder. Be careful when doing this. Brake fluid that is dripped on painted surfaces will quickly destroy the paint.
4. The level should be maintained approximately 1/2 in. below the top of the reservoir.
5. If brake fluid is needed, use only a good quality brake fluid meeting the specifications under "'Recommended Fluids and Lubricants."
6. If necessary, add fluid to maintain the proper level and replace the top on the master cylinder securely.

NOTE: *If the fluid level is constantly low, it would be a good idea to look into the matter. This is a good indication of problems elsewhere in the system.*

Clutch Master Cylinder

The clutch master cylinder is located at the left rear corner of the engine compartment.

1. Check the level in the clutch master cylinder in the same manner as the brake master cylinder. The level should be kept approximately 1/2 in. from the top of the cylinder. Be sure that the truck is on a level surface.

Coolant

CAUTION: *To avoid injury when working on a hot engine, cover the radiator cap with a thick cloth and turn it slowly counterclockwise until the pressure begins to escape. After the pressure is completely removed, remove the cap. Never remove the cap until the pressure is gone. Never remove the radiator cap until the expansion tank cap is removed.*

Check the coolant level when the engine is cold. The radiator coolant level should be kept above the bottom of the filler housing elbow and below the bottom of the filler neck.

When adding coolant, a mixture of permanent antifreeze and water is recommended for year around operation. It is not recommended that different brands of antifreeze be mixed, nor that any other than permanent types be used.

Freeze protection should be maintained at a level for the temperatures which may occur in the area in which the truck is to be operated. It should be maintained to at least 0° F to provide adequate corrosion and boil-over protection.

If the truck is operated in areas where the temperature is always above freezing, water with an anti-rust inhibitor can be used in place of antifreeze. However, before using any rust inhibitors, be sure that they are recommended for aluminum parts. The water and rust inhibitor should be replaced every six months.

Tap water can be used in the engine as long as it is known to have a low alkaline content.

CLEANING AND FLUSHING THE COOLING SYSTEM

1. Open the radiator and engine block drain cocks and drain the coolant. Remove the radiator cap.
2. Close the drain cocks and fill the system with clean water.
3. Drive the truck for about an hour, be careful not to overheat the engine.
4. Completely drain the water from the system again and flush clean water through the cooling system.
5. Close the drain cocks and add antifreeze solution or corrosion inhibitor solution according to seasonal require-

GENERAL INFORMATION AND MAINTENANCE

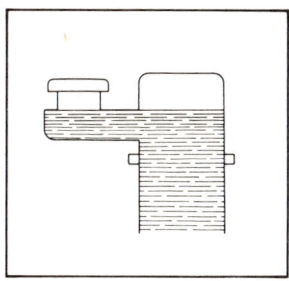

Radiator coolant level (© Toyo Kogyo Co., Ltd.)

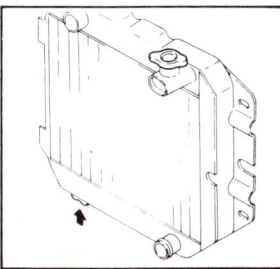

Radiator drain cock (© Toyo Kogyo Co., Ltd.)

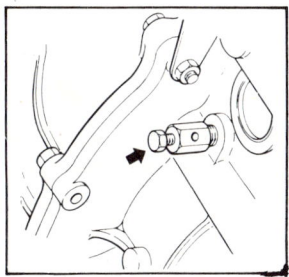

Engine block drain cock (© Toyo Kogyo Co., Ltd.)

ments. During a complete refill of the system, always operate the engine until it reaches normal temperature to remove air from the system. Let the system cool, recheck the fluid level and refill as necessary.

Rear Axle

The rear axle fluid level is checked from underneath the truck.

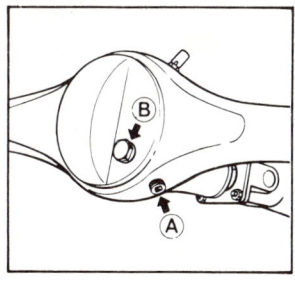

Rear axle fill plug (B) and drain plug (A) (© Toyo Kogyo Co., Ltd.)

1. Clean the dirt and grease away from the area of the filler (top) plug.
2. Remove the filler plug. The lubricant level should be even with the bottom of the filler plug hole.
3. If lubricant is required, use only the specified type. It will probably have to be pumped in through the filler hole. Hypoid SAE 90 lubricant usually does not pour very well.

Steering Gear

1. Clean the area around the plug and remove the plug from the top of the gear housing.
2. The oil level should just reach the plug hole.

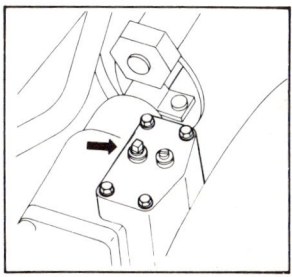

Steering gear lubricant level plug (arrow) (© Toyo Kogyo Co., Ltd.)

3. If necessary, add gear oil until the fluid is at the proper level.
4. Reinstall the plug.

Battery

Check the battery electrolyte level at least once a month, more often in hot weather or during periods of extended vehicle operation. The electrolyte in each cell should be kept filled to the split ring. If the level is low, add only distilled water or colorless, odorless drinking water.

At least once a year check the specific gravity of the battery. It should be between 1.20–1.26 at room temperature. Clean and tighten the terminal clamps and apply a thin coating of petroleum jelly to the terminals. This will help to retard corrosion. The terminals can be cleaned with a stiff wire brush or with a terminal cleaner made for the purpose. These are inexpensive and can be purchased in most any decently equipped parts store.

If water is added during freezing weather, the truck should be driven sev-

GENERAL INFORMATION AND MAINTENANCE

eral miles to allow the water to mix with the electrolyte. Otherwise the battery could freeze.

If the battery becomes corroded, a mixture of baking soda and water will neutralize the corrosion. This should be washed off after making sure that the caps are tight and securely in place. Rinse the solution off with cold water.

If a "fast" charger is used to charge the battery while the battery is in the truck, disconnect the battery first.

NOTE: *Keep flame or sparks away from the battery; it gives off explosive hydrogen gas, while it is being charged.*

Battery State of Charge At Room Temperature

Specific Gravity Reading	Charged Condition
1.260–1.280	Fully Charged
1.230–1.250	¾ Charged
1.200–1.220	½ Charged
1.170–1.190	¼ Charged
1.140–1.160	Almost No Charge
1.110–1.130	No Charge

TIRES AND WHEELS

Inspect the tires at least weekly and at every oil change. Check for cuts, bruises, objects embedded in the tread, abnormal wear and proper inflation. It is important that correct tire pressure be maintained to ensure proper handling and the best ride and tire wear. It is normal for tires to build up pressure in excess of the specification on the side of the tire when they are warm. It is not wise to lower the tire pressure in this situation.

To equalize tread wear, the tires should be rotated every 4,000 miles. Do not rotate the tires if different sizes are used on the front and rear.

Recommended Cold Inflation Pressure

Rotary Pick-Up

Tire Size	Inflation (psi)
7.35 x 14	24 front
	36 rear

B-1600

Tire Size	Inflation (psi)
6.00 x 14	25 front, normal speed
	45 rear, normal speed
	30 front, high-speed
	45 rear, high-speed

Tire Rotation

At the intervals specified, the tires should be rotated according to the dia-

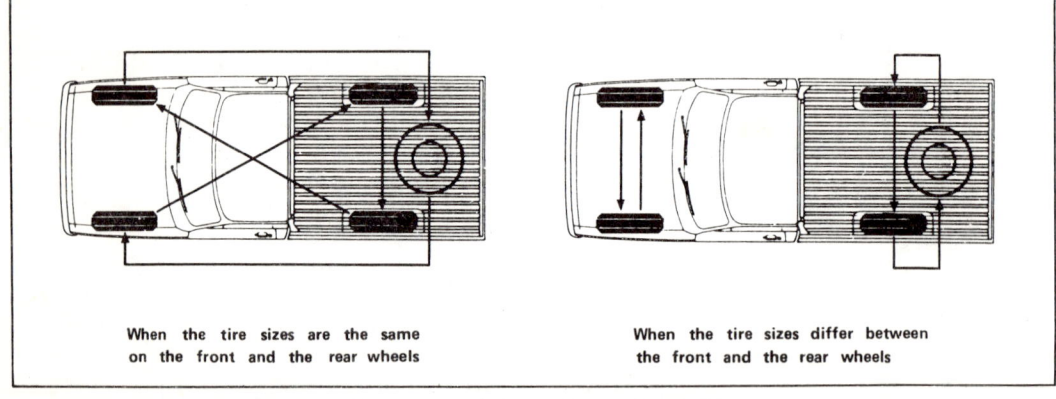

When the tire sizes are the same on the front and the rear wheels

When the tire sizes differ between the front and the rear wheels

Tire rotation (© Toyo Kogyo Co., Ltd.)

GENERAL INFORMATION AND MAINTENANCE

gram. The wheel lug nuts should be torqued to 58–65 ft lbs in the proper sequence.

FUEL FILTER

The fuel filter is located on the center of the left frame member near the fuel tank on B-1600s and under the left-side of the cargo bed, just forward of the rear wheel on Rotary Pick-Ups. Both trucks use a cartridge fuel filter that is replaceable.

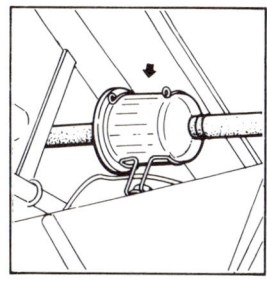

Fuel filter (© Toyo Kogyo Co., Ltd.)

To replace the filter, loosen the clamps at both ends of the filter and pop the filter from its clamp.

OUTSIDE VEHICLE MAINTENANCE

Lock Cylinders

Apply graphite lubricant sparingly through the key slot. Insert the key and operate the lock several times to be sure that the lubricant is worked into the lock cylinder.

Door Hinges and Hinge Checks

Spray a silicone lubricant on the hinge pivot points to eliminate any binding conditions. Open and close the door several times to be sure that the lubricant is evenly and thoroughly distributed.

Tailgate

Spray a silicone lubricant on all of the pivot and friction surfaces to eliminate any squeaks or binds. Work the tailgate to distribute the lubricant.

Body Drain Holes

Be sure that the drain holes in the doors and rocker panels are clear of obstruction. A small screwdriver can be used to clear them of any debris.

Windshield Washer Adjustment

The washer spray direction can be adjusted by inserting a pin into the nozzle and turning it to the desired position.

Wiper Blade Replacement

Wiper blade replacement will vary with the amount of use, type of weather, etc. Generally, if the wiper pattern across the screen is streaked over clean glass, the blades should be replaced.

1. To remove the wiper blade, press down on the arm to unlatch the locking stud. Depress the tab on the saddle and pull the blade from the arm.

2. To install a new blade, slip the blade connector over the end of the wiper arm so that the locking stud snaps into place.

Capacities

Year	Model	Engine Displacement Cu in. (cc)	Engine Crankcase (qts) With Filter	Engine Crankcase (qts) Without Filter	Transmission (pts) Manual 3-spd	Transmission (pts) Manual 4-spd	Transmission (pts) Automatic	Drive Axle (pts)	Gasoline Tank (gals)	Cooling System (qts) w/heater
1972–1975	B-1600	96.8 (1586)	4.0	3.0	——	①	——	2.8	11.7	6.8
1974–1975	Rotary Pick-Up	40.0 (654) x 2 rotors	5.5	4.5	——	3.6	13.2	2.8	20.4	10.8

①—Up to No. 49824: 3.0 pts
From No. 49825: 3.2 pts

GENERAL INFORMATION AND MAINTENANCE

Lubrication

OIL AND FUEL RECOMMENDATIONS

Engine Oil

The SAE grade number indicates the viscosity of the engine oil, or its ability to lubricate under a given temperature. The lower the SAE grade number, the lighter the oil; the lower the viscosity, the easier it is to crank the engine in cold weather.

The API (American Petroleum Institute) designation indicates the classification of engine oil for use under given operating conditions. Only oils designated for "Service SE" (old designation MS) should be used. These oils provide maximum engine protection. Both the SAE grade number and the API designation can be found on the top of a can of oil.

NOTE: *Non-detergent or straight mineral oils should not be used.*

Oil viscosities should be chosen from those oils recommended for the lowest anticipated temperatures during the oil change interval.

OIL RECOMMENDATIONS

The following lubricants are recommended for use in your Mazda truck.

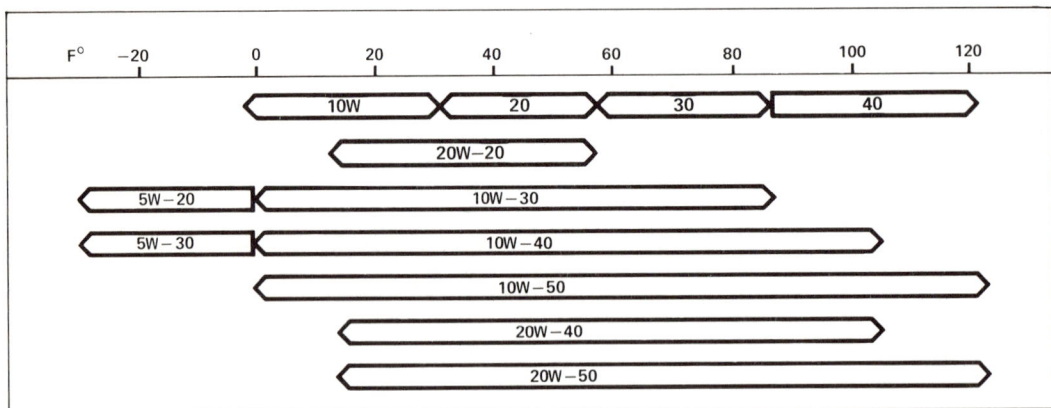

Oil viscosities—B-1600 (© Toyo Kogyo Co., Ltd.)

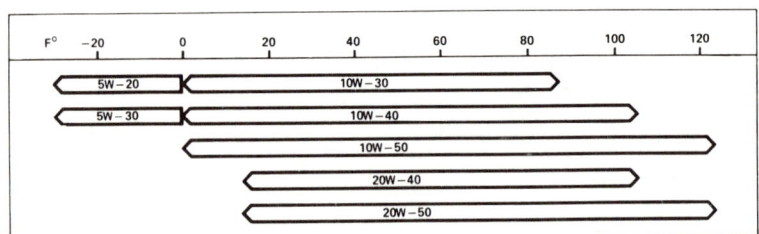

Oil viscosities—Rotary Pick-Up (© Toyo Kogyo Co., Ltd.)

Lubricant Recommendations

Rotary Pick-Up

Item		Lubricant	
Transmission	Automatic	ATF Type "F"	
	Manual	Above 0° F SAE 90 Below 0° F SAE 80	SAE 80

GENERAL INFORMATION AND MAINTENANCE

Lubricant Recommendations (cont.)

Rotary Pick-Up

Item	Lubricant
Rear axle	Above 0° F SAE 90 SAE 80 Below 0° F SAE 80
Steering gear	SAE 90
Upper and lower arm ball joints, upper arm shafts	Disulphide Molybdenum Grease NLGI No. 2
Idler arm, front wheel bearings	Lithium Grease NLGI No. 2
Body pivot points	
Brake and clutch fluid reservoirs	SAE J1703a or MVSS 116, DOT-3 or DOT-4

B-1600

Item	Lubricant
Manual Transmision	Above 0° F SAE 90 Below 0° F SAE 80
Rear axle	Above 0° F SAE 90 Below 0° F SAE 80
Steering gear	SAE 90
Upper and lower arm ball joints, upper arm shafts	Disulphide Molybdenum Grease NLGI No. 2
Idler arm, front wheel bearings, body pivot points	Lithium Grease NLGI No. 2
Brake and clutch fluid reservoirs	MVSS 116, DOT-3 or DOT-4

OIL AND FLUID CHANGES

Engine Oil

Engine oil should be changed according to the maintenance schedule. Under such conditions as:
—Driving in dusty conditions;
—Continuous trailer pulling or RV use;
—Extensive or prolonged idling;
—Extensive short trip operation in freezing temperatures (when the engine is not thoroughly warmed);
—Frequent long runs at high-speeds in high ambient temperatures, and;
—Stop-and-go service such as delivery trucks,
the oil change interval and filter change interval should be cut in half. Operation of the engine under severe conditions, such as dust storms, may require an immediate oil and filter change.

Except for the first oil change, it is recommended that the oil filter be replaced at every other oil change. But, if you do this, you are always leaving one quart of dirty oil in the system for at least 14,000 miles.

To change the engine oil, the truck should be parked on a level surface and the engine should be at operating temperature. This is to ensure that foreign matter will be drained away with the oil and not left behind in the engine to form sludge, which will happen if the engine is drained cold. Oil that is slightly brownish when drained is a good sign that the contaminants are being drained away. You should have available a container that will hold at least five quarts, a wrench to fit the oil drain plug, a spout for pouring in new oil and some rags to clean up the inevitable mess. If the filter is being replaced, you will also need a band wrench to fit the filter.

1. Position the truck on a level surface and set the parking brake or block the wheels. Slide a drain pan under the oil drain plug.

2. From under the truck, loosen, but do not remove the oil drain plug. Cover your hand with a heavy rag or glove and slowly unscrew the drain plug. Push the plug against the threads to prevent oil from leaking past the threads.

CAUTION: *The engine oil will be hot. Keep your arms, face and hands away from the oil as it drains out.*

3. As the plug comes to the end of the threads, whisk it away from the hole, letting the oil drain into the pan, which hopefully is still under the drain plug. This method usually avoids the messy task of reaching into a tub full of hot, dirty oil to retrieve a usually elusive drain plug. Crawl out from under the truck and wait for the oil to drain.

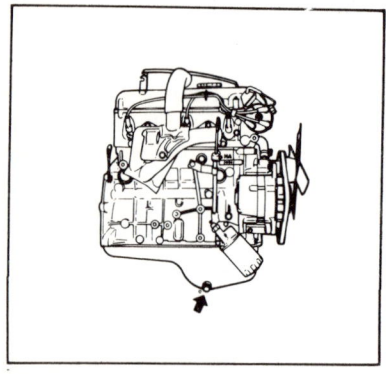

Oil drain plug (arrow) on the B-1600. The drain plug for the Rotary Pick-Up is similar, but on the driver's side of the oil pan. (© Toyo Kogyo Co., Ltd.)

4. When the oil is drained, reinstall the drain plug. If you are replacing the filter on a Rotary Pick-Up, leave the plug out.

5. Change the engine oil filter as necessary or desired. On the B-1600, the filter is located at the right front of the engine, down below and behind the alternator. Loosen the filter with a band wrench and spin the filter off by hand. Be careful of the one quart of hot, dirty oil that inevitably overflows the filter. On Rotary Pick-Ups, the engine oil filter is on top of the engine, next to the dipstick. To remove it, punch a hole in the top of the filter to allow the oil in the filter to drain out through the engine. After the oil is drained from the filter, loosen it with a band wrench and remove it. When oil ceases to flow from the engine, replace the drain plug.

6. Coat the rubber gasket on a new filter with engine oil and install the filter. Screw the filter onto the mounting stud and tighten according to the directions on the filter.

7. Refill the engine with the specified amount of clean engine oil. Be sure to use the proper viscosity. Pour the oil in through the capped opening.

Oil is added through the capped opening in the valve cover on the B-1600. On the rotary engine it is added through the capped pipe just above the dipstick. (© Toyo Kogyo Co., Ltd.)

8. Run the engine for several minutes, checking for oil pressure and leaks. Check the level of the oil and add if necessary.

Manual Transmission

The same instructions apply to manual transmissions as apply to engines. The truck should be on a level surface and the lubricant should be at operating temperature.

GENERAL INFORMATION AND MAINTENANCE

1. Position the truck on a level surface.
2. Place a pan of sufficient capacity under the transmission drain plug.
3. Remove the upper (fill) plug to provide a vent opening.
4. Remove the lower (drain) plug and let the lubricant drain out. Be sure to clean the magnetic drain plug.
5. Replace the drain plug.
6. Pump in sufficient lubricant of the proper type to bring the level to the bottom of the filler plug opening.
7. Reinstall the filler plug. Run the engine and check for leaks.

Automatic Transmission

The automatic transmission fluid is a long-lasting type and the manufacturer does not specify that it need be changed. However, should you wish to change the fluid, use the following procedure.
1. Run the engine for one minute prior to draining the fluid.
2. Be sure that the truck is on a level surface.
3. There is no drain plug, so the transmission oil pan must be removed to drain the fluid.
4. Carefully remove the screws from the oil pan and carefully lower the transmission oil pan at the corner. Allow the fluid to drain into a suitable container.
5. Remove the old gasket and install a new one. Replace the transmission oil pan.
6. Refill the transmission with the specified type and quantity of transmission fluid. Fluid is added by removing the dipstick and pouring the fluid through a funnel with a flexible spout inserted in the dipstick tube.
7. After adding fluid, lower the truck to the ground and run the engine at idle, shifting into all gears to allow the fluid to fill all the passages.
8. Run the engine at fast idle to allow the fluid to reach operating temperature. Check the fluid level and add as necessary.

Rear Axle

The Mazda uses a removable carrier axle which has a drain and fill plug.
1. Jack the rear of the vehicle and support it with jackstands.
2. Position a suitable container under the axle drain plug. Remove the fill plug to provide a vent.
3. Remove the drain plug and allow the lubricant to drain out.
NOTE: *Do not confuse the drain and fill plugs. The drain plug is magnetic to attract fine particles of metal which are inevitably present.*
4. Clean the magnetic drain plug.
5. Install the drain plug.
6. Fill the rear axle with the specified amount and type of fluid. Install the filler plug.
7. Lower the truck to the ground and drive the truck, checking for leaks after the fluid is warm.

• WHEEL BEARINGS

See Chapter 9.

Pushing, Towing and Jump Starting

PUSHING

Mazda trucks with manual transmissions can be push started, but this is not recommended if you value the appearance of your truck. Mazda trucks with automatic transmissions cannot be push started.

To push start trucks with manual transmissions, make sure that both bumpers are in reasonable alignment and protected with old blankets or something similar. Be careful in judging the alignment of bumpers as bent sheet metal and inflamed tempers are both predictable results of misaligned bumpers. Turn the ignition key to ON and engine High gear. Turn off all accessories. Depress the clutch pedal. When a speed of about 10 mph is reached, lightly depress the gas pedal and slowly release the clutch pedal. Do not attempt to engage the clutch while both vehicles are in contact.

Never get a starting assist by having your truck towed.

TOWING

Manual Transmission

If the transmission and rear axle are not damaged, the vehicle may be towed from the front. Otherwise it should be

GENERAL INFORMATION AND MAINTENANCE

lifted and towed from the rear. Be sure that the parking brake is OFF and the transmission is in Neutral.

Automatic Transmission

With the automatic transmission, the rear wheels must be lifted off the ground or the driveshaft must be disconnected. If this is not done, the transmission may be damaged.

Manual or Automatic Transmission

Do not attach chains to the bumpers or bracketing. All attachments should be made to structural members. Safety chains should also be used. If you are flat towing, remember that the power steering and power brake assists will not work with the engine OFF.

Jump Starting

To jump start the truck when the battery is discharged, use a booster battery of the same voltage and grounded terminal as your battery. Observe the correct polarity when connecting the two batteries (negative-to-negative and positive-to-positive).

The following procedure is recommended to jump start the truck.
1. Position the two vehicles so that they are not touching.
2. Set the parking brake and place automatic transmissions in Park and manual transmissions in Neutral. Turn off the lights, radio, heater and all other electrical loads.
3. Remove the vent caps from the discharged and booster battery. Lay a cloth over the open cells of each battery.
4. Attach one cable to the positive terminal of the booster battery and the positive terminal of the discharged battery.
5. Attach one end of the remaining cable to the negative terminal of the booster battery and the discharged battery.
6. Start the engine in the vehicle with the booster battery. Then, start the engine in your truck. Reverse the above steps to disconnect the batteries. Reinstall the vent caps. Dispose of the cloths; they may have battery acid on them.

Hoisting and Jacking

The jack supplied with your truck was meant for changing tires. It was not meant to support the truck while you work under it. Whenever it is necessary to get under your truck to perform service operations, be sure that it is adequately supported on jackstands.

Do not lift the truck by the front bumper. Be careful when lifting the truck on a two-post hoist. Damage to the suspension may occur if care is not exercised in positioning the hoist adapters.

FRAME CONTACT HOIST

Adapters are necessary to lift the truck. Position the adapters so that the frame is centered on the adapter contact area. All four contact points must contact the adapters.

DRIVE-ON HOIST

Check for possible interference between the flanges of the hoist area and the truck.

TWIN-POST HOIST

The adapters for the front end post must be positioned under the front suspension lower arms and centered on the

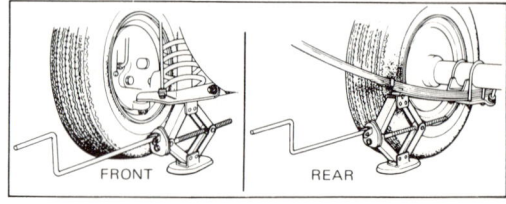

Jack locations for scissors type jack (© Toyo Kogyo Co., Ltd.)

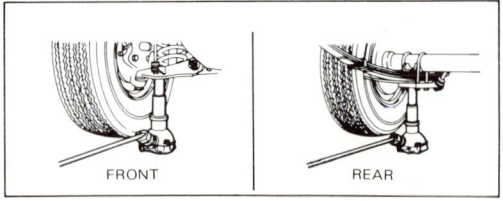

Jack locations for hydraulic jack (© Toyo Kogyo Co., Ltd.)

GENERAL INFORMATION AND MAINTENANCE

coil springs or slightly outboard of the coil spring center.

The rear forks should be positioned under the axle housing near the springs. Be sure that the forks do not interfere with the shock absorbers or the shock absorber brackets.

NOTE: *To support your Mazda with the jack supplied with the truck, refer to the accompanying illustrations.*

10 years of rotary engine development (© Toyo Kogyo Co., Ltd.)

Chapter Two
Tune-Up and Troubleshooting

Tune-Up Procedures

NOTE: *The procedures contained in this section are specific procedures applicable to your Mazda. More general procedures that would apply to* almost any vehicle are contained in the "Tune-Up and Troubleshooting" section at the end of this chapter.

Neither tune-up nor troubleshooting can be considered independently since each has direct bearing on the other. An engine tune-up is a service designed to restore the maximum capabil-

Rotary Pick-Up Tune-Up Specifications

Year	Engine Displacement Cu in. (cc)	Spark Plugs Type	Spark Plugs Gap (in.)	Distributor Point Dwell (deg)	Distributor Point Gap (in.)	Ignition Timing Leading Plug (deg)	Ignition Timing Trailing Plug (deg)	Port Timing Intake Opens (deg)	Fuel Pump Pressure (psi)	Idle Speed (rpm) MT (N)	Idle Speed (rpm) AT (D)
1974–1975	40.0 (654) x 2 rotors	①	0.024–0.028	55–61	0.016–0.020	5A	15A	32A	3.6–5.0	900–970	750–825

① Recommended spark plugs:

Standard	Cold Type
B7EM	B8EM
BR7EM	BR8EM
B7EMV	B8EMV
BR7EMV	BR8EMV
W22EA	W25EA
W22EAR	W25EAR
W22EA-G	W25EA-G
W22EAR-G	W25EAR-G
N-80B	N-78B
RN-80B	RN-78B

(N)—Transmission in Neutral
(D)—Transmission in Drive
A—ATDC (After Top Dead Center)
CO concentration at idle—0.1–2.0%
HC concentration at idle—less than 200 ppm (parts per million)
Idle Fuel Adjustment:

	Throttle Opening Angle (deg)	Idle Fuel Flow (gals/hr)	Time Required to consume 50 cc
Manual Trans	1.5–2.5	0.57–0.62	75–82 sec
Auto Trans	1.5–2.5	0.59–0.63	73–80 sec

TUNE-UP AND TROUBLESHOOTING

B-1600 Tune-Up Specifications

Year	Engine Displacement Cu in. (cc)	Spark Plug Type	Spark Plug Gap (in.)	Distributor Point Dwell (deg)	Distributor Point Gap (in.)	Ignition Timing (deg) MT	Ignition Timing (deg) AT	Intake Valve Opens (deg)	Fuel Pump Pressure (psi)	Compression Pressure (psi)	Idle Speed (rpm) MT	Idle Speed (rpm) AT	Valve Clearance (in.)▲ In	Valve Clearance (in.)▲ Ex
1972–1975	96.8 (1586)	BP-6ES	0.031	49–55	0.020	5B	—	13B	2.8–3.6	170 (new) 120 (low limit)	①	—	0.012	0.012

▲ At the valve (warm engine)
— Not Applicable
① 1972: 775–825 rpm
All others: 800–850 rpm
CO % at idle: 1972–75—1.5–2.5%
B—BTDC (Before Top Dead Center)

TUNE-UP AND TROUBLESHOOTING

ity of power, performance, economy and reliability in an engine, and, at the same time, assure the owner of a complete check and more lasting results in efficiency and trouble-free performance. Engine tune-up becomes increasingly important each year, to ensure that pollutant levels are in compliance with federal emissions standards.

It is advisable to follow a definite and thorough tune-up procedure. Tune-up consists of three separate steps: Analysis, the process of determining whether normal wear is responsible for performance loss, and whether parts require replacement or service; Parts Replacement or Service; and Adjustment, where engine adjustments are returned to the original factory specifications.

The extent of an engine tune-up is usually determined by the length of time since the previous service, although the type of driving and the general mechanical condition of the engine must be considered. Specific maintenance should also be performed at regular intervals, depending on operating conditions.

Troubleshooting is a logical sequence of procedures designed to lead the owner or service man to the particular cause of trouble. The troubleshooting section of this manual is general in nature, yet specific enough to locate the problem. Service usually comprises two areas; diagnosis and repair. While the apparent cause of trouble, in many cases, is worn or damaged parts, performance problems are less obvious. The first job is to locate the problem and cause. Once the problem has been isolated, refer to the appropriate section for repair, removal or adjustment procedures.

It is advisable to read the entire chapter before beginning a tune-up, although those who are more familiar with tune-up procedures may wish to go directly to the instructions.

SPARK PLUGS

The function of a spark plug is to ignite the air/fuel mixture in the cylinder as the mixture is compressed by the piston. The expansion of the ignited mixture forces the piston down, which turns the crankshaft and supplies power to the drive train.

Spark plugs should be checked frequently (approximately 5,000 miles) depending on use. All the recommendations are based on the ambient conditions as well as driving conditions. If you drive at high-speeds constantly, the plugs will probably not need as much attention as those used for constant stop-and-start driving.

The electrode end of the plug (the end with the threads) is a good indicator of the internal condition of your engine. If a spark plug has fouled and caused the engine to misfire, the problem will have to be found and corrected. Often, "reading" the spark plugs will lead you to the cause of the problem. Spark plug conditions and probable causes are listed in the "Troubleshooting" section of this chapter. It is a good idea to pull the plugs once in a while just to get an idea of the internal condition of your engine.

NOTE: *A small amount of light tan-colored deposits on the electrode end of the spark plug is quite normal. These plugs need not be replaced unless they are severely worn.*

Heat range is a term used to describe the cooling characteristics of spark plugs. Plugs with longer-nosed insulators take a longer time to dissipate heat effectively, and are termed "hot" plugs. The reverse is also true, shorter-nosed plugs dissipate heat rapidly, and are thus called "cold" plugs. It is generally advisable to use the factory-specified spark plugs. However, in conditions of extremely hard usage (e.g., driving cross country in August), going to the next cooler heat range is all right. The same is true if most driving is done in the city or over short distances, go to the next hotter range spark plug to eliminate spark plug fouling. If in doubt concerning spark plug substitution, consult a Mazda dealer.

Spark plugs should be gapped when installed new and when they are checked periodically.

To gap the spark plugs, remove each one in turn and measure the gap with a round feeler gauge of the appropriate thickness. The round feeler gauge is inserted between the center and side electrode, as illustrated. To adjust the gap, bend the side electrode with the tool on

TUNE-UP AND TROUBLESHOOTING 27

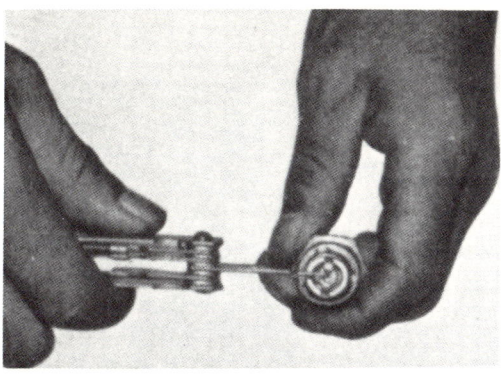

Checking spark plug gap—B-1600 (© Toyo Kogyo Co., Ltd.)

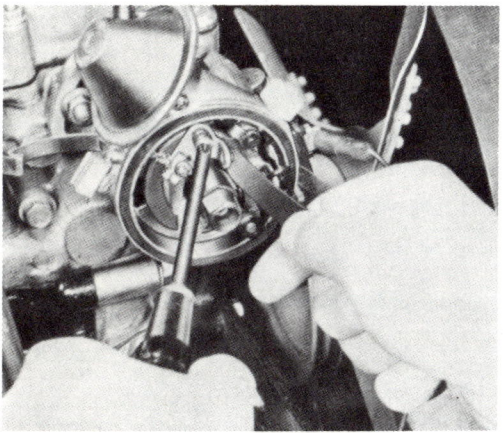

Checking spark plug gap—Rotary Pick-Up. Note the dual side electrodes. (© Toyo Kogyo Co., Ltd.)

the end of the feeler gauge until the specified gap is obtained.

REMOVAL

1. Raise the hood and locate all the spark plugs.
2. If the spark plug wires are not numbered, mark each one with a small piece of masking tape. Print the number of the cylinder on the piece of tape.
3. Disconnect the wire from the plug by grasping, twisting and pulling the molded cap from the plug. Do not simply yank the wire from the plug as the connection inside the cap can become damaged.
4. Using a spark plug socket, loosen the plug a few turns.
5. If compressed air is available, blow out the area around the base of the spark plug to remove foreign matter.
6. Remove the plug the rest of the way and inspect them. It is a good idea to inspect the plugs whether or not they are going to be reused.

Inspection

1. Compare the condition of the spark plugs to the plugs shown in the accompanying illustration (see "Troubleshooting," subject 4.6). It should be remembered that any type of deposit will decrease the efficiency of the plug. If the plugs are not to be replaced, they should be thoroughly cleaned before installation. If the electrode ends of the plugs are not worn or damaged and if they are to be reused, wipe off the porcelain insulator on each plug and check for cracks or breaks. If either condition exists, the plug must be replaced.
2. If the plugs are judged reusable, have them cleaned on a plug cleaning machine (found in most service stations) or remove the deposits with a stiff wire brush.
3. Check the plug gap on both new and used plugs before installing them in the engine. The ground electrode must be parallel to the center electrode and the specified size wire gauge should pass through the opening with a slight drag. If the center or ground electrode has worn unevenly, level them off with a file. If the air gap between the two electrodes is not correct, open or close the ground electrode, with the proper tool, to bring it to specifications. Such a tool is usually provided with a gap gauge.

INSTALLATION

1. Coat the threads of new plugs with Moly-paste. Insert the plugs into the engine and tighten them finger-tight.
2. Be sure that the plugs are not cross-threaded. If the plugs use metal gaskets, new gaskets should be installed each time the plugs are removed and installed.
3. Tighten the spark plugs to 9–13 ft. lbs (Rotary Pick-Up) or 11–15 ft lbs (B-1600).
4. Install the spark plug wires on their respective plugs. Be sure that each wire is firmly connected.
5. While you are about the task of checking the spark plugs, the spark plug wires should also be checked. Any wires

TUNE-UP AND TROUBLESHOOTING

that are cracked or brittle should be replaced.

BREAKER POINTS AND CONDENSER

Operation

When the breaker points are closed, current flows from the battery through the ignition switch and ballast type resistor to the primary windings in the coil, then to ground through the closed breaker points. When the points open, the magnetic field built up in the primary windings of the coil, moves through the secondary windings of the coil, producing high voltage. The high voltage flows through the coil high tension lead to the distributor cap, where the rotor distributes it to the spark plug terminals. This process is repeated for every power stroke of the engine.

Removal and Installation

ALL MODELS

NOTE: *Because of engine design, the rotary engine uses 2 sets of points in the distributor. Removal and installation is basically the same as for a single set of points.*

1. Raise the hood and locate the distributor. It is on the front of the engine.
2. Scribe an alignment mark on the distributor cap and the distributor body. This way you will get the cap on the right way.
3. Remove the distributor cap and rotor. The rotor only goes on the shaft one way.
4. Disconnect the primary and condenser wires from the breaker point terminal. Note the position of the wires before removing them from the terminal.
5. Remove the screws attaching the breaker points to the base plate. If possible, it is best to use a magnetic screwdriver to do this. The screws are very small and can be dropped easily.
6. Lift the breaker point(s) assemblies from the distributor. Remove the condenser.

To install the points:

7. Place the breaker point(s) assemblies on the base plate. Install the attaching screws, again using a magnetic screwdriver, if you have one.
8. Install the condenser. It is always best to install a new condenser each time you replace the points. It is just cheap insurance against condenser failure.
9. Connect the primary and condenser wires to the point(s) terminal and tighten the connection.
10. Be sure that the points are aligned.
11. Set the point gap or dwell angle and install the rotor and distributor cap. Use the alignment marks made previously to get the cap on correctly.

DWELL ANGLE

When setting ignition contact points, it is advisable to observe the following general rules:

1. If the points are used, they should not be adjusted using a feeler gauge. The gauge will not give an accurate reading on a pitted surface.
2. Never file the points—this removes their protective coating and results in rapid pitting.
3. When using a feeler gauge to set new points, be certain that the points are fully open. The fiber rubbing block must rest on the highest point of the cam lobe.
4. Always make sure that a feeler gauge is free of oil or grease before setting the points.
5. Make sure that the points are properly aligned and that the feeler gauge is not tilted. If points are misaligned, bend the fixed contact support only, never the movable breaker arm.

A dwell meter virtually eliminates errors in point gap caused by the distributor cam lobes being unequally worn, or human error. In any case, point dwell should be checked as soon as possible after setting with a feeler gauge because it is a far more accurate check of point operation under normal operating conditions. The dwell meter is also capable of detecting high point resistance (oxidation) or poor connections within the distributor.

The dwell meter, actually a modified voltmeter, depends on the nature of contact point operation for its usefulness. In this electro-mechanical system, a fiber block slides under tension, over a cam. The angle that the block traverses on the

TUNE-UP AND TROUBLESHOOTING

cam, during which time current is made available to the coil primary winding, is an inverse function of point gap. In other words, the wider the gap, the smaller the "dwell" (expressed in degrees); the closer the gap, the greater the "dwell."

Because the fiber block wears down gradually in service, it is a good practice to set the dwell on the low side of any dwell range (smaller number of degrees) given in specifications. As the block wears, the dwell becomes greater (toward the center of the range) and point life is increased between adjustments.

To connect the dwell meter, switch the meter to the six-, four- or eight-cylinder range, as the case may be, and connect one lead to ground. The other lead should be connected to the coil distributor terminal (the one having the wire going to contact points). Follow the manufacturer's instructions if they differ from those listed. Zero the meter, start the engine and gradually allow it to assume normal idle speed. (See "Tune-Up Specifications.") The meter should agree with the specifications. Any excessive variation in dwell indicates a worn distributor shaft or bushings, or perhaps a worn distributor cam or breaker plate.

It is obvious from the above procedure that some means of measuring engine rpm must also be employed when checking dwell. An external tachometer should be employed. Hook-up is the same as for the dwell meter and both can be used in conjunction. Most commercial dwell meters have a tachometer scale built in and switching between them is possible.

Adjustment—Single Point Distributors (B-1600)

There are two methods to adjust the breaker point gap. By far the more accurate is the method of measuring dwell angle electronically.

FEELER BLADE METHOD

1. Check and adjust the breaker point alignment. Bend the fixed contact support only.
2. Crank the engine in short bursts until the rubbing block rests on a peak of a cam lobe.
3. Insert a feeler blade of the speci-

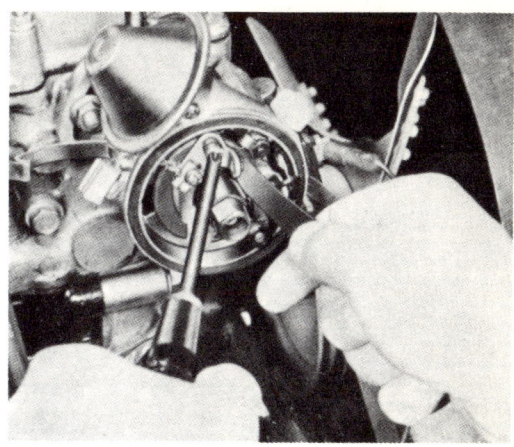

Adjusting the point gap—B-1600 (© Toyo Kogyo Co., Ltd.)

fied thickness between the breaker points. Adjust the gap until the feeler blade will slide through the gap with a slight drag, by loosening the adjustment screw and moving the point base. When the correct gap is obtained, tighten the adjustment screw.

4. Clean the breaker cam and apply a thin coating of distributor cam lubricant to the cam. Do not use engine oil.
5. After setting the breaker point gap, set the ignition timing.
6. Install the distributor rotor and cap.

DWELL METER METHOD

1. Connect a dwell meter and tachometer or a dwell/tach to the engine following the manufacturer's instructions.
2. Remove the distributor cap and rotor.
3. Crank the engine and note the dwell reading.
4. If the dwell angle is not as specified, adjust the point gap. Crank the engine again and note the dwell reading. Repeat this process until the dwell is within specifications.
5. Lock the points in position.
6. Install the rotor and distributor cap. Disconnect the instruments and adjust the ignition timing.

Adjustment—Dual Point Distributors (Rotary Pick-Up)

There are two methods to adjust the points. By far the most accurate and preferable, on used points, is the dwell meter method.

TUNE-UP AND TROUBLESHOOTING

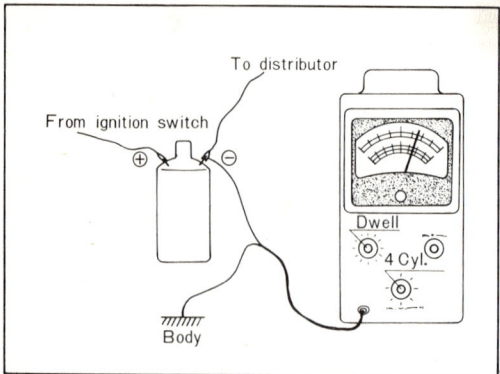

Dwell meter connections (© Toyo Kogyo Co., Ltd.)

FEELER BLADE METHOD

1. Remove the distributor high tension lead and the distributor cap and rotor.
2. Check the breaker point alignment. If necessary, align the points by bending the stationary contact. Never bend the movable contact.
3. Crank the engine in short bursts until the rubbing block on the breaker arm rests on the high point of the cam lobe. This is the maximum point opening.

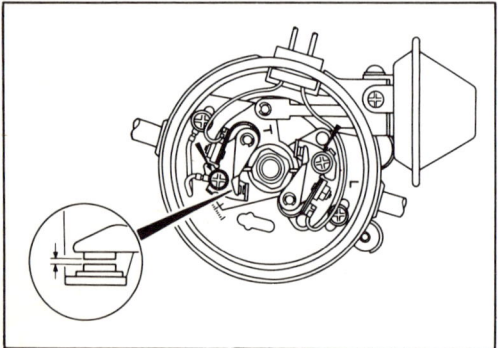

Adjusting the point gap—Rotary Pick-Up. Arrows indicate the lockscrews to be loosened. (© Toyo Kogyo Co., Ltd.)

4. Insert a feeler blade of the specified thickness between each set of breaker points in turn.
5. If adjustment is required, loosen the setscrews and move the stationary contact and base until the correct gap is obtained.
6. Tighten the setscrews and recheck the gap.
7. Install the rotor and distributor cap. Reconnect the high tension lead.

DWELL METER METHOD

1. Disconnect the vacuum line from the distributor and plug it with a pencil or a golf tee.
2. Connect the dwell meter in accordance with the manufacturer's instructions.
3. Run the engine at idle, after it has warmed up.
4. Observe the dwell meter reading. It should be according to specifications.
5. If it is not within specifications, adjust the dwell.

NOTE: *If dwell angle is above the specified amount, the point gap is too small; if it is below, the gap is too large.*

Remove the high tension leads and ground them. Remove the distributor cap. Loosen the breaker point attaching screws and crank the engine. Adjust the dwell to specifications and tighten the setscrews. Install the distributor cap and high tension leads.

6. If both the dwell angle and the contact point gap cannot be brought to within specifications, check for one or more of the following:
    a. Worn distributor cam;
    b. Worn rubbing block;
    c. Bent movable contact arm.

Replace any of the parts, as necessary.

7. When the dwell angle check is completed, disconnect the meter and reconnect the vacuum line.

IGNITION TIMING

B-1600

1. Raise the hood and clean and mark the timing marks. Chalk or fluorescent paint makes a good, visible mark.
2. Disconnect the vacuum line to the distributor and plug the disconnected line. Disconnect the line at the vacuum source, not at the distributor.
3. Connect a timing light to the front (No. 1) cylinder, a power source and ground. Follow the manufacturer's instructions.
4. Connect a tachometer to the engine.
5. Start the engine and reduce the idle to 700–750 rpm to be sure that the centrifugal advance mechanism is not working.

TUNE-UP AND TROUBLESHOOTING

Checking ignition timing—B-1600 (© Toyo Kogyo Co., Ltd.)

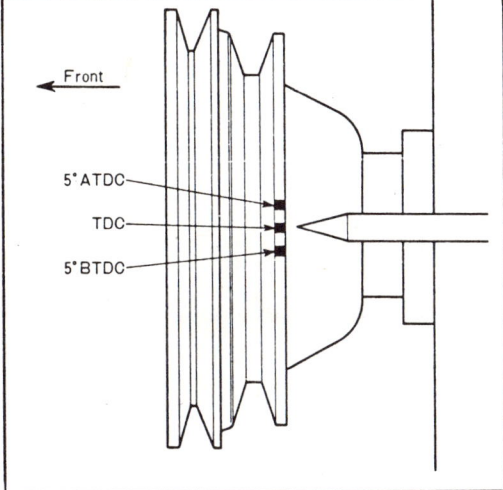

Schematic view of the timing marks—B-1600 (© Toyo Kogyo Co., Ltd.)

6. With the engine running, shine the timing light at the timing pointer and observe the position of the pointer in relation to the timing mark on the crankshaft pulley.

7. If the timing is not as specified, adjust the timing by loosening the distributor hold-down bolt and rotating the distributor in the proper direction. When the proper ignition timing is obtained, tighten the hold-down bolt on the distributor.

8. Check the centrifugal advance mechanism by accelerating the engine to about 2,000 rpm. If the ignition timing advances, the mechanism is working properly.

9. Stop the engine and remove the timing light.

10. Reset the idle to specifications.

11. Remove the tachometer.

Rotary Pick-Up

1. Connect a tachometer to the engine.

2. Disconnect and plug the vacuum tube on the distributor.

3. Connect a timing light to the wire from the leading (lower) plug of the front rotor housing.

4. Start the engine and run it idle speed.

5. Shine the timing light on the indicator pin located on the front cover.

6. If the leading timing mark is not correctly aligned with the pointer, stop the engine.

7. Loosen the distributor locknut and rotate the distributor housing (with the engine running) until the timing marks align. Stop the engine and tighten the distributor locknut.

8. Recheck the timing.

9. Change the connection of the timing light to the wire from the trailing (top) plug in the front rotor housing.

10. Start the engine and shine the timing light at the indicator pin. If the trail-

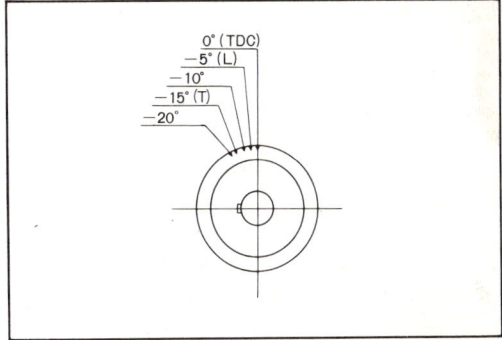

Ignition timing marks—Rotary Pick-Up. The (−) minus sign corresponds to a reading of ATDC. (© Toyo Kogyo Co., Ltd.)

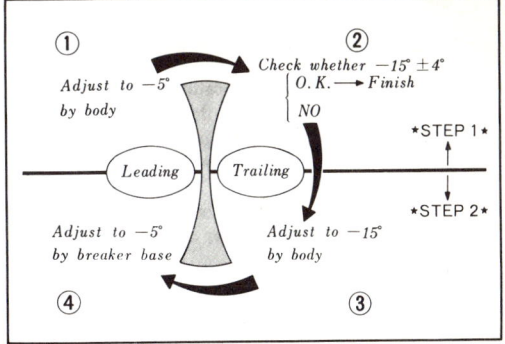

Diagram of ignition timing procedures—Rotary Pick-Up (© Toyo Kogyo Co., Ltd.)

TUNE-UP AND TROUBLESHOOTING

Adjustment of ignition timing (© Toyo Kogyo Co., Ltd.)

ing timing falls within the specifications, no further adjustments are necessary.

11. If the trailing timing is not within specifications, proceed with the rest of the procedure.
12. If the trailing timing is not within specifications, adjust the trailing and leading timing as follows:
13. Adjust the trailing timing to specification by rotating the distributor body, as in Step 7.
14. Check the leading timing again and record how much it differs from specification.
15. Remove the distributor cap and rotor.
16. Loosen the breaker base setscrews (the ones directly opposite each other near the outside of the distributor body) and turn the distributor base plate until the correct leading plug timing is obtained again.
17. Recheck the timing. If the leading and trailing plug timing marks should both be aligned (or within specifications). If not, repeat the procedure until they are.

VALVE LASH

B-1600

1. Run the engine until normal operating temperature is reached.

2. Shut off the engine and remove the rocker cover.
3. Torque the cylinder head bolts to 70 ft lbs.
4. Rotate the crankshaft so that the No. 1 cylinder (front) is in the firing position. This can be determined by removing the spark plug from the No. 1 cylinder and putting your thumb over the spark plug port. When compression is felt, the No. 1 cylinder is on the compression stroke. Rotate the engine with a wrench on the crankshaft pulley and stop it at TDC of the compression stroke on the No. 1 cylinder.

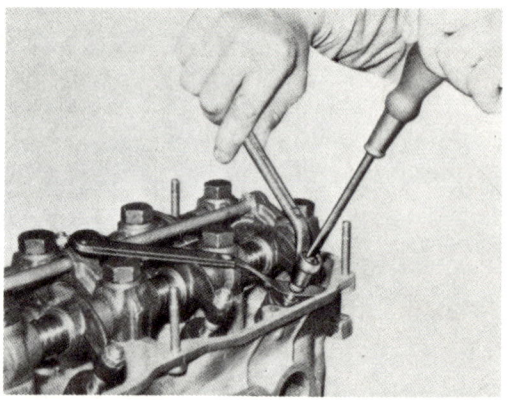

Adjusting the valve clearance—B-1600 (© Toyo Kogyo Co., Ltd.)

5. Check the valve clearance with a feeler blade. The clearance can be checked at the camshaft or at the valve.
6. If the valve clearance is incorrect, loosen the adjusting screw locknut and adjust the clearance by turning the adjusting screw with the feeler blade inserted. Hold the adjusting screw in the correct position and tighten the locknut.
7. Rotate the crankshaft (in the normal direction of rotation), adjusting the valves for each cylinder at TDC of the compression stroke. Adjust the valves for each cylinder, in the firing order, 1–3–4–2.
8. Install the rocker arm cover and torque the nuts to 18 in. lbs.

Rotary Pick-Up

Because of its unique design, there are no valves to adjust on the rotary engine.

TUNE-UP AND TROUBLESHOOTING

CARBURETOR

Idle Speed and Mixture

B-1600

1. Thoroughly warm the engine to normal operating temperature. The water temperature gauge will tell you when normal operating temperature is reached.
2. Make sure that the choke valve is fully open.
3. Connect a tachometer according to the manufacturer's instructions.
4. Adjust the idle speed screw to specifications.
5. The mixture should be checked by, at least, a CO meter. The carbon monoxide percentage at idle should be as specified.
6. Disconnect the tachometer.

ROTARY PICK-UP

1. Warm the engine to normal operating temperature.

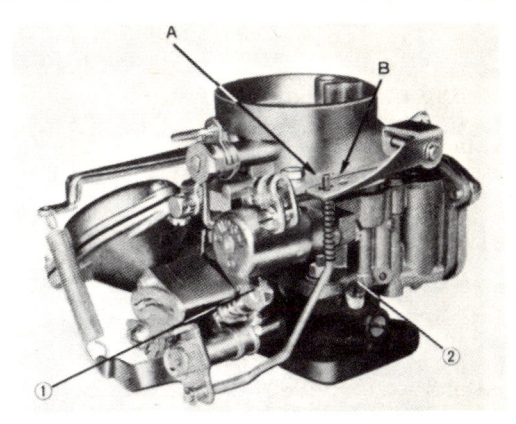

B-1600 carburetor showing throttle adjusting screw (1) and idle adjusting screw (2) (© Toyo Kogyo Co., Ltd.)

2. Be sure that the secondary throttle valve is fully returned.
3. Set the parking brake and block the front wheels.
4. Connect a tachometer according to the manufacturer's instructions.
5. Adjust the idle speed to specifica-

Rotary Pick-Up carburetor (© Toyo Kogyo Co., Ltd.)

1. Primary stage
2. Secondary stage
3. Primary air vent
4. Choke valve
5. Secondary air vent
6. Fuel inlet fitting (return side)
7. Fuel inlet fitting (inlet side)
8. Bimetal spring housing
9. Vacuum break diaphragm
10. Safety return spring
11. Throttle return spring
12. Fast idle connecting rod
13. Fuel bowl sight glass
14. Throttle lever
15. Choke lever
16. Throttle adjust screw (locked)
17. To altitude compensator
18. Idle adjust screw (locked)
19. Air adjust screw (for idle adjustment)
20. To distributor vacuum control diaphragm
21. From metering oil pmp
22. From sub-zero starting assist fluid tank
23. Accelerator pump lever
24. Accelerator pump piston
25. Lead wire of bimetal

tions. The idle speed should ONLY be adjusted with the idle air screw. Never use the idle fuel jet screw to adjust the idle. This screw is preset at the factory and should not be moved.

6. After idle speed adjustment, you should also have the mixture checked with a CO analyzer.

Idle and Throttle Screw Adjustment

If for some reason (tampering or carburetor overhaul) the idle and throttle screws need adjustment, use the following procedures. Two procedures are given; one for a HC/CO analyzer and one for a fuel flow meter.

Fuel Flow Meter

It is best to use this procedure to set the idle and throttle screws after they have been disturbed. After you are finished, check the adjustment with a HC/CO analyzer.

1. Adjust the throttle angle opening to specifications with the throttle adjustment screw. The adjustment should be made from the fully closed position. Tighten the locknut after the adjustment is complete.
2. Connect a fuel flow meter.
3. Start the engine and set the approximate idle speed with the idle air screw.
4. Adjust the idle fuel flow to specifications with the idle fuel screw.
5. Use the idle air screw to set the idle speed again.
6. Repeat this procedure (Steps 4 and 5) until both the idle fuel flow and the idle speed are within specifications.
7. Disconnect the fuel flow meter.

HC/CO Analyzer

1. If you have not already done so, adjust the throttle angle opening to specifications. Make the adjustment from the fully closed position.
2. Lock the nut after adjustment.
3. Start the engine and adjust the idle speed with the idle air screw.
4. Using the gas analyzer, check the HC (hydrocarbon) and CO (carbon monoxide) readings. If the HC is less than 200 ppm (parts per million) and the CO is between 0.1–2.0%, no further adjustment is needed.
5. If the HC and CO are not within specifications, adjust the CO reading to as close to 0.1% as possible, keeping the HC reading below 200 ppm. Use the idle fuel screw to make this adjustment.
6. Recheck the idle speed and adjust, if necessary, using the idle air screw.
7. Recheck the HC and CO readings to be sure that they are within limits. Repeat Steps 5 and 6 until the HC, CO and idle speed are all within specifications.

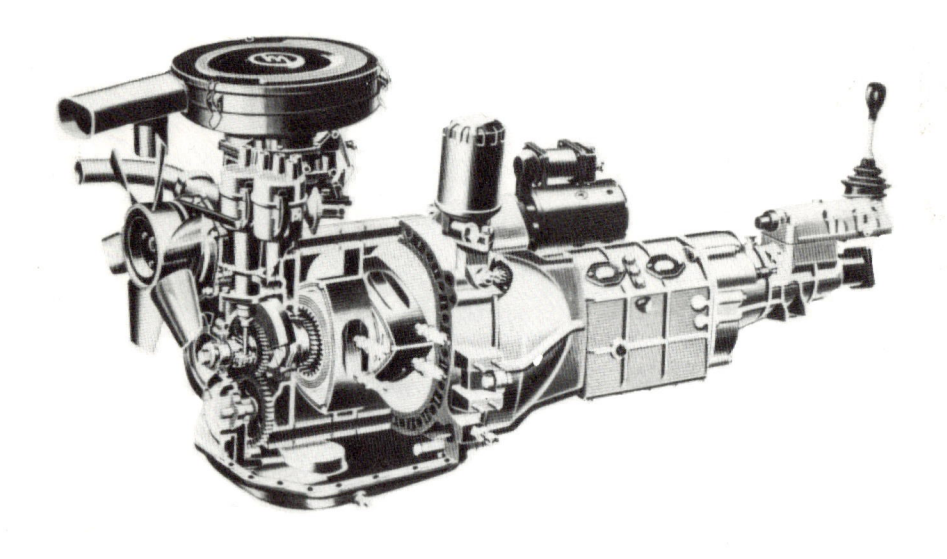

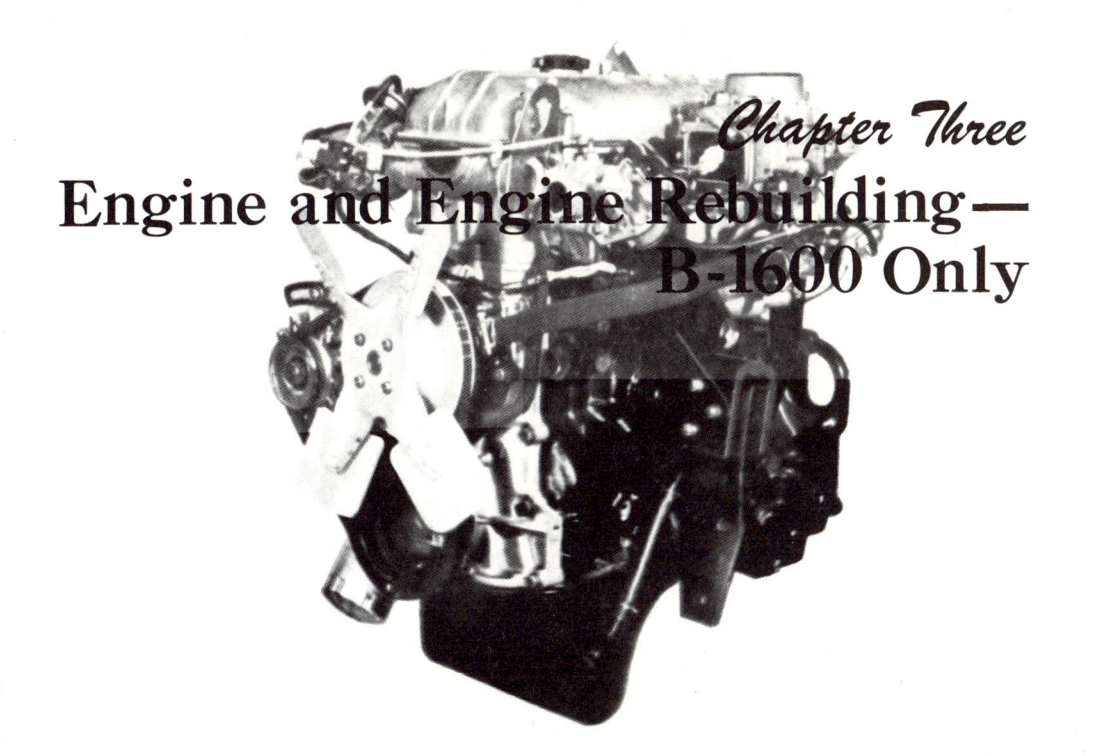

Chapter Three
Engine and Engine Rebuilding—B-1600 Only

Engine Electrical

DISTRIBUTOR

The distributor is located on the right front side of the engine. A single point distributor is used on all Mazda B-1600's through 1975.

Removal and Installation

1. Matchmark the distributor cap and the body of the distributor. Remove the distributor cap.
2. Disconnect the vacuum hose from the diaphragm.
3. Scribe matchmarks on the distributor body and the cylinder block to indicate the relative positions.
4. Scribe another mark on the distributor body indicating the position of the rotor.
5. Disconnect the primary wires from the distributor.
6. Remove the distributor hold-down nut, lockwasher and flat washer.
7. Remove the distributor from the engine.
   NOTE: *Do not crank the engine while the distributor is removed.*
   To install the distributor:
8. Align the matchmarks on the distributor gear and body.
9. If the engine was cranked while the distributor was removed, turn the crankshaft until the No. 1 cylinder is at the top of the compression stroke. This can be determined by feeling compression with your thumb over the spark plug port. The 5° BTDC mark on the crankshaft pulley should also be aligned with the timing pointer. Slide the distributor into the engine with the rotor pointing to the No. 1 cylinder firing position (see "Firing Order").
10. If the engine has not been cranked while the distributor was removed, slide the distributor (with the O-

Firing Order

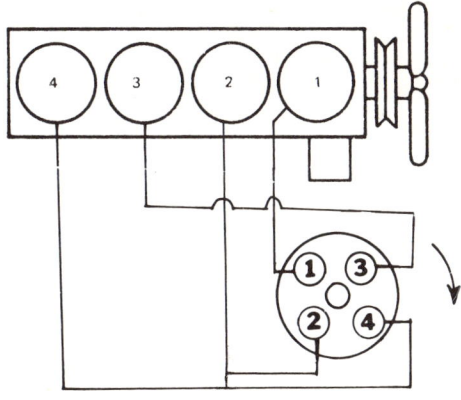

Firing order—B-1600 (© Toyo Kogyo Co., Ltd.)

ENGINE AND ENGINE REBUILDING—B-1600 ONLY

ring) into the engine, aligning the matchmarks made during removal.

11. Install the flat washer, lockwasher and hold-down nut, but do not tighten the nut.
12. Install the distributor cap and connect the primary wires.
13. Set the ignition timing, and tighten the hold-down nut.
14. Connect the vacuum line.

ALTERNATOR

Alternator Precautions

Some precautions should be taken when working on this, or any other, AC charging system.

1. Never switch battery polarity.
2. When installing a battery, always connect the grounded terminal first.
3. Never disconnect the battery while the engine is running.
4. If the molded connector is disconnected from the alternator, never ground the hot wire.
5. Never run the alternator with the main output cable disconnected.
6. Never electric weld around the truck without disconnecting the alternator.
7. Never apply any voltage in excess of battery voltage while testing.
8. Never "jump" a battery for starting purposes with more than 12 volts.

Removal and Installation

1. Open the hood and remove the battery. Disconnect the negative (ground) cable first.
2. Remove the nut holding the alternator wire to the terminal at the rear of the alternator.
3. Pull the multiple connector from the rear of the alternator.
4. Remove the alternator adjusting arm bolt. Swing the alternator in and disengage the fan belt.
5. Remove the distributor cap and rotor from the distributor.
6. Remove the alternator pivot bolt

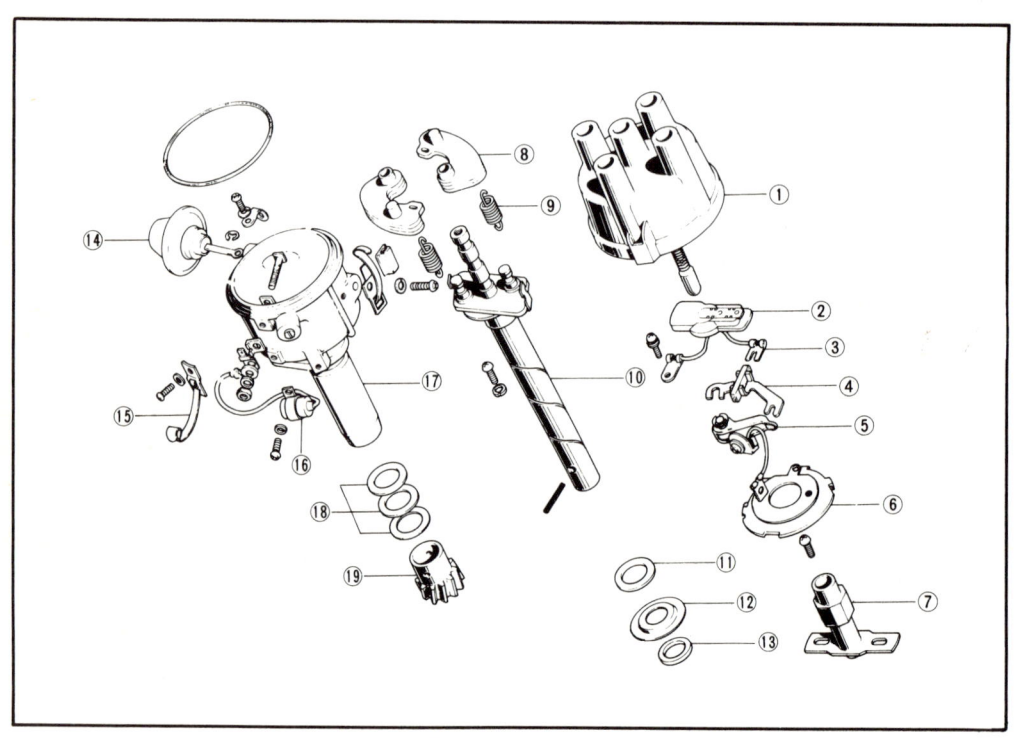

Exploded view of B-1600 distributor (© Toyo Kogyo Co., Ltd.)

1. Cap	6. Breaker plate	11. Washer	15. Retaining clip
2. Rotor	7. Cam	12. Spacer	16. Condenser
3. Ground wire	8. Governor weight	13. Felt	17. Housing
4. Cam lubricating felt	9. Governor spring	14. Vacuum control unit	18. Washer
5. Point assembly	10. Shaft		19. Driven gear

ENGINE AND ENGINE REBUILDING—B-1600 ONLY

and remove the alternator from the truck.

7. Installation is the reverse of removal. Be sure to adjust the drive belt tension and to connect the battery properly.

REGULATOR

The Mazda uses an external regulator located on the fender splash shield.

Removal and Installation

1. Raise the hood and disconnect the negative battery cable.
2. Disconnect the regulator wires at the multiple connector.
3. Remove the two regulator attaching screws and remove the regulator from the splash shield.

To install the regulator:

4. Position the regulator on the fender splash shield and install the two attaching screws.
5. Connect the regulator wires at the multiple connector.
6. Connect the negative battery cable.
7. Start the engine and be sure that the charging system indicator light goes out.

Regulator Test

The alternator regulator is composed of two control units: a constant voltage relay and a pilot lamp relay.

CHECKING THE CONSTANT VOLTAGE RELAY

1. Use an almost fully charged battery and connect a voltmeter between the "A" and "E" terminals of the regulator.
2. Run the engine at 2,000 rpm and read the voltmeter. It should read from 14–15 volts.
3. If not, adjust the voltage relay.

CHECKING THE PILOT LAMP RELAY

1. Using a voltmeter and variable resistor, construct a circuit as shown.
2. Light the pilot lamp.
3. Slide the knob of the variable resistor so that the voltage gradually increases.
4. Read the voltage between the "N" and "E" terminals of the regulator. If the voltage is 3.7–5.7 volts, it is operating properly.

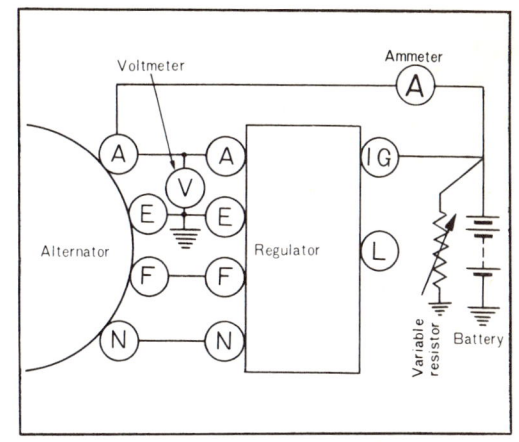

Checking the constant voltage relay (© Toyo Kogyo Co., Ltd.)

5. Slide the knob of the variable resistor to decrease the voltage. Note the point on the voltmeter where the light will light again. If the reading is less than 3.5 volts, the unit is working properly.
6. Disconnect the test instruments.

Adjusting the Regulator

1. Check the air gap, back gap and point gap with a wire gauge. If they are

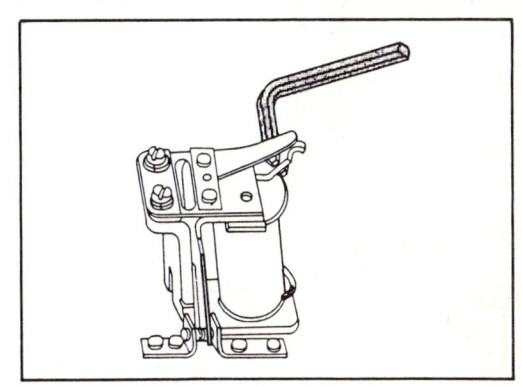

Adjusting the voltage regulator (© Toyo Kogyo Co., Ltd.)

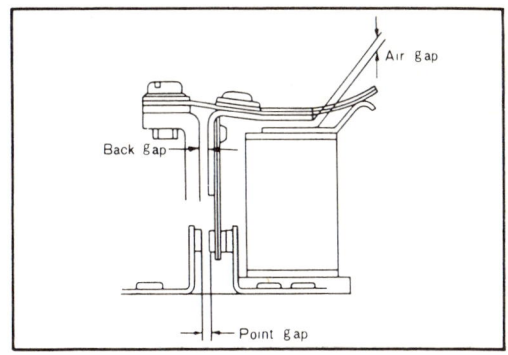

Regulator air gaps (© Toyo Kogyo Co., Ltd.)

ENGINE AND ENGINE REBUILDING—B-1600 ONLY

not within specification, adjust the gap by bending the stationary bracket.

2. After the gaps are correctly set, adjust the voltage setting. Bend the upper plate down to increase the voltage setting, or bend it up to increase the voltage setting.

Constant Voltage Relay

Air Gap	0.028–0.043 in.
Point Gap	0.012–0.016 in.
Back Gap	0.028–0.043 in.

Pilot Lamp Relay

Air Gap	0.035–0.047 in.
Point Gap	0.028–0.043 in.
Back Gap	0.028–0.043 in.

STARTER

The Mazda starter is a 4-brush, 4-field, 4-pole wound unit. Engine cranking occurs when the starter solenoid (mounted on the starter) is energized through the ignition switch. The solenoid shifts the starter pinion into mesh with the flywheel ring gear. At the same time, the main contacts of the solenoid are closed and the battery current is directed to the starter causing the armature to rotate. After the engine starts, the starter is disengaged when the ignition switch is returned to the "run" position. This opens the circuit to the starter solenoid and the solenoid return spring causes the shift lever to disengage the starter drive from the flywheel ring gear.

Removal and Installation

1. Raise the hood and disconnect the battery ground cable.
2. Remove the carburetor air cleaner and air intake tube.
3. Disconnect the battery cable from the starter solenoid battery terminal.
4. Pull the ignition switch wire from the solenoid terminal.
5. Raise and support the truck on jackstands.
6. Working under the truck, remove the two starter attaching bolts, washers and nuts.
7. Tilt the drive end of the starter and remove the starter by working it out below the emission system hoses.

To install the starter:

8. Install the starter and two bolts, washers and nuts.
9. Connect the ignition switch wire to the solenoid terminal.
10. Connect the battery cable to the solenoid battery terminal.
11. Install the carburetor air cleaner and air intake tube.
12. Connect the ground cable to the battery.

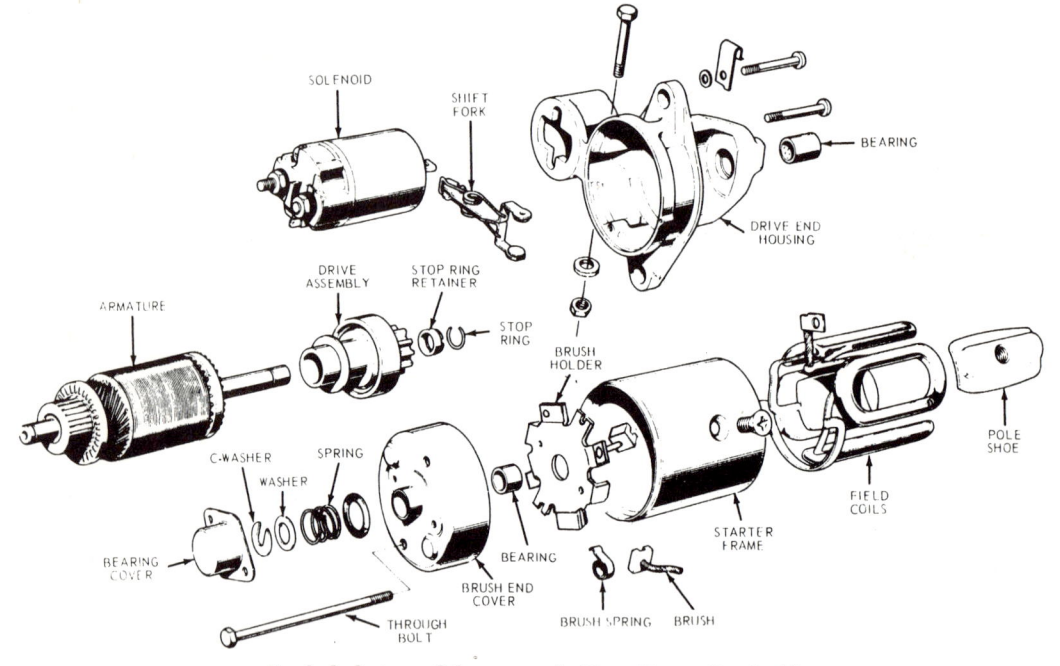

Exploded view of the starter (© Toyo Kogyo Co., Ltd.)

ENGINE AND ENGINE REBUILDING—B-1600 ONLY

13. Lower the truck to the ground and check the operation of the starter.

Starter Overhaul

1. Remove the starter from the truck.
2. Disconnect the field strap from the solenoid.
3. Remove the screws attaching the solenoid to the drive end housing. Disengage the solenoid plunger hook from the shift fork and remove the solenoid.
4. Remove the shift fork pivot bolt, nut and lockwasher.
5. Remove the through-bolts and separate the drive end housing from the starter frame. At the same time, disengage the shift fork from the drive assembly.
6. Remove the two screws attaching the brush end bearing cover to the brush end cover.
7. Remove the C-washer, washer and spring from the brush end of the armature shaft.
8. Pull the brush end cover from the starter frame.
9. Slide the armature from the starter frame and brushes.
10. Slide the drive stop-ring retainer toward the armature and remove the stop-ring. Slide the retainer and drive assembly off the armature shaft.
11. Remove the field brushes from the brush holder and separate the brush holder from the starter frame.

To assemble the starter:

12. Position the drive assembly on the armature shaft.
13. Position the drive stop-ring retainer on the armature shaft and install the drive stop-ring. Slide the stop-ring retainer over the stop-ring to secure the stop-ring on the shaft.
14. Position the armature in the starter frame. Install the brush holder on the armature and starter frame. Install the brushes in the brush holder.
15. Install the drive end housing on the armature shaft and starter housing. Engage the shift fork with the starter drive assembly as you move the drive end housing toward the starter frame.
16. Install the brush end cover on the starter frame making sure that the rear tabs of the brush holder are aligned with the through-bolt holes.
17. Install the through-bolts.
18. Install the rubber washer, spring, washer and C-washer on the armature shaft at the brush end. Install the brush end bearing cover on the brush end cover and install the attaching screws. If the brush end cover is not properly positioned, the bearing cover screws cannot be installed.
19. Align the shift fork with the pivot bolt hole and install the pivot bolt, lockwasher and nut. Tighten the nut securely.
20. Position the solenoid on the drive end housing. Be sure that the solenoid plunger hook is engaged with the shift fork.
21. Install the two solenoid retaining screws and washers.
22. Apply 12 volts to the solenoid S terminal (ground the M terminal) and check the clearance between the starter drive and the stop-ring retainer. The clearance should be 0.080–0.020 in. If not, the solenoid plunger is not properly adjusted. The clearance can be adjusted by inserting an adjusting shim between the solenoid body and drive end housing.
23. Install the field strap and tighten the nut.
24. Install the starter. Check the operation of the starter.

Brush Replacement

1. Remove the starter. Remove the two screws attaching the brush end bearing cover and remove the bearing cover.
2. Remove the through-bolts.
3. Remove the C-washer, washer and spring from the brush end of the armature shaft.
4. Pull the brush end cover from the starter frame.
5. Unsolder the two brushes from the field terminals and slide the brush holder from the armature shaft.
6. Cut the two brush wires at the brush holder and solder two new brushes to the brush holder.
7. Install the brush holder on the armature shaft and install the brushes in the brush holder.
8. Install the brush end cover on the starter frame and be sure that the ear tabs of the brush holder are aligned with the through-bolt holes.
9. Install the through-bolts.

ENGINE AND ENGINE REBUILDING—B-1600 ONLY

10. Install the rubber gasket, spring, washer and C-washer on the armature shaft.

11. Install the brush end bearing cover on the brush end cover and install the two screws. If the brush holder tabs are not aligned with the through-bolts, the bearing cover screws cannot be installed.

Solenoid Replacement

1. Remove the starter from the truck.
2. Disconnect the field strap from the solenoid terminal.
3. Remove the two solenoid attaching screws.
4. Disengage the solenoid plunger from the shift fork and remove the solenoid.

To install the solenoid:

5. Install the solenoid on the drive end housing, making sure that the solenoid plunger hook is engaged with the shift fork.
6. Apply 12 volts to the solenoid S terminal and measure the clearance between the starter drive and the stop-ring retainer. It should be 0.080–0.020 in. If not, remove the solenoid and adjust the clearance by inserting an adjusting shim between the solenoid body and drive end housing.
7. Check the solenoid for proper operation and install the starter.
8. Check the operation of the starter.

BATTERY

The battery is located under the hood at the front corner of the engine compartment, on the passenger's side. It can be removed by disconnecting the two battery cables and removing the hold-down clamps. Installation is the reverse of removal.

Engine Mechanical

Mazda piston engines are 1586 cc (96.8 cu in.), single overhead camshaft, four-cylinder engines. Water cools the thin cast iron block and cast aluminum alloy cylinder head with multispherical type combustion chambers.

The camshaft bearing caps are machined with the cylinder head and are not interchangeable. The cylinder head bolts also retain the camshaft bearing caps and the rocker arm shaft supports.

Exhaust valves are free rotating to prevent uneven valve wear. Intake rocker arm shafts are a two-piece unit, while the exhaust rocker arm shafts are single piece units.

The timing chain is a dual cog type encircling the crankshaft and camshaft sprockets. The crankshaft sprocket also holds the rotor type oil pump drive chain.

Battery and Starter Specifications

Year	Engine Displacement cu in. (cc)	Battery Amp Hour Capacity	Volts	Ground	Starter Lock Test Amps	Volts	Torque (ft lbs)	No Load Test Amps	Volts	RPM	Brush Spring Tension (oz)
1972–75	96.8 (1586)	60	12	Neg	560 or less	7.5	9.4 or more	60 or less	11.5	6000 or more	35–46

General Engine Specifications

Year	Engine Displacement cu in. (cc)	Carb Type	Advertised Horsepower (@ rpm)	Advertised Torque @ rpm (ft lbs)	Bore and Stroke (in.)	Advertised Compression Ratio	Oil Pressure
1972–75	96.8 (1586)	2-bbl	70 @ 5000	82 @ 3400	3.07 x 3.27	8.6 : 1	50–64 @ 3000

Valve Specifications

Year	Engine Displacement cu in. (cc)	Seat Angle (deg)	Face Angle (deg)	Spring Test Pressure (lbs @ in.)	Spring Installed Height (in.)	Stem-to-Guide Clearance (in.) Intake	Stem-to-Guide Clearance (in.) Exhaust	Stem Diameter (in.) Intake	Stem Diameter (in.) Exhaust
1972-75	96.8 (1586)	45	45	NA	1.339	0.0007-0.0021	0.0007-0.0023	0.3150	0.3150

NA—Not Available

Crankshaft and Connecting Rod Specifications
(All measurements given in in.)

Year	Engine Displacement cu in. (cc)	Crankshaft Main Brg Journal Dia	Crankshaft Main Brg Oil Clearance	Crankshaft Shaft End-Play	Thrust on No.	Connecting Rod Journal Dia	Connecting Rod Oil Clearance	Connecting Rod Side Clearance
1972-75	96.8 (1586)	2.4804	0.001-0.002	0.003-0.009	4	2.0866	0.001-0.003	0.004-0.008

Piston Clearance

Year	Engine Displacement cu in. (cc)	Minimum (in.) ①	Maximum (in.) ①
1972-75	96.8 (1586)	0.0022	0.0028

① Wear limit—0.006 in.

Ring Gaps

Year	Engine Displacement cu in. (cc)	Top Compression (in.) Min	Top Compression (in.) Max	Bottom Compression (in.) Min	Bottom Compression (in.) Max	Oil Control (in.) Min	Oil Control (in.) Max
1972-75	96.8 (1586)	0.008	0.016	0.008	0.016	0.008	0.016

Ring Side Clearance

Year	Engine Displacement cu in. (cc)	Top Compression (in.) Min	Top Compression (in.) Max	Top Compression (in.) Replace	Bottom Compression (in.) Min	Bottom Compression (in.) Max	Bottom Compression (in.) Replace	Oil Control (in.) Min	Oil Control (in.) Max
1972-75	96.8 (1586)	0.137	0.145	0.145	0.137	0.145	0.145	0.114	0.122

ENGINE AND ENGINE REBUILDING—B-1600 ONLY

B-1600 Torque Specifications
(All figures given in ft lbs)

Engine	
Main bearing caps	61–65
Connecting rod caps	36–40
Oil pump sprocket	22–25
Oil pan	5–7
Cylinder head	
Cold engine	56–60
Warm engine	69–72
Camshaft sprocket	51–58
Distributor drive gear	51–58
Valve rocker arm cover	1.1–1.4
Crankshaft pulley	101–108
Inlet manifold	14–19
Exhaust manifold	12–17
Spark plugs	11–15
Oil filter cartridge	7–11
Oil pressure switch	9–13
Temperature gauge unit	4–7
Clutch	
Flywheel	112–118
Clutch cover	13–20
Transmission	
Shift lock spring caps	33–40
Plug for interlock pin hole	7–11
Reverse lock spring cap	33–40
Control lever-to-control rod	13–20
Shift fork set bolts	6–9
Mainshaft locknut	116–174
Reverse lamp switch	20–33
Driveshaft	
Yoke-to-rear axle companion flange	40–47
Yoke-to-front driveshaft	116–130
Center bearing support	14–21
Rear axle	
Ring gear bolts	40–47
Differential side bearing caps	47–56
Companion flange-to-pinion	145–253
Steering	
Steering gear housing-to-frame	33–41
Steering wheel nut	22–29
Pitman arm-to-selector shaft	108–130
Idler arm bracket-to-frame	33–41
Center link-to-pitman arm	21–28
Center link-to-idler arm	33–47
Tie-rod-to-center link	18–25
Tie-rod-to-knuckle arm	21–28
Tie-rod clamps	13–18
Wheels	
Wheel nuts	58–65
Suspension	
Ball joints-to-knuckle	51–65
Upper suspension arm shaft-to-frame	61–76
Lower suspension arm shaft-to-frame	54–69
U-bolts	46–58
Spring pin nuts	61–76
Spring pin-to-frame bracket	14–18
Shackle pin nuts	43–58

Unspecified Torques

6T	
6 mm bolt/nut	5–7
8 mm bolt/nut	12–17
10 mm bolt/nut	23–34
12 mm bolt/nut	41–59
14 mm bolt/nut	56–76
8T	
6 mm bolt/nut	6–9
8 mm bolt/nut	13–20
10 mm bolt/nut	27–40
12 mm bolt/nut	46–69
14 mm bolt/nut	75–101

Removal and Installation

The engine is removed through the engine compartment, leaving the transmission in place.

1. Scribe the locations of the hood hinges and remove the hood.
2. Remove the engine splash shield.
3. Drain the coolant.
4. Drain the engine oil.
5. Disconnect the battery cables and remove the battery.
6. Disconnect the primary wire and coil wire from the distributor.
7. Disconnect the wire at the "B" terminal of the alternator and disconnect the plug from the rear of the alternator.
8. Disconnect the wire from the oil pressure switch.
9. Disconnect the engine ground wire.
10. Remove the air cleaner and heat insulator.
11. Disconnect the breather hose from the rocker cover.
12. Disconnect the water temperature gauge wire and solenoid valve wire.
13. Disconnect the starter wires.
14. Remove the upper and lower radiator hoses.
15. Remove the bolts attaching the radiator cowling. The cowling can only be removed after the radiator has been removed.
16. Unbolt and remove the radiator and cowling.
17. Disconnect the heater hoses from the intake manifold.
18. Disconnect the throttle cable from the carburetor and remove the throttle linkage from the rocker cover attaching point.
19. Disconnect the choke cable from the carburetor.
20. Disconnect the fuel ventilation hose from the oil separator.
21. Disconnect the fuel line at the carburetor and plug the fuel line.

ENGINE AND ENGINE REBUILDING—B-1600 ONLY

22. Remove the starter.
23. Disconnect the exhaust pipe from the manifold.
24. Remove the clutch cover plate.
25. Support the transmission with a jack and remove the bolts attaching the engine to the transmission.
26. Unbolt the right and left engine mounts.
27. Attach a lifting sling to the engine and pull the engine forward until it clears the clutch shaft.
28. Lift the engine from the truck.
29. Installation is the reverse of removal. Be sure to check all fluid levels.

CYLINDER HEAD

Removal and Installation

Be sure that the cylinder head is cold before removal. This will prevent warpage.

1. Drain the cooling system.
2. Scribe alignment marks around the hood hinges and remove the hood.
3. Remove the air cleaner.
4. Disconnect the coil wire and vacuum line from the distributor.
5. Rotate the crankshaft to put the No. 1 cylinder at TDC on the compression stroke.
6. Remove the plug wires and distributor cap as a unit.
7. Remove the distributor.
8. Remove the rocker arm cover.
9. Raise and support the truck. Disconnect the exhaust pipe from the manifold.
10. Remove the accelerator linkage.
11. Remove the nut, washer and the distributor gear from the camshaft.
12. Remove the nut washer and camshaft gear. Support the timing chain from falling into the timing chain case. Do not remove the cam gear from the timing chain. The relationship between the chain and gear teeth should not be disturbed.
13. Remove the cylinder head bolts, and cylinder head-to-front cover bolt.
14. Remove the rocker arm assembly.
15. Remove the camshaft and camshaft gear.
16. Lift off the cylinder head.
17. Remove all tension from the timing chain.

To install the cylinder head:

18. Clean the rocker cover gasket surface at the head and the cover. Clean the head gasket surface at the head and the block. Clean the water pump gasket surface at the head gasket surface and the front cover.
19. Check the cylinder head flatness with a straightedge and feeler blades. It should not exceed 0.003 in. in any six in. span or 0.006 in. overall. If necessary, the cylinder head can be milled, not to exceed 0.008 in.

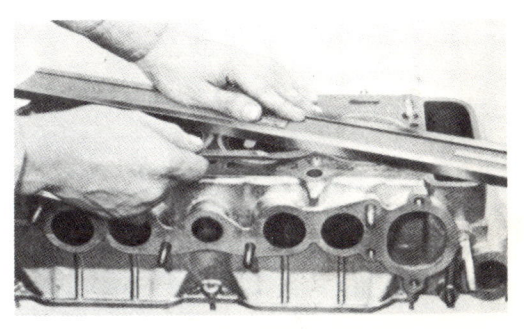

Checking the cylinder head distortion (© Toyo Kogyo Co., Ltd.)

20. Clean the cylinder head bolt holes of oil and dirt.
21. Position a new head gasket on the cylinder block.
22. Install the cylinder head on the block using the guides at either end of the block.

Removing or installing the cylinder head (© Toyo Kogyo Co., Ltd.)

23. Install the camshaft on the head and camshaft gear.
24. Install the rocker arm assembly.
25. Install the head bolts. Torque the bolts to specifications.
26. Install the camshaft gear washer and nut.
27. Install the distributor gear, washer and nut.

28. Time the engine. Follow the instructions under "Timing Chain and Sprocket Installation."
29. Adjust the timing chain tension. See "Timing Chain Tensioner Adjustment."
30. Connect the exhaust pipe to the exhaust manifold. Lower the truck.
31. Install the distributor, distributor cap and plug wires.
32. Install the lower intake bracket bolt.
33. Install the accelerator linkage.
34. Connect the vacuum line and coil wire.
35. Adjust the valve clearance cold.
36. Install the rocker arm cover. Fill the cooling system.
37. Run the engine until normal operating temperature is reached, and check for leaks. Adjust the valve clearance hot.
38. Adjust the carburetor and ignition timing. Install the air cleaner and install the hood.

Torque Sequences

B-1600 cylinder head torque sequence (© Toyo Kogyo Co., Ltd.)

Valve Guide Removal and Installation

Before attempting this, consult the "Engine Rebuilding" section for general procedures that will apply.
1. Remove the cylinder head.
2. Remove the deposits from the combustion chambers with a stiff wire brush and scraper before removing the valves. Do not scratch the cylinder head surface.
3. Compress the valve springs with a valve spring compressor. Remove the valve spring retainer locks and release the springs.
4. Keep the exhaust and intake valve retainers separate. They should be reassembled to the valve from which they were removed.
5. Remove the spring retainer, springs and valve.
6. Remove the valve stem seals. Identify all parts so that they can be reinstalled in their original locations.
7. Drive out the valve guides.

Removing the valve guide (© Toyo Kogyo Co., Ltd.)

8. Check the cylinder head flatness as described under "Cylinder Head Removal and Installation."

Assemble the cylinder head using new parts where applicable:

a. Lubricate all valves, valve stems, and valve guides with heavy-duty oil (SE). The valve tips should be lubricated with Lubriplate® or the equivalent. Apply this before installation.

b. Press new valve guides into each bore until the ring on the guide touches the cylinder head. Note that the intake and exhaust valve guides are different.

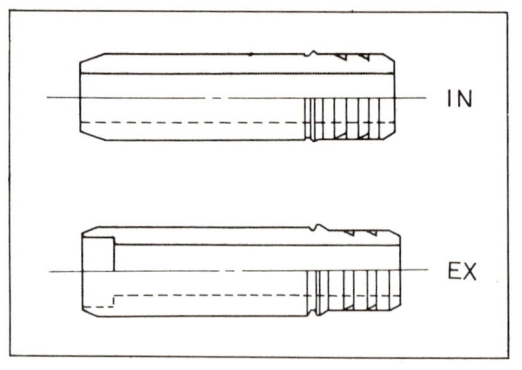

Intake (IN) and exhaust (EX) valve guides (© Toyo Kogyo Co., Ltd.)

ENGINE AND ENGINE REBUILDING—B-1600 ONLY

c. Install new valve seals on the valve guides.

d. Install each valve into the valve from which it was removed or fitted.

e. Install the valve springs over the valve. Install the spring retainer.

f. Compress the springs and install the retainer locks. Be sure that the exhaust and intake locks are assembled to the correct valves.

9. Install the cylinder head. See "Cylinder Head Installation." Adjust the valves and set the timing and carburetor.

ROCKER SHAFTS

Removal and Installation

This operation should only be performed on a cold engine; the bolts which hold the rocker shafts in place also hold the cylinder head to the block.

1. Raise the hood and cover the fenders.
2. Disconnect the choke cable.
3. If equipped, disconnect the air by-pass valve cable.
4. Disconnect the spark plug wires. Remove the wires from the spark plug wire clips on the rocker covers and position them out of the way.
5. Remove the rocker cover and discard the gasket.
6. Remove the rocker arm shaft attaching bolts evenly and remove the rocker arm shafts.

To install the rocker shafts:

a. Install the rocker arm assemblies on the cylinder head. Install the balls on each rocker arm as shown. Temporarily tighten the cylinder head bolts to specifications and offset each rocker arm support 0.04 in. from the valve

Removing or installing the rocker arms (© Toyo Kogyo Co., Ltd.)

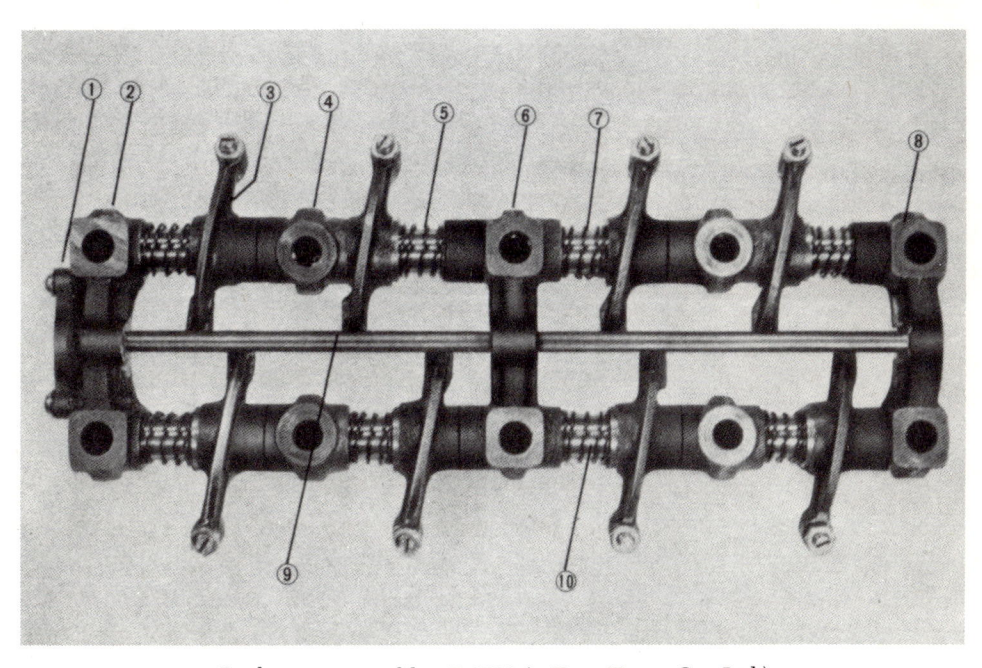

Rocker arm assembly—B-1600 (© Toyo Kogyo Co., Ltd.)

1. Thrust plate
2. Front bearing cap
3. Rocker arm (Exhaust)
4. Supporter
5. Rocker arm shaft (Exhaust)
6. Center bearing cap
7. Spring
8. Rear bearing cap
9. Oil pipe
10. Rocker arm shaft (Intake)

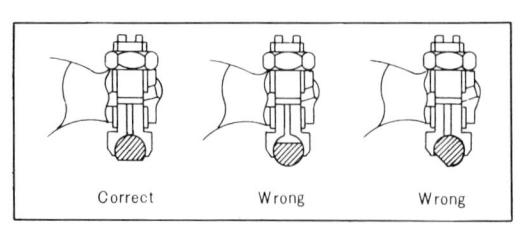

Installing the rocker arm balls (© Toyo Kogyo Co., Ltd.)

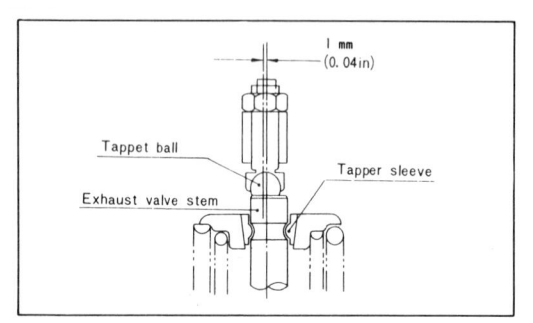

Offset of the exhaust rocker arm (© Toyo Kogyo Co., Ltd.)

stem center. Torque the bolts to specifications.
7. Adjust the valves cold.
8. Clean the mating surfaces of the cylinder head and rocker cover.
9. Install the rocker cover with a new gasket.
10. Install the spark plug wires on the plugs. Place the wires in the clips on the rocker cover. Connect the choke and air by-pass valve cable.
11. Start the engine and check for leaks.
12. Allow the engine to reach operating temperature, torque the head bolts to specifications and adjust the valves hot.

INTAKE MANIFOLD

Removal and Installation

1. Drain the cooling system.
2. Remove the air cleaner.
3. Remove the accelerator linkage.
4. Disconnect the choke cable and fuel line. Plug the fuel line.
5. Disconnect the PCV valve hose.
6. Disconnect the heater return hose and by-pass hose.
7. Remove the intake manifold-to-cylinder head attaching nuts.
8. Remove the manifold and carburetor as an assembly.
To install the manifold:
9. Clean the gasket mating surfaces.

10. Install a new gasket and the manifold on the studs. Torque the attaching nuts to specification, working from the center outward.
11. Connect the PCV valve hose to the manifold.
12. Connect the by-pass and heater return hoses.
13. Install the accelerator linkage.
14. Connect the fuel line and choke cable.
15. Replace the air cleaner.
16. Fill the cooling system. Run the engine and check for leaks.

EXHAUST MANIFOLD

Removal and Installation

1. Raise and support the truck.
2. Remove the two attaching nuts from the exhaust pipe at the manifold.
3. Remove the manifold attaching nuts.
4. Remove the manifold.
To install the manifold:
5. Apply a light film of graphite grease to the exhaust manifold mating surfaces before installation.
6. Install the manifold on the studs and install the attaching nuts. Torque the attaching nuts to specifications.
7. Install a new exhaust pipe gasket. Connect the exhaust pipe and torque the nuts to specifications.

CYLINDER FRONT COVER

Removal and Installation

1. Scribe alignment marks on the hood hinges and remove the hood.
2. Drain the cooling system.
3. Disconnect the upper and lower radiator hoses. Remove the radiator.

Removing the crankshaft pulley bolt (© Toyo Kogyo Co., Ltd.)

ENGINE AND ENGINE REBUILDING—B-1600 ONLY

Cylinder head-to-front cover bolt (© Toyo Kogyo Co., Ltd.)

4. Remove the accessory drive belts.
5. Remove the crankshaft pulley and the water pump.
6. Remove the cylinder head-to-front cover bolt.
7. Raise and support the truck.
8. Remove the engine skid plate.
9. Disconnect the emission line from the oil pan. Drain the oil from the engine.
10. Remove the oil pan.
11. Remove the alternator and bracket and lay the alternator aside.
12. Remove the steel tube from the front of the engine.
13. Unbolt and remove the front cover.

To install the front cover:

14. Clean all the gasket mating surfaces.
15. Clean the crankshaft pulley.
16. Use contact cement to cement a new front cover gasket on the block.
17. Install the front cover and torque the attaching bolts to specifications.
18. Install the air pump (if equipped).
19. Install the alternator and bracket.
20. Install the water pump and a new gasket. Torque the bolts to specifications.
21. Connect the by-pass hose and heater hose to the water pump.
22. Install the crankshaft pulley and attaching bolt. Torque the bolt to specifications.
23. Install the alternator belts, and the water pump pulley.
24. Install the fan. Adjust the tension of the belt(s).
25. Install the radiator and the upper and lower hoses.
26. Install the air cleaner.
27. Install the oil pan and the emission line.
28. Install the engine skid plate.
29. Lower the truck to the ground.
30. Fill the engine with oil and fill the cooling system. Run the engine and check for leaks.
31. Install the hood.

FRONT COVER OIL SEAL

Removal and Installation

The front cover oil seal can be removed and a new one installed without removing the front cover.

1. Scribe alignment marks on the hood hinges and remove the hood.
2. Drain the cooling system.
3. Disconnect the upper and lower radiator hoses and remove the radiator.
4. Remove the drive belt(s).
5. Remove the crankshaft pulley.
6. Pry the front oil seal from the front cover.

To install a new oil seal:

7. Clean the pulley and seal area.
8. Press a new front seal into position (flush).
9. Install the crankshaft pulley and torque the bolt to specifications.
10. Install the drive belt(s) and adjust the tension.
11. Install the radiator and connect the upper and lower hoses. Fill the cooling system.
12. Start the engine and check for leaks.
13. Install the hood.

TIMING CHAIN AND TENSIONER

Removal and Installation

1. Remove the cylinder head and front cover. It is not necessary that the intake and exhaust manifolds be removed from the head.
2. Remove the oil pump and chain.
3. Remove the timing chain tensioner.
4. Loosen the timing chain guide strip screws.
5. Remove the oil slinger.
6. Remove the oil pump gear and chain as an assembly.
7. Remove the timing chain, crank-

ENGINE AND ENGINE REBUILDING—B-1600 ONLY

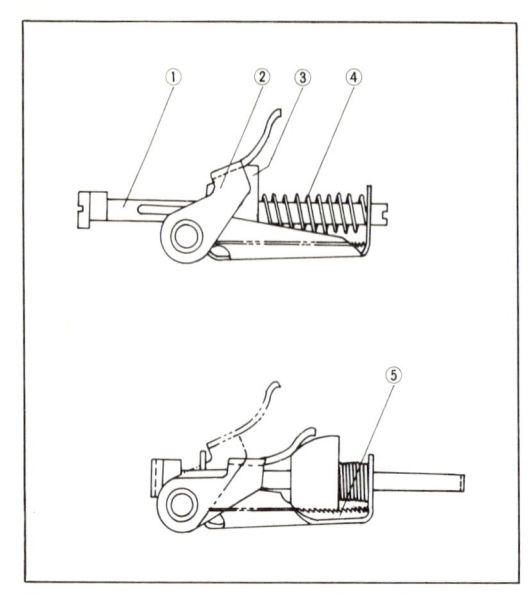

Chain tensioner (© Toyo Kogyo Co., Ltd.)

1. Slide pin
2. Arm
3. Wedge
4. Spring
5. Wedge plate

Removing or installing the oil slinger (© Toyo Kogyo Co., Ltd.)

shaft gear and camshaft gears from the engine.

To install the timing chain, timing gears and tensioner:

8. Position the crankshaft gear in the timing chain.
9. Position the oil pump chain and gear on the crankshaft and oil pump. Check the oil pump drive chain slack. It should be 0.15 in. Adjusting shims (between the oil pump body and cylinder block) are available in thickness of 0.006 in.
10. Install the oil slinger.
11. Install the oil pump washer and nut. Bend the washer over the nut.
12. Install the timing chain tensioner. Fully compress the snubber spring

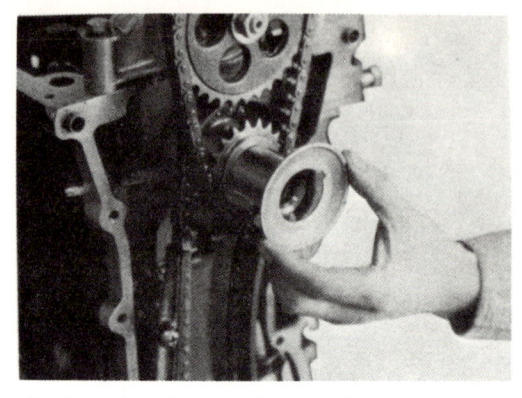

Checking the oil pump chain slack (© Toyo Kogyo Co., Ltd.)

and wedge a screwdriver into the tensioner release mechanism. Without removing the screwdriver, install the tensioner.

13. Install the cylinder head and camshaft. Be sure that the valve timing is as illustrated. It must be exact. You may have to move the cam gear one or two teeth to obtain the correct alignment.

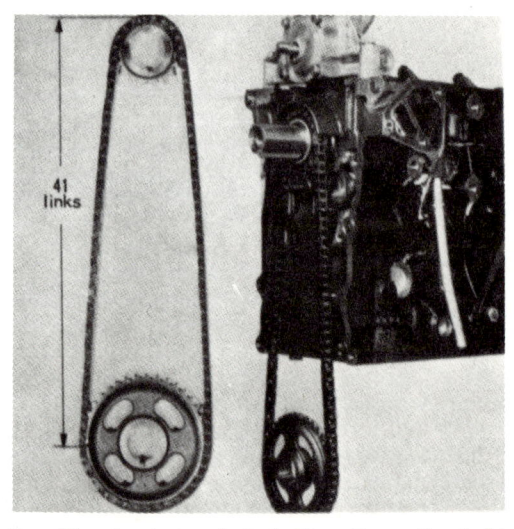

Installing the timing chain (© Toyo Kogyo Co., Ltd.)

14. Install the rocker arm shafts and cam bearing caps.
15. Install and torque the cylinder head bolts.
16. Adjust the timing chain tension. Press in on the chain guide strip. Tighten the guide strip attaching screws. Remove the screwdriver from the tensioner, allowing the snubber to take up the chain slack.
17. Replace the front cover.
18. Adjust the valve clearance cold.

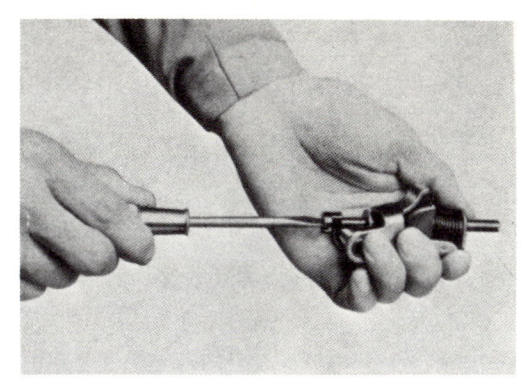

ENGINE AND ENGINE REBUILDING—B-1600 ONLY

Depressing the chain tensioner slide pin (© Toyo Kogyo Co., Ltd.)

Run the engine. Torque the cylinder head bolts and adjust the valve clearance hot.

TIMING CHAIN TENSIONER
Removal and Installation
FRONT COVER INSTALLED

1. Remove the water pump.
2. Remove the tensioner cover.
3. Remove the attaching bolts from the tensioner. Remove the tensioner.

To install the tensioner.

4. Fully compress the snubber spring. Insert a screwdriver into the tensioner release mechanism.
5. Without removing the screwdriver, insert the tensioner and align the bolt holes. Install and torque the bolts.
6. Adjust the chain tension as follows:
 a. Remove the two blind plugs and aluminum washers from the front cover.
 b. Loosen the guide strip attaching screws.
 c. Press the top of the chain guide strip through the adjusting hole in the cylinder head.
 d. Tighten the guide strip attaching screws.
 e. Remove the screwdriver from the tensioner and let the snubber take up the slack in the chain.
 f. Install the blind plugs and aluminum washers.
 g. Install the tensioner cover and gasket.
 h. Install a new gasket and water pump. Install the crankshaft pulley and drive belt and adjust the tension. Check the cooling system level.

Timing Chain Tensioner Adjustment

Perform Steps 1 and 4 through 6h of the preceding procedure.

CAMSHAFT
Removal and Installation

Perform this operation on a cold engine only.

1. Scribe alignment marks on the hood hinges and remove the hood.
2. Remove the water pump.
3. Disconnect the coil wire and vacuum line from the distributor.
4. Rotate the crankshaft to place the No. 1 cylinder on TDC of the compression stroke. This can be determined by removing the spark plug and feeling compression with your thumb. When compression is felt, rotate the crankshaft until the pointer aligns with the TDC mark on the pulley.
5. Remove the plug wires and distributor cap. Remove the distributor.
6. Remove the valve cover.
7. Release the tension on the timing chain.
8. Remove the cylinder head bolts. Only do this on a cold engine.
9. Remove the rocker arm assembly.
10. Remove the nut, washer and distributor gear from the camshaft.
11. Remove the nut and washer holding the camshaft gear.
12. Remove the camshaft. Do not remove the camshaft gear from the timing chain. Be sure that the gear teeth and chain relationship is not disturbed. Wire

Removing or installing the camshaft (© Toyo Kogyo Co., Ltd.)

ENGINE AND ENGINE REBUILDING—B-1600 ONLY

the chain and cam gear to a place so that they will not fall into the front cover.

To install the camshaft:

13. Clean all the gasket surfaces.
14. Clean the cylinder head bolt holes.
15. Install the camshaft on the head and install the camshaft gear.
16. Check the valve timing.
17. Install the rocker arm assembly.
18. Install and torque the head bolts.
19. Install the cam gear washer and nut.
20. Install the distributor gear, washer and nut.
21. Adjust the timing chain tension.
22. Check the camshaft end-play. It should be 0.001–0.007 in. If it exceeds 0.008 in., replace the thrust plate with a new one.

Checking the camshaft end-play (© Toyo Kogyo Co., Ltd.)

23. Install the distributor, distributor cap and plug wires.
24. Connect the vacuum line and coil wire.
25. Adjust the valve clearance cold. Install the valve cover and fill the cooling system.
26. Run the engine and check for leaks. When normal operating temperature is reached, adjust the hot valve clearance.
27. Adjust the carburetor and ignition timing.
28. Install the air cleaner and hood.

PISTONS AND CONNECTING RODS

Removal and Installation

In addition to the procedures below, refer to the "Engine Rebuilding" section for general engine service.

1. Drain the cooling system and the crankcase.
2. Remove the cylinder head.
3. Remove the oil pan.
4. Remove the oil pump inlet tube and the oil pump.
5. Turn the crankshaft until the piston to be removed is at the top of its travel. Place a cloth over the piston to protect it.
6. Using a ridge reamer, remove the ridge from the top of the cylinder. Never cut into the ring travel area in excess of $1/32$ in. when removing the ridges.
7. Be sure that all the connecting rod caps are marked so that they can be reinstalled in their original locations. If all the pistons are being removed, number the pistons as to which cylinder they came out of.
8. Remove the connecting rod cap.
9. Push the connecting rod and piston out of the cylinder with a wooden rod. Be careful not to scratch the connecting rod journal on the crankshaft or the cylinder wall.

To install the piston and rod:

10. Clean the oil pump inlet tube screen and the oil pan and block gasket surfaces.

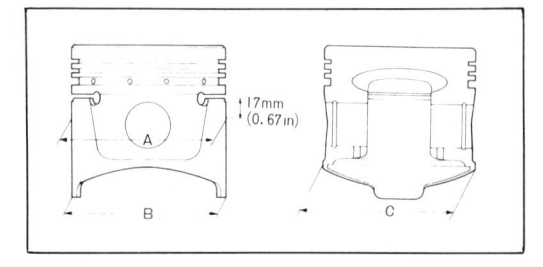

Piston measurements (© Toyo Kogyo Co., Ltd.)

11. Install the piston rings and check the gaps. Oil the piston rings, pistons and cylinder walls with light engine oil.
12. Install the piston(s) in the cylinder(s) from which they were removed, or fitted. The connecting rod bearing caps are numbered 1 through 4 beginning at the front of the engine. The numbers on the connecting rods and bearing caps must be on the same side when installed in the cylinder(s). If a connecting rod is ever transposed from one engine to another, new bearings should be installed and the rod renumbered to correspond with the new cylinder number.

ENGINE AND ENGINE REBUILDING—B-1600 ONLY

13. Make sure that the ring gaps are properly spaced around the piston. They should be placed so that the gaps are 120° apart and so that no gap is on the thrust side or on the piston pin side.

Installing the piston ring. The mark (inset) should face upward. (© Toyo Kogyo Co., Ltd.)

14. Install a ring compressor and push the piston into the cylinder until it is just below the top of the cylinder. Cover the connecting rod bolts with short pieces of rubber hose to protect the connecting rod journals. The piston should be installed so that the "F" in the piston head is toward the front of the engine.

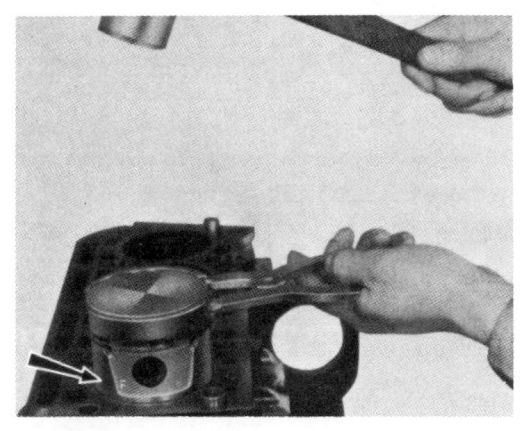

The "F" marks on the piston face the front of the engine (© Toyo Kogyo Co., Ltd.)

Piston and cylinder mating marks (© Toyo Kogyo Co., Ltd.)

Installing the connecting rod cap. Be sure that the numbers are on the same side. (© Toyo Kogyo Co., Ltd.)

15. Check the clearance of each bearing with Plastigage®.
16. Lightly coat the bearings and journals with engine oil.
17. Turn the crankshaft throw to the bottom of the stroke and push the piston all the way down until the connecting rod bearing seats on the journals. Install the connecting rod cap and torque the nuts to specifications.
18. Check the connecting rod side clearance on each crankshaft journal.

Checking connecting rod side-play (© Toyo Kogyo Co., Ltd.)

19. Prime and install the oil pump.
20. Install the oil pan and oil pump inlet tube.
21. Install the cylinder head. Adjust the valve clearance cold.
22. Fill the cooling system and crankcase.
23. Start the engine and check for oil pressure. Check for oil and coolant leaks.
24. When the engine temperature stabilizes, check and, if necessary, adjust the ignition timing. Adjust the idle speed and fuel mixture. Adjust the valve clearance hot.

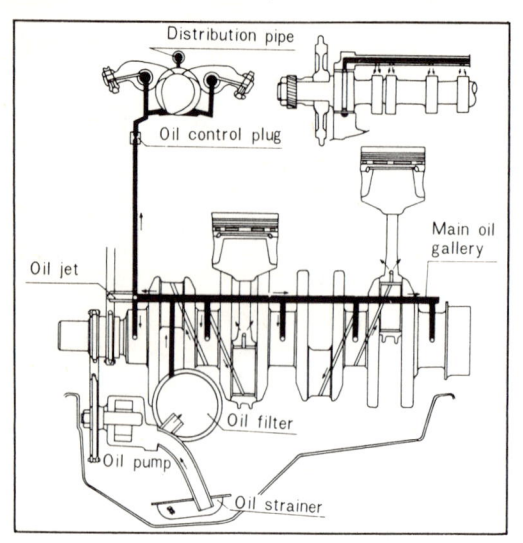

Engine lubrication schematic (© Toyo Kogyo Co., Ltd.)

Engine Lubrication

OIL PAN

Removal and Installation

1. Raise and support the truck.
2. Remove the engine skid plate.
3. Drain the engine oil.
4. Remove the clutch release cylinder attaching nuts. Let the cylinder hang.
5. Remove the engine rear brace attaching bolts and loosen the bolts on the left-side.
6. Disconnect the emission line from the oil pan.
7. Remove the oil pan nuts and bolts and let the oil pan rest on the crossmember.
8. Remove the oil pump pickup tube from the pump.
9. Remove the oil pan.
  To install the oil pan:
10. Clean all the gasket surfaces.
11. Clean the oil pan, oil pump pickup tube and oil pump screen.
12. Install a new oil pan gasket with oil-resistant sealer.
13. Install the oil pump pickup tube and screen.
14. Install the oil pan on the block. Torque the nuts and bolts to specifications.
15. Connect the emission line to the oil pan.
16. Attach the rear engine bracket. Torque the bolts to specifications.
17. Reinstall the clutch release cylinder. Torque the nuts to specifications.
18. Replace the engine skid plate.
19. Lower the truck. Fill the crankcase, and run the engine. Check for leaks and oil pressure.

REAR MAIN OIL SEAL

Replacement

If the rear main oil seal is being replaced independently of any other parts, it can be done with the engine in place. If the rear main oil seal and the rear main bearing are being replaced, together, the engine must be removed from the truck.

1. Remove the transmission.
2. Remove the clutch disc, pressure plate and flywheel.
3. Using an awl, punch two holes in the crankshaft rear oil seal. They should be punched on opposite sides of the crankshaft, just above the bearing cap-to-cylinder block split line.
4. Install a sheet metal screw in each hole. Pry against both screws at the same time to remove the oil seal. Do not scratch the oil seal surface on the crankshaft.
5. Clean the oil recess in the cylinder block and bearing cap. Clean the oil seal surface on the crankshaft.
6. Coat the oil seal surfaces with oil. Coat the oil surface and the seal surface on the crankshsaft with Lubriplate®. Install the oil seal and be sure that it is not cocked. Be sure that the seal surface was not damaged.
7. Install the flywheel. Coat the threads of the flywheel attaching bolts with oil-resistant sealer. Torque the bolts to specifications in sequence across from each other.
8. Install the clutch, pressure plate and transmission.

OIL PUMP

Removal and Installation

1. Remove the oil pan.
2. Remove the oil pump gear attaching nut.
3. Remove the bolts attaching the oil

ENGINE AND ENGINE REBUILDING—B-1600 ONLY

pump to the block. Loosen the gear on the pump.
4. Remove the oil pump and gear.

To install the oil pump:
5. Install the oil pump gear in the chain.

Installing the oil pump (© Toyo Kogyo Co., Ltd.)

6. Prime the oil pump and install it on the gear and cylinder block. Install the bolts and torque them to specifications.

7. Install the washer, gear and nut. Bend the locktab on the washer.
8. Install the oil pan. Fill the engine with oil. Start the engine and check for oil pressure. Check for leaks.

Engine Cooling

The completely sealed cooling system consists of a radiator with pressure cap, centrifugal water pump, thermostat and a fan.

RADIATOR

Removal and Installation

1. Drain the cooling system.
2. If equipped, remove the fan shroud.
3. Remove the fan. On California cars, remove the fan clutch.

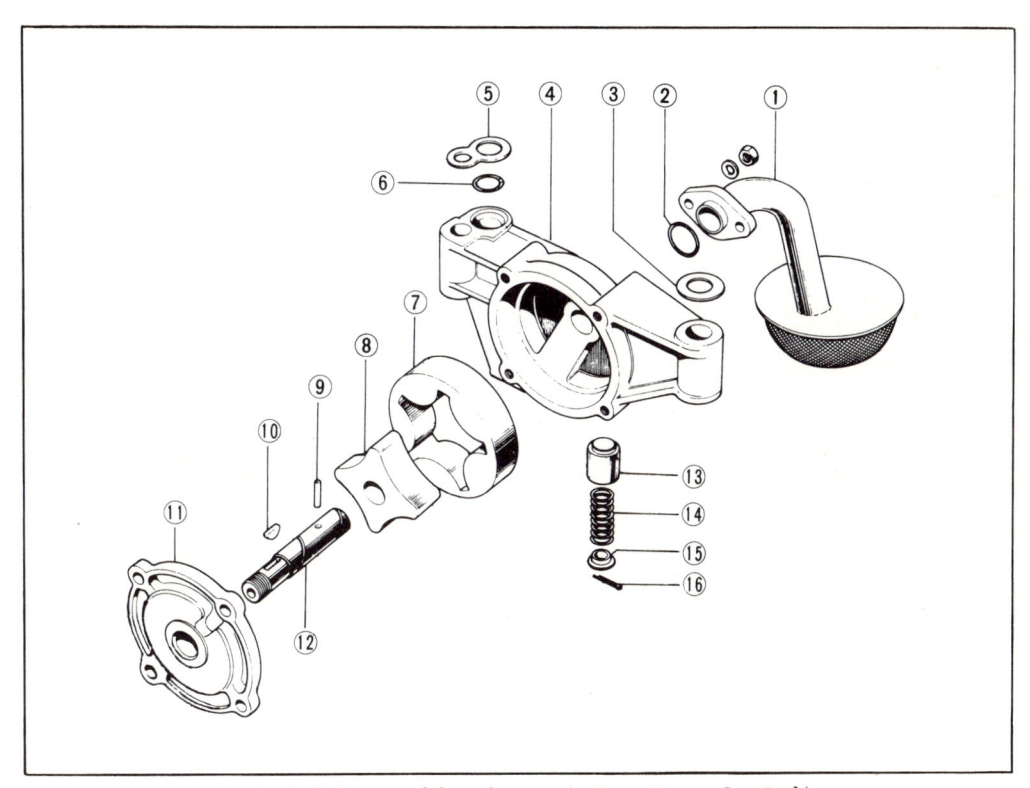

Exploded view of the oil pump (© Toyo Kogyo Co., Ltd.)

1. Oil strainer
2. O-ring
3. Adjusting shim
4. Body
5. Adjusting shim
6. O-ring
7. Outer rotor
8. Inner rotor
9. Pin
10. Key
11. Cover
12. Shaft
13. Plunger
14. Spring
15. Spring seat
16. Cotter pin

4. Disconnect the upper and lower radiator hoses.
5. Unbolt and remove the radiator.

To install the radiator:

6. Install the radiator against the supports and torque the mounting bolts to specifications.
7. Install the hoses on the radiator. Tighten the clamps.
8. Install the fan and fan clutch (California cars).
9. If equipped, install the fan shroud.
10. Refill the cooling system with the specified amount and type of coolant. Run the engine and check for leaks.

WATER PUMP

Removal and Installation

1. Scribe alignment marks on the hood hinges and remove the hood.
2. Drain the cooling system.
3. Remove the lower hose from the water pump.
4. Disconnect the upper radiator hose from the engine and the lower radiator hose at the radiator.
5. Remove the radiator.
6. Remove the drive belts.
7. Remove the fan and pulley. Remove the crankshaft pulley.
8. Unbolt and remove the water pump.

To install the water pump:

9. Clean the gasket surfaces of the water pump and cylinder block.
10. Install the water pump and new gasket on the block. Torque the bolts to specifications.
11. Install the lower hose on the water pump.
12. Install the fan and pulley. Install the crankshaft pulley.
13. Install the drive belts and adjust the tension.
14. Install the radiator.
15. Refill the cooling system with the specified amount and type of coolant. Install the radiator cap and start the engine. Check for leaks.
16. Install the hood.

THERMOSTAT

Removal and Installation

1. Drain enough coolant to bring the coolant level down below the thermostat housing. The thermostat housing is located on the left front side of the cylinder block. Disconnect the temperature sending unit wire.
2. Remove the coolant outlet elbow. If so equipped, position the vacuum control valve out of the way. The vacuum control valve is not used on California cars.
3. Disconnect the coolant by-pass hose from the thermostat housing.
4. Remove the thermostat and housing from the engine.
5. Remove the thermostat from the housing and note the position of the jiggle pin.

To install the thermostat:

6. Remove all gasket material from the parts.
7. Install the thermostat housing using a new gasket with water-resistant sealer.
8. Position the thermostat in the housing with the jiggle pin up. Coat a new gasket with sealer and install it on the thermostat housing.
9. Install the coolant outlet elbow and vacuum control valve (if equipped).
10. Connect the by-pass and radiator hoses.
11. Connect the temperature sending unit wire.
12. Fill the cooling system with the proper coolant. Operate the engine and check the coolant level. Check for leaks.

Engine Rebuilding

This section describes, in detail, the procedures involved in rebuilding a typical engine. The procedures specifically refer to an inline engine, however, they are basically identical to those used in rebuilding engines of nearly all design and configurations. Procedures for servicing atypical engines (i.e., horizontally opposed) are described in the appropriate section, although in most cases, cylinder head reconditioning procedures described in this chapter will apply.

The section is divided into two sections. The first, Cylinder Head Reconditioning, assumes that the cylinder head is removed from the engine, all manifolds are removed, and the cylinder head is on a workbench. The camshaft should be removed from overhead cam cylinder heads. The second section, Cylinder Block Reconditioning, covers the block, pistons, connecting rods and crankshaft. It is assumed that the engine is mounted on a work stand, and the cylinder head and all accessories are removed.

Procedures are identified as follows:

Unmarked—Basic procedures that must be performed in order to successfully complete the rebuilding process.

Starred (*)—Procedures that should be performed to ensure maximum performance and engine life.

Double starred (**)—Procedures that may be performed to increase engine performance and reliability. These procedures are usually reserved for extremely heavy-duty or competition usage.

In many cases, a choice of methods is also provided. Methods are identified in the same manner as procedures. The choice of method for a procedure is at the discretion of the user.

The tools required for the basic rebuilding procedure should, with minor exceptions, be those

TORQUE (ft. lbs.)*

U.S.

Bolt Diameter (inches)	Bolt Grade (SAE) 1 and 2	5	6	8	Wrench Size (inches) Bolt	Nut
1/4	5	7	10	10.5	3/8	7/16
5/16	9	14	19	22	1/2	9/16
3/8	15	25	34	37	9/16	5/8
7/16	24	40	55	60	5/8	3/4
1/2	37	60	85	92	3/4	13/16
9/16	53	88	120	132	7/8	7/8
5/8	74	120	167	180	15/16	1
3/4	120	200	280	296	1-1/8	1-1/8
7/8	190	302	440	473	1-5/16	1-5/16
1	282	466	660	714	1-1/2	1-1/2

Metric

Bolt Diameter (mm)	Bolt Grade 5D	8G	10K	12K	Wrench Size (mm) Bolt and Nut
6	5	6	8	10	10
8	10	16	22	27	14
10	19	31	40	49	17
12	34	54	70	86	19
14	55	89	117	137	22
16	83	132	175	208	24
18	111	182	236	283	27
22	182	284	394	464	32
24	261	419	570	689	36

*—Torque values are for lightly oiled bolts. CAUTION: Bolts threaded into aluminum require much less torque.

General Torque Specifications

ENGINE AND ENGINE REBUILDING—B-1600 ONLY

Heli-Coil installation
(© Chrysler Corp.)

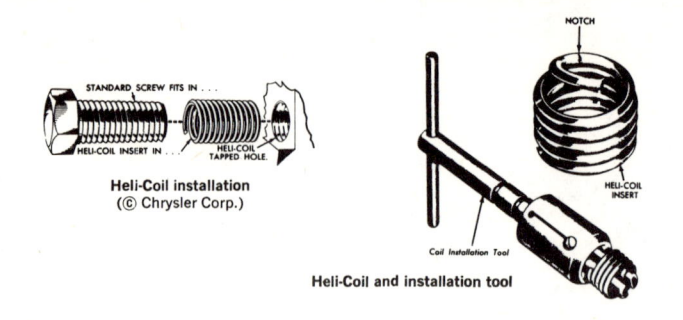

Heli-Coil and installation tool

Heli-Coil Specifications

Heli-Coil Insert Thread Size	Part No.	Insert Length (In.)	Drill Size	Tap Part No.	Insert Tool Part No.	Extracting Tool Part No.
1/2 -20	1185-4	3/8	17/64(.266)	4 CPB	528-4N	1227-6
5/16-18	1185-5	15/32	Q(.332)	5 CPB	528-5N	1227-6
3/8 -16	1185-6	9/16	X(.397)	6 CPB	528-6N	1227-6
7/16-14	1185-7	21/32	29/64(.453)	7 CPB	528-7N	1227-16
1/2 -13	1185-8	3/4	33/64(.516)	8 CPB	528-8N	1227-16

included in a mechanic's tool kit. An accurate torque wrench, and a dial indicator (reading in thousandths) mounted on a universal base should be available. Bolts and nuts with no torque specification should be tightened according to size (see chart). Special tools, where required, all are readily available from the major tool suppliers (i.e., Craftsman, Snap-On, K-D). The services of a competent automotive machine shop must also be readily available.

When assembling the engine, any parts that will be in frictional contact must be pre-lubricated, to provide protection until initial start-up. Vortex Pre-Lube, STP, or any product specifically formulated for this purpose may be used. NOTE: *Do not use engine oil.* Where semi-permanent (locked but removable) installation of bolts or nuts is desired, threads should be cleaned and coated with Loctite. Studs may be permanently installed using Loctite Stud and Bearing Mount.

Aluminum has become increasingly popular for use in engines, due to its low weight and excellent heat transfer characteristics. The following precautions must be observed when handling aluminum engine parts:

—Never hot-tank aluminum parts.

—Remove all aluminum parts (identification tags, etc.) from engine parts before hot-tanking (otherwise they will be removed during the process).

—Always coat threads lightly with engine oil or anti-seize compounds before installation, to prevent seizure.

—Never over-torque bolts or spark plugs in aluminum threads. Should stripping occur, threads can be restored according to the following procedure, using Heli-Coil thread inserts:

Tap drill the hole with the stripped threads to the specified size (see chart). Using the specified tap (NOTE: *Heli-Coil tap sizes refer to the size thread being replaced, rather than the actual tap size*), tap the hole for the Heli-Coil. Place the insert on the proper installation tool (see chart). Apply pressure on the insert while winding it clockwise into the hole, until the top of the insert is one turn below the surface. Remove the installation tool, and break the installation tang from the bottom of the insert by moving it up and down. If the Heli-Coil must be removed, tap the removal tool firmly into the hole, so that it engages the top thread, and turn the tool counter-clockwise to extract the insert.

Snapped bolts or studs may be removed, using a stud extractor (unthreaded) or Vise-Grip pliers (threaded). Penetrating oil (e.g., Liquid Wrench) will often aid in breaking frozen threads. In cases where the stud or bolt is flush with, or below the surface, proceed as follows:

Drill a hole in the broken stud or bolt, approximately 1/2 its diameter. Select a screw extractor (e.g., Easy-Out) of the proper size, and tap it into the stud or bolt. Turn the extractor counter-clockwise to remove the stud or bolt.

Magnaflux and Zyglo are inspection techniques used to locate material flaws, such as stress cracks. Magnafluxing coats the part with fine magnetic particles, and subjects the part to a magnetic field. Cracks cause breaks

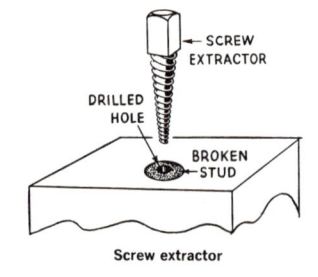

Screw extractor

in the magnetic field, which are outlined by the particles. Since Magnaflux is a magnetic process, it is applicable only to ferrous materials. The Zyglo process coats the material with a fluorescent dye penetrant, and then subjects it to blacklight inspection, under which cracks glow bright-

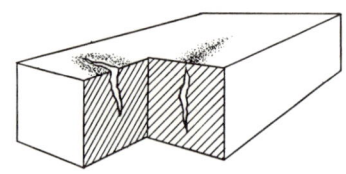

Magnaflux indication of cracks

ENGINE AND ENGINE REBUILDING—B-1600 ONLY

ly. Parts made of any material may be tested using Zyglo. While Magnaflux and Zyglo are excellent for general inspection, and locating hidden defects, specific checks of suspected cracks may be made at lower cost and more readily using spot check dye. The dye is sprayed onto the suspected area, wiped off, and the area is then sprayed with a developer. Cracks then will show up brightly. Spot check dyes will only indicate surface cracks; therefore, structural cracks below the surface may escape detection. When questionable, the part should be tested using Magnaflux or Zyglo.

CYLINDER HEAD RECONDITIONING

Procedure	Method
Identify the valves: *Valve identification* (© SAAB)	Invert the cylinder head, and number the valve faces front to rear, using a permanent felt-tip marker.
Remove the rocker arms:	Remove the rocker arms with shaft(s) or balls and nuts. Wire the sets of rockers, balls and nuts together, and identify according to the corresponding valve.
Remove the valves and springs:	Using an appropriate valve spring compressor (depending on the configuration of the cylinder head), compress the valve springs. Lift out the keepers with needlenose pliers, release the compressor, and remove the valve, spring, and spring retainer.
Check the valve stem-to-guide clearance: *Checking the valve stem-to-guide clearance* (© American Motors Corp.)	Clean the valve stem with lacquer thinner or a similar solvent to remove all gum and varnish. Clean the valve guides using solvent and an expanding wire-type valve guide cleaner. Mount a dial indicator so that the stem is at 90° to the valve stem, as close to the valve guide as possible. Move the valve off its seat, and measure the valve guide-to-stem clearance by moving the stem back and forth to actuate the dial indicator. Measure the valve stems using a micrometer, and compare to specifications, to determine whether stem or guide wear is responsible for excessive clearance.
De-carbon the cylinder head and valves: *Removing carbon from the cylinder head* (© Chevrolet Div. G.M. Corp.)	Chip carbon away from the valve heads, combustion chambers, and ports, using a chisel made of hardwood. Remove the remaining deposits with a stiff wire brush. NOTE: *Ensure that the deposits are actually removed, rather than burnished.*

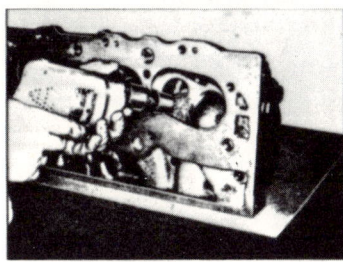

ENGINE AND ENGINE REBUILDING—B-1600 ONLY

Procedure	Method
Hot-tank the cylinder head:	Have the cylinder head hot-tanked to remove grease, corrosion, and scale from the water passages. NOTE: *In the case of overhead cam cylinder heads, consult the operator to determine whether the camshaft bearings will be damaged by the caustic solution.*
Degrease the remaining cylinder head parts:	Using solvent (i.e., Gunk), clean the rockers, rocker shaft(s) (where applicable), rocker balls and nuts, springs, spring retainers, and keepers. Do not remove the protective coating from the springs.
Check the cylinder head for warpage: Checking the cylinder head for warpage (© Ford Motor Co.)	Place a straight-edge across the gasket surface of the cylinder head. Using feeler gauges, determine the clearance at the center of the straight-edge. Measure across both diagonals, along the longitudinal centerline, and across the cylinder head at several points. If warpage exceeds .003″ in a 6″ span, or .006″ over the total length, the cylinder head must be resurfaced. NOTE: *If warpage exceeds the manufacturers maximum tolerance for material removal, the cylinder head must be replaced.* When milling the cylinder heads of V-type engines, the intake manifold mounting position is altered, and must be corrected by milling the manifold flange a proportionate amount.
** Porting and gasket matching: Marking the cylinder head for gasket matching (© Petersen Publishing Co.) Port configuration before and after gasket matching (© Petersen Publishing Co.)	** Coat the manifold flanges of the cylinder head with Prussian blue dye. Glue intake and exhaust gaskets to the cylinder head in their installed position using rubber cement and scribe the outline of the ports on the manifold flanges. Remove the gaskets. Using a small cutter in a hand-held power tool (i.e., Dremel Moto-Tool), gradually taper the walls of the port out to the scribed outline of the gasket. Further enlargement of the ports should include the removal of sharp edges and radiusing of sharp corners. Do not alter the valve guides. NOTE: *The most efficient port configuration is determined only by extensive testing. Therefore, it is best to consult someone experienced with the head in question to determine the optimum alterations.*

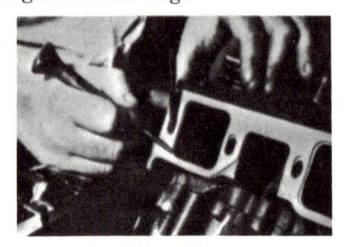

ENGINE AND ENGINE REBUILDING—B-1600 ONLY

Procedure	Method
** Polish the ports: *Relieved and polished ports* (© Petersen Publishing Co.) *Polished combustion chamber* (© Petersen Publishing Co.)	** Using a grinding stone with the above mentioned tool, polish the walls of the intake and exhaust ports, and combustion chamber. Use progressively finer stones until all surface imperfections are removed. NOTE: *Through testing, it has been determined that a smooth surface is more effective than a mirror polished surface in intake ports, and vice-versa in exhaust ports.*
* Knurling the valve guides: *Cut-away view of a knurled valve guide* (© Petersen Publishing Co.)	* Valve guides which are not excessively worn or distorted may, in some cases, be knurled rather than replaced. Knurling is a process in which metal is displaced and raised, thereby reducing clearance. Knurling also provides excellent oil control. The possibility of knurling rather than replacing valve guides should be discussed with a machinist.
Replacing the valve guides: NOTE: *Valve guides should only be replaced if damaged or if an oversize valve stem is not available.* A-VALVE GUIDE I.D. B-SLIGHTLY SMALLER THAN VALVE GUIDE O.D. **Valve guide removal tool** WASHERS A-VALVE GUIDE I.D. B-LARGER THAN THE VALVE GUIDE O.D. **Valve guide installation tool (with washers used during installation)**	Depending on the type of cylinder head, valve guides may be pressed, hammered, or shrunk in. In cases where the guides are shrunk into the head, replacement should be left to an equipped machine shop. In other cases, the guides are replaced as follows: Press or tap the valve guides out of the head using a stepped drift (see illustration). Determine the height above the boss that the guide must extend, and obtain a stack of washers, their I.D. similar to the guide's O.D., of that height. Place the stack of washers on the guide, and insert the guide into the boss. NOTE: *Valve guides are often tapered or beveled for installation.* Using the stepped installation tool (see illustration), press or tap the guides into position. Ream the guides according to the size of the valve stem.

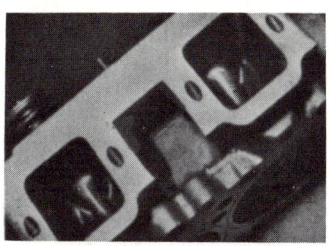

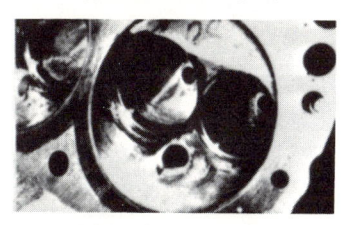

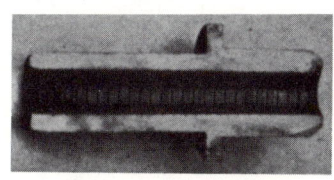

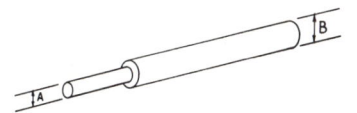

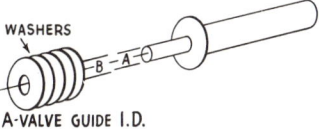

ENGINE AND ENGINE REBUILDING—B-1600 ONLY

Procedure	Method
Replacing valve seat inserts:	Replacement of valve seat inserts which are worn beyond resurfacing or broken, if feasible, must be done by a machine shop.
Resurfacing (grinding) the valve face: *Grinding a valve (© Subaru)* *Critical valve dimensions (© Ford Motor Co.)*	Using a valve grinder, resurface the valves according to specifications. CAUTION: *Valve face angle is not always identical to valve seat angle.* A minimum margin of 1/32" should remain after grinding the valve. The valve stem tip should also be squared and resurfaced, by placing the stem in the V-block of the grinder, and turning it while pressing lightly against the grinding wheel.
Resurfacing the valve seats using reamers: *Reaming the valve seat (© S.p.A. Fiat)* *Valve seat width and centering (© Ford Motor Co.)*	Select a reamer of the correct seat angle, slightly larger than the diameter of the valve seat, and assemble it with a pilot of the correct size. Install the pilot into the valve guide, and using steady pressure, turn the reamer clockwise. CAUTION: *Do not turn the reamer counter-clockwise.* Remove only as much material as necessary to clean the seat. Check the concentricity of the seat (see below). If the dye method is not used, coat the valve face with Prussian blue dye, install and rotate it on the valve seat. Using the dye marked area as a centering guide, center and narrow the valve seat to specifications with correction cutters. NOTE: *When no specifications are available, minimum seat width for exhaust valves should be 5/64", intake valves 1/16".* After making correction cuts, check the position of the valve seat on the valve face using Prussian blue dye.
* Resurfacing the valve seats using a grinder: *Grinding a valve seat (© Subaru)*	Select a pilot of the correct size, and a coarse stone of the correct seat angle. Lubricate the pilot if necessary, and install the tool in the valve guide. Move the stone on and off the seat at approximately two cycles per second, until all flaws are removed from the seat. Install a fine stone, and finish the seat. Center and narrow the seat using correction stones, as described above.

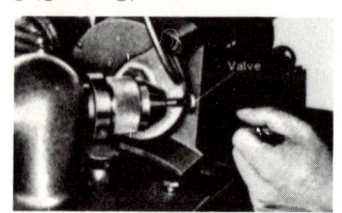

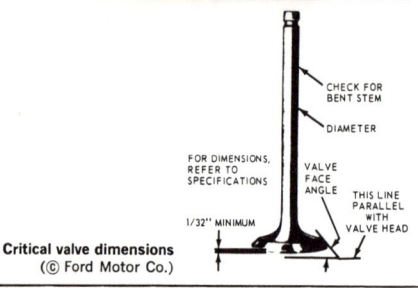

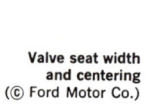

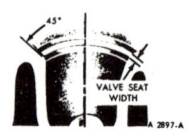

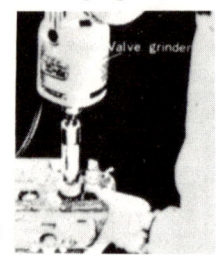

ENGINE AND ENGINE REBUILDING—B-1600 ONLY

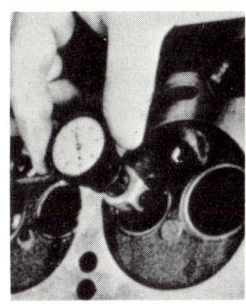

Procedure	Method
Checking the valve seat concentricity:	Coat the valve face with Prussian blue dye, install the valve, and rotate it on the valve seat. If the entire seat becomes coated, and the valve is known to be concentric, the seat is concentric.
Checking the valve seat concentricity using a dial gauge (© American Motors Corp.)	* Install the dial gauge pilot into the guide, and rest the arm on the valve seat. Zero the gauge, and rotate the arm around the seat. Run-out should not exceed .002″.
* Lapping the valves: NOTE: *Valve lapping is done to ensure efficient sealing of resurfaced valves and seats. Valve lapping alone is not recommended for use as a resurfacing procedure.*	* Invert the cylinder head, lightly lubricate the valve stems, and install the valves in the head as numbered. Coat valve seats with fine grinding compound, and attach the lapping tool suction cup to a valve head (NOTE: *Moisten the suction cup*). Rotate the tool between the palms, changing position and lifting the tool often to prevent grooving. Lap the valve until a smooth, polished seat is evident. Remove the valve and tool, and rinse away all traces of grinding compound.
Hand lapping the valves	** Fasten a suction cup to a piece of drill rod, and mount the rod in a hand drill. Proceed as above, using the hand drill as a lapping tool. CAUTION: *Due to the higher speeds involved when using the hand drill, care must be exercised to avoid grooving the seat.* Lift the tool and change direction of rotation often.
Home made mechanical valve lapping tool	
Check the valve springs:	Place the spring on a flat surface next to a square. Measure the height of the spring, and rotate it against the edge of the square to measure distortion. If spring height varies (by comparison) by more than 1/16″ or if distortion exceeds 1/16″, replace the spring.
Checking the valve spring free length and squareness (© Ford Motor Co.) Checking the valve spring tension (© Chrysler Corp.)	** In addition to evaluating the spring as above, test the spring pressure at the installed and compressed (installed height minus valve lift) height using a valve spring tester. Springs used on small displacement engines (up to 3 liters) should be ± 1 lb. of all other springs in either position. A tolerance of ± 5 lbs. is permissible on larger engines.

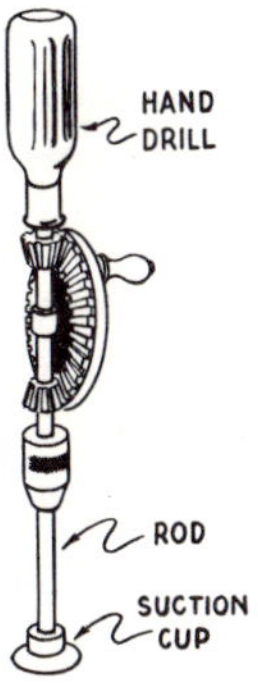

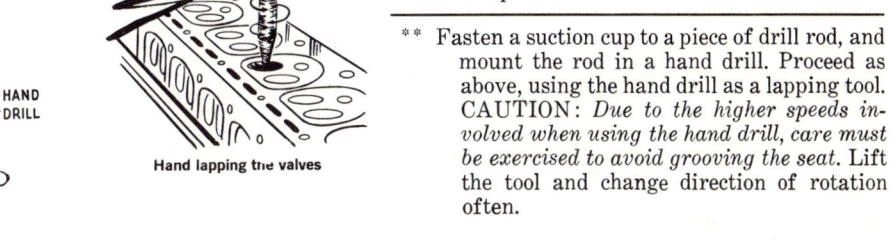

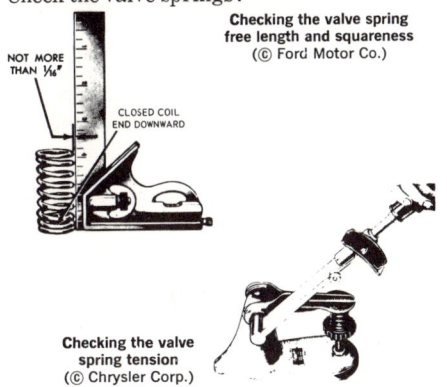

ENGINE AND ENGINE REBUILDING—B-1600 ONLY

Procedure	Method
* Install valve stem seals: 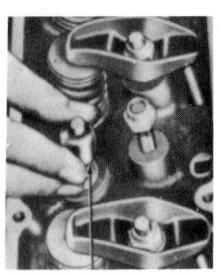 *Valve stem seal installation* (© Ford Motor Co.) SEAL	* Due to the pressure differential that exists at the ends of the intake valve guides (atmospheric pressure above, manifold vacuum below), oil is drawn through the valve guides into the intake port. This has been alleviated somewhat since the addition of positive crankcase ventilation, which lowers the pressure above the guides. Several types of valve stem seals are available to reduce blow-by. Certain seals simply slip over the stem and guide boss, while others require that the boss be machined. Recently, Teflon guide seals have become popular. Consult a parts supplier or machinist concerning availability and suggested usages. NOTE: *When installing seals, ensure that a small amount of oil is able to pass the seal to lubricate the valve guides; otherwise, excessive wear may result.*
Install the valves:	Lubricate the valve stems, and install the valves in the cylinder head as numbered. Lubricate and position the seals (if used, see above) and the valve springs. Install the spring retainers, compress the springs, and insert the keys using needlenose pliers or a tool designed for this purpose. NOTE: *Retain the keys with wheel bearing grease during installation.*
Checking valve spring installed height: 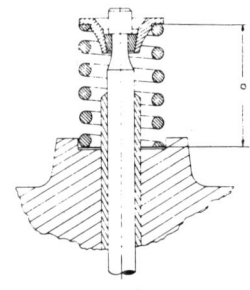 *Valve spring installed height dimension* (© Porsche) 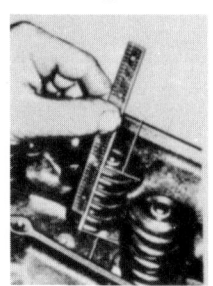 *Measuring valve spring installed height* (© Petersen Publishing Co.)	Measure the distance between the spring pad and the lower edge of the spring retainer, and compare to specifications. If the installed height is incorrect, add shim washers between the spring pad and the spring. CAUTION: *Use only washers designed for this purpose.*
** CC'ing the combustion chambers:	** Invert the cylinder head and place a bead of sealer around a combustion chamber. Install an apparatus designed for this purpose (burette mounted on a clear plate; see illustration) over the combustion chamber, and fill with the specified fluid to an even mark on the burette. Record the burette reading, and fill the combustion chamber with fluid. (NOTE: *A hole drilled in the plate will permit air to escape*). Subtract the burette reading, with the combustion chamber filled, from the previous reading, to determine combustion chamber volume in cc's. Duplicate this procedure in all combustion

ENGINE AND ENGINE REBUILDING—B-1600 ONLY 63

Procedure	Method
 **CC'ing the combustion chamber** (© Petersen Publishing Co.)	chambers on the cylinder head, and compare the readings. The volume of all combustion chambers should be made equal to that of the largest. Combustion chamber volume may be increased in two ways. When only a small change is required (usually), a small cutter or coarse stone may be used to remove material from the combustion chamber. NOTE: *Check volume frequently.* Remove material over a wide area, so as not to change the configuration of the combustion chamber. When a larger change is required, the valve seat may be sunk (lowered into the head). NOTE: *When altering valve seat, remember to compensate for the change in spring installed height.*
Inspect the rocker arms, balls, studs, and nuts (where applicable): **Stress cracks in rocker nuts** (© Ford Motor Co.) SMALL FRACTURES	Visually inspect the rocker arms, balls, studs, and nuts for cracks, galling, burning, scoring, or wear. If all parts are intact, liberally lubricate the rocker arms and balls, and install them on the cylinder head. If wear is noted on a rocker arm at the point of valve contact, grind it smooth and square, removing as little material as possible. Replace the rocker arm if excessively worn. If a rocker stud shows signs of wear, it must be replaced (see below). If a rocker nut shows stress cracks, replace it. If an exhaust ball is galled or burned, substitute the intake ball from the same cylinder (if it is intact), and install a new intake ball. NOTE: *Avoid using new rocker balls on exhaust valves.*
Replacing rocker studs: **Reaming the stud bore for oversize rocker studs** (© Buick Div. G.M. Corp.) **Extracting a pressed in rocker stud** (© Buick Div. G.M. Corp.)	In order to remove a threaded stud, lock two nuts on the stud, and unscrew the stud using the lower nut. Coat the lower threads of the new stud with Loctite, and install. Two alternative methods are available for replacing pressed in studs. Remove the damaged stud using a stack of washers and a nut (see illustration). In the first, the boss is reamed .005-.006" oversize, and an oversize stud pressed in. Control the stud extension over the boss using washers, in the same manner as valve guides. Before installing the stud, coat it with white lead and grease. To retain the stud more positively, drill a hole through the stud and boss, and install a roll pin. In the second method, the boss is tapped, and a threaded stud installed. Retain the stud using Loctite Stud and Bearing Mount.

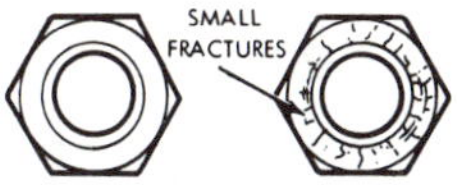

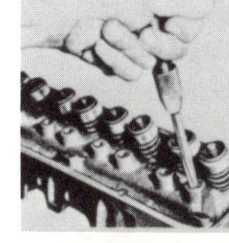

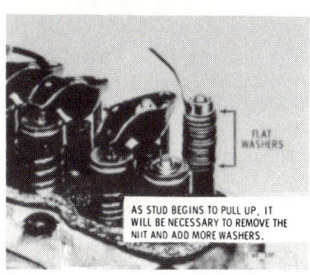

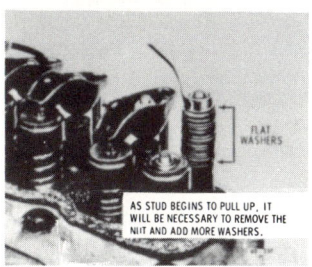

64 ENGINE AND ENGINE REBUILDING—B-1600 ONLY

Procedure	Method
Inspect the rocker shaft(s) and rocker arms (where applicable):  *Disassembled rocker shaft parts arranged for inspection* (© American Motors Corp.) 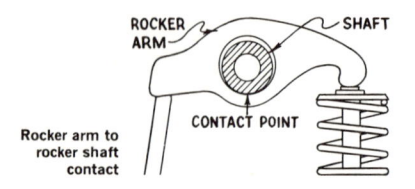 *Rocker arm to rocker shaft contact*	Remove rocker arms, springs and washers from rocker shaft. NOTE: *Lay out parts in the order they are removed.* Inspect rocker arms for pitting or wear on the valve contact point, or excessive bushing wear. Bushings need only be replaced if wear is excessive, because the rocker arm normally contacts the shaft at one point only. Grind the valve contact point of rocker arm smooth if necessary, removing as little material as possible. If excessive material must be removed to smooth and square the arm, it should be replaced. Clean out all oil holes and passages in rocker shaft. If shaft is grooved or worn, replace it. Lubricate and assemble the rocker shaft.
Inspect the camshaft bushings and the camshaft (overhead cam engines):	See next section.
Inspect the pushrods:	Remove the pushrods, and, if hollow, clean out the oil passages using fine wire. Roll each pushrod over a piece of clean glass. If a distinct clicking sound is heard as the pushrod rolls, the rod is bent, and must be replaced.
	* The length of all pushrods must be equal. Measure the length of the pushrods, compare to specifications, and replace as necessary.
Inspect the valve lifters: *Checking the lifter face* (© American Motors Corp.)	Remove lifters from their bores, and remove gum and varnish, using solvent. Clean walls of lifter bores. Check lifters for concave wear as illustrated. If face is worn concave, replace lifter, and carefully inspect the camshaft. Lightly lubricate lifter and insert it into its bore. If play is excessive, an oversize lifter must be installed (where possible). Consult a machinist concerning feasibility. If play is satisfactory, remove, lubricate, and reinstall the lifter.
* Testing hydraulic lifter leak down: 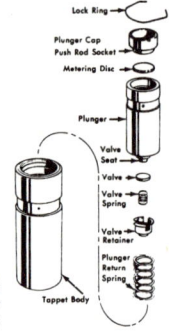 *Exploded view of a typical hydraulic lifter* (© American Motors Corp.)	Submerge lifter in a container of kerosene. Chuck a used pushrod or its equivalent into a drill press. Position container of kerosene so pushrod acts on the lifter plunger. Pump lifter with the drill press, until resistance increases. Pump several more times to bleed any air out of lifter. Apply very firm, constant pressure to the lifter, and observe rate at which fluid bleeds out of lifter. If the fluid bleeds very quickly (less than 15 seconds), lifter is defective. If the time exceeds 60 seconds, lifter is sticking. In either case, recondition or replace lifter. If lifter is operating properly (leak down time 15-60 seconds), lubricate and install it.

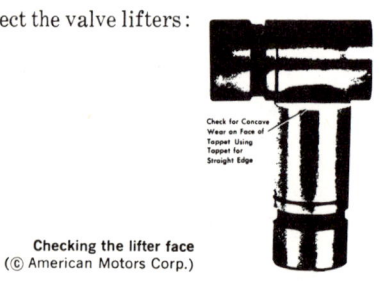

ENGINE AND ENGINE REBUILDING—B-1600 ONLY

CYLINDER BLOCK RECONDITIONING

Procedure	Method
Checking the main bearing clearance: *Plastigage installed on main bearing journal* (© Chevrolet Div. G.M. Corp.) *Measuring Plastigage to determine main bearing clearance* (© Chevrolet Div. G.M. Corp.) *Causes of bearing failure* (© Ford Motor Co.)	Invert engine, and remove cap from the bearing to be checked. Using a clean, dry rag, thoroughly clean all oil from crankshaft journal and bearing insert. NOTE: *Plastigage is soluble in oil; therefore, oil on the journal or bearing could result in erroneous readings.* Place a piece of Plastigage along the full length of journal, reinstall cap, and torque to specifications. Remove bearing cap, and determine bearing clearance by comparing width of Plastigage to the scale on Plastigage envelope. Journal taper is determined by comparing width of the Plastigage strip near its ends. Rotate crankshaft 90° and retest, to determine journal eccentricity. NOTE: *Do not rotate crankshaft with Plastigage installed.* If bearing insert and journal appear intact, and are within tolerances, no further main bearing service is required. If bearing or journal appear defective, cause of failure should be determined before replacement. * Remove crankshaft from block (see below). Measure the main bearing journals at each end twice (90° apart) using a micrometer, to determine diameter, journal taper and eccentricity. If journals are within tolerances, reinstall bearing caps at their specified torque. Using a telescope gauge and micrometer, measure bearing I.D. parallel to piston axis and at 30° on each side of piston axis. Subtract journal O.D. from bearing I.D. to determine oil clearance. If crankshaft journals appear defective, or do not meet tolerances, there is no need to measure bearings; for the crankshaft will require grinding and/or undersize bearings will be required. If bearing appears defective, cause for failure should be determined prior to replacement.
Checking the connecting rod bearing clearance: *Plastigage installed on connecting rod bearing journal* (© Chevrolet Div. G.M. Corp.)	Connecting rod bearing clearance is checked in the same manner as main bearing clearance, using Plastigage. Before removing the crankshaft, connecting rod side clearance also should be measured and recorded. * Checking connecting rod bearing clearance, using a micrometer, is identical to checking main bearing clearance. If no other service

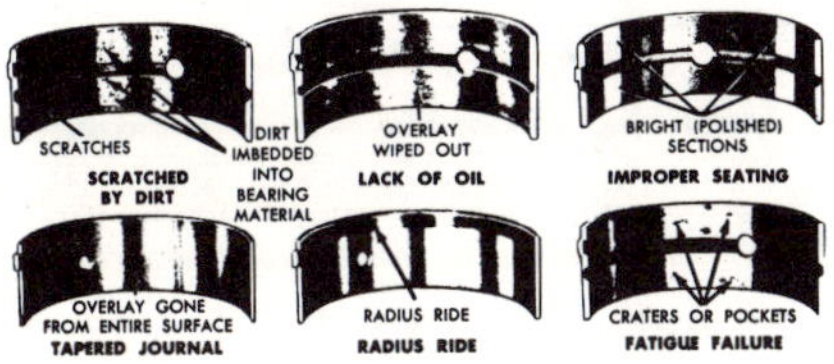

ENGINE AND ENGINE REBUILDING—B-1600 ONLY

Procedure	Method
 *Measuring Plastigage to determine connecting rod bearing clearance* (© Chevrolet Div. G.M. Corp.)	is required, the piston and rod assemblies need not be removed.
Removing the crankshaft:  *Connecting rod matching marks* (© Ford Motor Co.)	Using a punch, mark the corresponding main bearing caps and saddles according to position (i.e., one punch on the front main cap and saddle, two on the second, three on the third, etc.). Using number stamps, identify the corresponding connecting rods and caps, according to cylinder (if no numbers are present). Remove the main and connecting rod caps, and place sleeves of plastic tubing over the connecting rod bolts, to protect the journals as the crankshaft is removed. Lift the crankshaft out of the block.
Remove the ridge from the top of the cylinder: 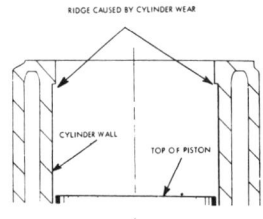 *Cylinder bore ridge* (© Pontiac Div. G.M. Corp.)	In order to facilitate removal of the piston and connecting rod, the ridge at the top of the cylinder (unworn area; see illustration) must be removed. Place the piston at the bottom of the bore, and cover it with a rag. Cut the ridge away using a ridge reamer, exercising extreme care to avoid cutting too deeply. Remove the rag, and remove cuttings that remain on the piston. CAUTION: *If the ridge is not removed, and new rings are installed, damage to rings will result.*
Removing the piston and connecting rod:  *Removing the piston* (© SAAB)	Invert the engine, and push the pistons and connecting rods out of the cylinders. If necessary, tap the connecting rod boss with a wooden hammer handle, to force the piston out. CAUTION: *Do not attempt to force the piston past the cylinder ridge* (see above).

ENGINE AND ENGINE REBUILDING—B-1600 ONLY

Procedure	Method
Service the crankshaft:	Ensure that all oil holes and passages in the crankshaft are open and free of sludge. If necessary, have the crankshaft ground to the largest possible undersize.
	** Have the crankshaft Magnafluxed, to locate stress cracks. Consult a machinist concerning additional service procedures, such as surface hardening (e.g., nitriding, Tuftriding) to improve wear characteristics, cross drilling and chamfering the oil holes to improve lubrication, and balancing.
Removing freeze plugs:	Drill a hole in the center of the freeze plugs, and pry them out using a screwdriver or drift.
Remove the oil gallery plugs:	Threaded plugs should be removed using an appropriate (usually square) wrench. To remove soft, pressed in plugs, drill a hole in the plug, and thread in a sheet metal screw. Pull the plug out by the screw using pliers.
Hot-tank the block:	Have the block hot-tanked to remove grease, corrosion, and scale from the water jackets. NOTE: *Consult the operator to determine whether the camshaft bearings will be damaged during the hot-tank process.*
Check the block for cracks:	Visually inspect the block for cracks or chips. The most common locations are as follows: Adjacent to freeze plugs. Between the cylinders and water jackets. Adjacent to the main bearing saddles. At the extreme bottom of the cylinders. Check only suspected cracks using spot check dye (see introduction). If a crack is located, consult a machinist concerning possible repairs.
	** Magnaflux the block to locate hidden cracks. If cracks are located, consult a machinist about feasibility of repair.
Install the oil gallery plugs and freeze plugs:	Coat freeze plugs with sealer and tap into position using a piece of pipe, slightly smaller than the plug, as a driver. To ensure retention, stake the edges of the plugs. Coat threaded oil gallery plugs with sealer and install. Drive replacement soft plugs into block using a large drift as a driver.
	* Rather than reinstalling lead plugs, drill and tap the holes, and install threaded plugs.

ENGINE AND ENGINE REBUILDING—B-1600 ONLY

Procedure	Method
Check the bore diameter and surface:	Visually inspect the cylinder bores for roughness, scoring, or scuffing. If evident, the cylinder bore must be bored or honed oversize to eliminate imperfections, and the smallest possible oversize piston used. The new pistons should be given to the machinist with the block, so that the cylinders can be bored or honed exactly to the piston size (plus clearance). If no flaws are evident, measure the bore diameter using a telescope gauge and micrometer, or dial gauge, parallel and perpendicular to the engine centerline, at the top (below the ridge) and bottom of the bore. Subtract the bottom measurements from the top to determine taper, and the parallel to the centerline measurements from the perpendicular measurements to determine eccentricity. If the measurements are not within specifications, the cylinder must be bored or honed, and an oversize piston installed. If the measurements are within specifications the cylinder may be used as is, with only finish honing (see below). NOTE: *Prior to submitting the block for boring, perform the following operation(s).*

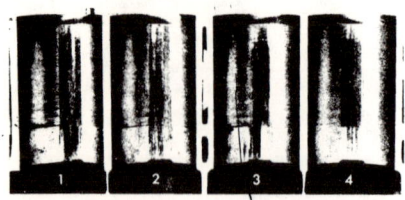

1, 2, 3 Piston skirt seizure resulted in this pattern. Engine must be rebored

4. Piston skirt and oil ring seizure caused this damage. Engine must be rebored

5, 6 Score marks caused by a split piston skirt. Damage is not serious enough to warrant reboring

7. Ring seized longitudinally, causing a score mark 1 3/16" wide, on the land side of the piston groove. The honing pattern is destroyed and the cylinder must be rebored

8. Result of oil ring seizure. Engine must be rebored

9. Oil ring seizure here was not serious enough to warrant reboring. The honing marks are still visible

Cylinder wall damage
(© Daimler-Benz A.G.)

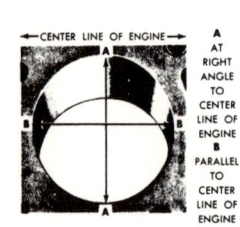

Cylinder bore measuring positions
(© Ford Motor Co.)

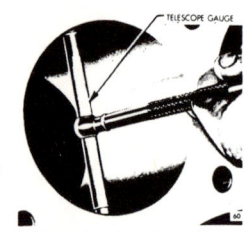

Measuring the cylinder bore with a telescope gauge
(© Buick Div. G.M. Corp.)

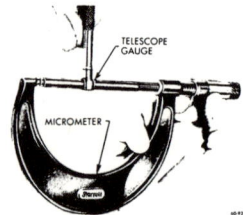

Determining the cylinder bore by measuring the telescope gauge with a micrometer
(© Buick Div. G.M. Corp.)

Measuring the cylinder bore with a dial gauge
(© Chevrolet Div. G.M. Corp.)

ENGINE AND ENGINE REBUILDING—B-1600 ONLY

Procedure	Method
Check the block deck for warpage:	Using a straightedge and feeler gauges, check the block deck for warpage in the same manner that the cylinder head is checked (see Cylinder Head Reconditioning). If warpage exceeds specifications, have the deck resurfaced. NOTE: *In certain cases a specification for total material removal (Cylinder head and block deck) is provided. This specification must not be exceeded.*
* Check the deck height:	The deck height is the distance from the crankshaft centerline to the block deck. To measure, invert the engine, and install the crankshaft, retaining it with the center main cap. Measure the distance from the crankshaft journal to the block deck, parallel to the cylinder centerline. Measure the diameter of the end (front and rear) main journals, parallel to the centerline of the cylinders, divide the diameter in half, and subtract it from the previous measurement. The results of the front and rear measurements should be identical. If the difference exceeds .005″, the deck height should be corrected. NOTE: *Block deck height and warpage should be corrected concurrently.*
Check the cylinder block bearing alignment: 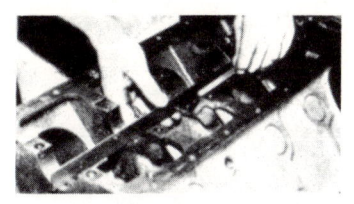 **Checking main bearing saddle alignment** (© Petersen Publishing Co.)	Remove the upper bearing inserts. Place a straightedge in the bearing saddles along the centerline of the crankshaft. If clearance exists between the straightedge and the center saddle, the block must be align-bored.
Clean and inspect the pistons and connecting rods: 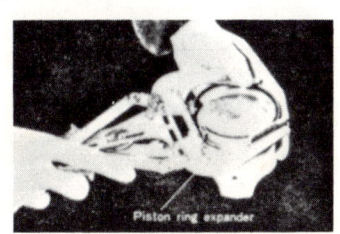 **Removing the piston rings** (© Subaru)	Using a ring expander, remove the rings from the piston. Remove the retaining rings (if so equipped) and remove piston pin. NOTE: *If the piston pin must be pressed out, determine the proper method and use the proper tools; otherwise the piston will distort.* Clean the ring grooves using an appropriate tool, exercising care to avoid cutting too deeply. Thoroughly clean all carbon and varnish from the piston with solvent. CAUTION: *Do not use a wire brush or caustic solvent on pistons.* Inspect the pistons for scuffing, scoring, cracks, pitting, or excessive ring groove wear. If wear is evident, the piston must be replaced. Check the connecting rod length by measuring the rod from the inside of the large end to the inside of the small end using calipers (see

ENGINE AND ENGINE REBUILDING—B-1600 ONLY

Procedure	Method
Cleaning the piston ring grooves (© Ford Motor Co.) *Connecting rod length checking dimension*	illustration). All connecting rods should be equal length. Replace any rod that differs from the others in the engine. * Have the connecting rod alignment checked in an alignment fixture by a machinist. Replace any twisted or bent rods. * Magnaflux the connecting rods to locate stress cracks. If cracks are found, replace the connecting rod.
Fit the pistons to the cylinders: *Measuring the cylinder with a telescope gauge for piston fitting* (© Buick Div. G.M. Corp.) *Measuring the piston for fitting* (© Buick Div. G.M. Corp.)	Using a telescope gauge and micrometer, or a dial gauge, measure the cylinder bore diameter perpendicular to the piston pin, $2\frac{1}{2}''$ below the deck. Measure the piston perpendicular to its pin on the skirt. The difference between the two measurements is the piston clearance. If the clearance is within specifications or slightly below (after boring or honing), finish honing is all that is required. If the clearance is excessive, try to obtain a slightly larger piston to bring clearance within specifications. Where this is not possible, obtain the first oversize piston, and hone (or if necessary, bore) the cylinder to size.
Assemble the pistons and connecting rods: *Installing piston pin lock rings* (© Nissan Motor Co., Ltd.)	Inspect piston pin, connecting rod small end bushing, and piston bore for galling, scoring, or excessive wear. If evident, replace defective part(s). Measure the I.D. of the piston boss and connecting rod small end, and the O.D. of the piston pin. If within specifications, assemble piston pin and rod. CAUTION: *If piston pin must be pressed in, determine the proper method and use the proper tools; otherwise the piston will distort.* Install the lock rings; ensure that they seat properly. If the parts are not within specifications, determine the service method for the type of engine. In some cases, piston and pin are serviced as an assembly when either is defective. Others specify reaming the piston and connecting rods for an oversize pin. If the connecting rod bushing is worn, it may in many cases be replaced. Reaming the piston and replacing the rod bushing are machine shop operations.

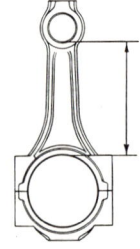

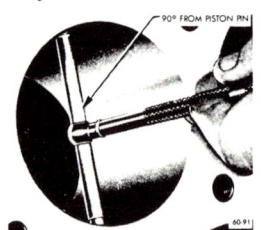

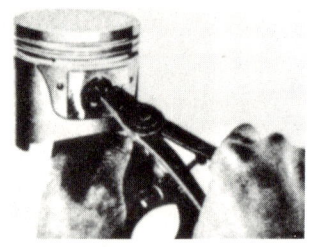

ENGINE AND ENGINE REBUILDING—B-1600 ONLY

Procedure	Method

Clean and inspect the camshaft:

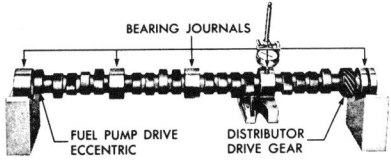

Checking the camshaft for straightness
(© Chevrolet Motor Div. G.M. Corp.)

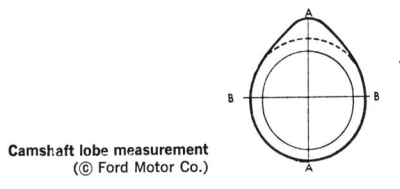

Camshaft lobe measurement
(© Ford Motor Co.)

Degrease the camshaft, using solvent, and clean out all oil holes. Visually inspect cam lobes and bearing journals for excessive wear. If a lobe is questionable, check all lobes as indicated below. If a journal or lobe is worn, the camshaft must be reground or replaced. NOTE: *If a journal is worn, there is a good chance that the bushings are worn.* If lobes and journals appear intact, place the front and rear journals in V-blocks, and rest a dial indicator on the center journal. Rotate the camshaft to check straightness. If deviation exceeds .001″, replace the camshaft.

* Check the camshaft lobes with a micrometer, by measuring the lobes from the nose to base and again at 90° (see illustration). The lift is determined by subtracting the second measurement from the first. If all exhaust lobes and all intake lobes are not identical, the camshaft must be reground or replaced.

Replace the camshaft bearings:

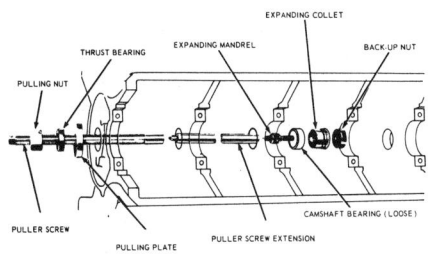

Camshaft removal and installation tool (typical)
(© Ford Motor Co.)

If excessive wear is indicated, or if the engine is being completely rebuilt, camshaft bearings should be replaced as follows: Drive the camshaft rear plug from the block. Assemble the removal puller with its shoulder on the bearing to be removed. Gradually tighten the puller nut until bearing is removed. Remove remaining bearings, leaving the front and rear for last. To remove front and rear bearings, reverse position of the tool, so as to pull the bearings in toward the center of the block. Leave the tool in this position, pilot the new front and rear bearings on the installer, and pull them into position. Return the tool to its original position and pull remaining bearings into position. NOTE: *Ensure that oil holes align when installing bearings.* Replace camshaft rear plug, and stake it into position to aid retention.

Finish hone the cylinders:

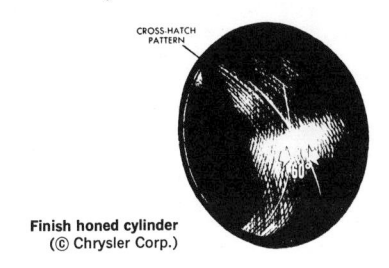

Finish honed cylinder
(© Chrysler Corp.)

Chuck a flexible drive hone into a power drill, and insert it into the cylinder. Start the hone, and move it up and down in the cylinder at a rate which will produce approximately a 60° cross-hatch pattern (see illustration). NOTE: *Do not extend the hone below the cylinder bore.* After developing the pattern, remove the hone and recheck piston fit. Wash the cylinders with a detergent and water solution to remove abrasive dust, dry, and wipe several times with a rag soaked in engine oil.

ENGINE AND ENGINE REBUILDING—B-1600 ONLY

Procedure	Method
Check piston ring end-gap: *Checking ring end-gap* (© Chevrolet Motor Div. G.M. Corp.)	Compress the piston rings to be used in a cylinder, one at a time, into that cylinder, and press them approximately 1" below the deck with an inverted piston. Using feeler gauges, measure the ring end-gap, and compare to specifications. Pull the ring out of the cylinder and file the ends with a fine file to obtain proper clearance. CAUTION: *If inadequate ring end-gap is utilized, ring breakage will result.*
Install the piston rings: *Checking ring side clearance* (© Chrysler Corp.) CORRECT INCORRECT Piston groove depth Correct ring spacer installation	Inspect the ring grooves in the piston for excessive wear or taper. If necessary, recut the groove(s) for use with an overwidth ring or a standard ring and spacer. If the groove is worn uniformly, overwidth rings, or standard rings and spacers may be installed without recutting. Roll the outside of the ring around the groove to check for burrs or deposits. If any are found, remove with a fine file. Hold the ring in the groove, and measure side clearance. If necessary, correct as indicated above. NOTE: *Always install any additional spacers above the piston ring.* The ring groove must be deep enough to allow the ring to seat below the lands (see illustration). In many cases, a "go-no-go" depth gauge will be provided with the piston rings. Shallow grooves may be corrected by recutting, while deep grooves require some type of filler or expander behind the piston. Consult the piston ring supplier concerning the suggested method. Install the rings on the piston, lowest ring first, using a ring expander. NOTE: *Position the ring markings as specified by the manufacturer (see car section).*
Install the camshaft:	Liberally lubricate the camshaft lobes and journals, and slide the camshaft into the block. CAUTION: *Exercise extreme care to avoid damaging the bearings when inserting the camshaft.* Install and tighten the camshaft thrust plate retaining bolts.
Check camshaft end-play: *Checking camshaft end-play with a feeler gauge* (© Ford Motor Co.)	Using feeler gauges, determine whether the clearance between the camshaft boss (or gear) and backing plate is within specifications. Install shims behind the thrust plate, or reposition the camshaft gear and retest end-play.

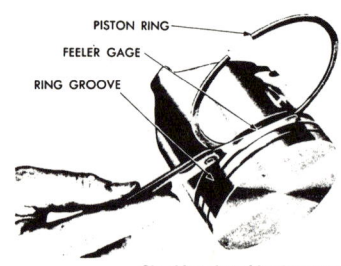

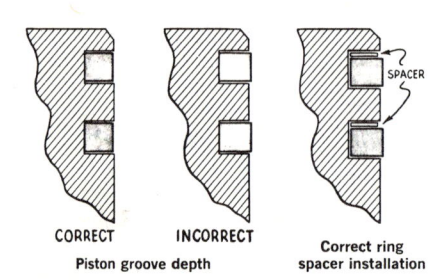

ENGINE AND ENGINE REBUILDING—B-1600 ONLY

Procedure	Method

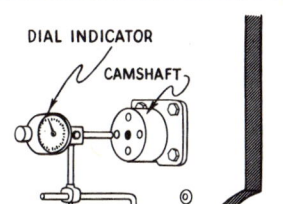

Checking camshaft end-play with a dial indicator

* Mount a dial indicator stand so that the stem of the dial indicator rests on the nose of the camshaft, parallel to the camshaft axis. Push the camshaft as far in as possible and zero the gauge. Move the camshaft outward to determine the amount of camshaft end-play. If the end-play is not within tolerance, install shims behind the thrust plate, or reposition the camshaft gear and retest.

Install the rear main seal (where applicable):

Seating the rear main seal
(© Buick Div. G.M. Corp.)

Position the block with the bearing saddles facing upward. Lay the rear main seal in its groove and press it lightly into its seat. Place a piece of pipe the same diameter as the crankshaft journal into the saddle, and firmly seat the seal. Hold the pipe in position, and trim the ends of the seal flush if required.

Install the crankshaft:

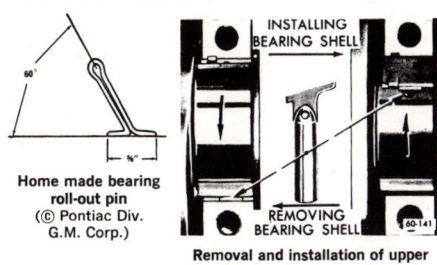

Home made bearing roll-out pin
(© Pontiac Div. G.M. Corp.)

Removal and installation of upper bearing insert using a roll-out pin
(© Buick Div. G.M. Corp.)

Thoroughly clean the main bearing saddles and caps. Place the upper halves of the bearing inserts on the saddles and press into position. NOTE: *Ensure that the oil holes align.* Press the corresponding bearing inserts into the main bearing caps. Lubricate the upper main bearings, and lay the crankshaft in position. Place a strip of Plastigage on each of the crankshaft journals, install the main caps, and torque to specifications. Remove the main caps, and compare the Plastigage to the scale on the Plastigage envelope. If clearances are within tolerances, remove the Plastigage, turn the crankshaft 90°, wipe off all oil and retest. If all clearances are correct, remove all Plastigage, thoroughly

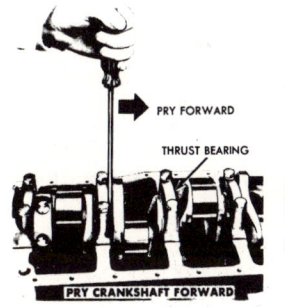

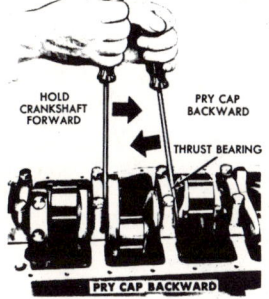

Aligning the thrust bearing
(© Ford Motor Co.)

ENGINE AND ENGINE REBUILDING—B-1600 ONLY

Procedure	Method
	lubricate the main caps and bearing journals, and install the main caps. If clearances are not within tolerance, the upper bearing inserts may be removed, without removing the crankshaft, using a bearing roll out pin (see illustration). Roll in a bearing that will provide proper clearance, and retest. Torque all main caps, excluding the thrust bearing cap, to specifications. Tighten the thrust bearing cap finger tight. To properly align the thrust bearing, pry the crankshaft the extent of its axial travel several times, the last movement held toward the front of the engine, and torque the thrust bearing cap to specifications. Determine the crankshaft end-play (see below), and bring within tolerance with thrust washers.
Measure crankshaft end-play: Checking crankshaft end-play with a dial indicator (© Ford Motor Co.) Checking crankshaft end-play with a feeler gauge (© Chevrolet Div. (G.M. Corp.)	Mount a dial indicator stand on the front of the block, with the dial indicator stem resting on the nose of the crankshaft, parallel to the crankshaft axis. Pry the crankshaft the extent of its travel rearward, and zero the indicator. Pry the crankshaft forward and record crankshaft end-play. NOTE: *Crankshaft end-play also may be measured at the thrust bearing, using feeler gauges* (see illustration).
Install the pistons:	Press the upper connecting rod bearing halves into the connecting rods, and the lower halves into the connecting rod caps. Position the piston ring gaps according to specifications (see car section), and lubricate the pistons. Install a ring compressor on a piston, and press two long (8") pieces of plastic tubing over the rod bolts. Using the plastic tubes as a guide, press the pistons into the bores and onto the crankshaft with a wooden hammer handle. After seating the rod on the crankshaft journal, remove the tubes and install the cap finger tight. Install the remaining pistons in the same man-

ENGINE AND ENGINE REBUILDING—B-1600 ONLY

Procedure	Method
 *Tubing used as guide when installing a piston* (© Oldsmobile Div. G.M. Corp.) 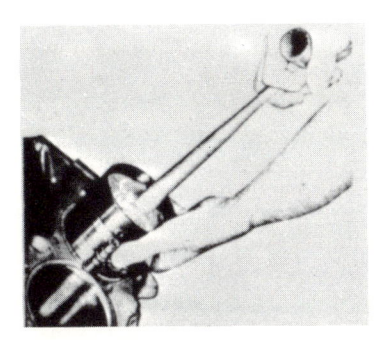 *Installing a piston* (© Chevrolet Div. G.M. Corp.)	ner. Invert the engine and check the bearing clearance at two points (90° apart) on each journal with Plastigage. NOTE: *Do not turn the crankshaft with Plastigage installed.* If clearance is within tolerances, remove *all* Plastigage, thoroughly lubricate the journals, and torque the rod caps to specifications. If clearance is not within specifications, install different thickness bearing inserts and recheck. CAUTION: *Never shim or file the connecting rods or caps.* Always install plastic tube sleeves over the rod bolts when the caps are not installed, to protect the crankshaft journals.
Check connecting rod side clearance: 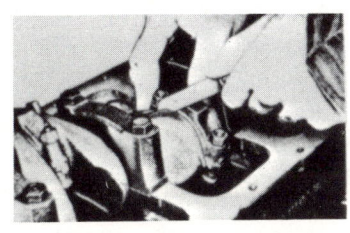 *Checking connecting rod side clearance* (© Chevrolet Div. G.M. Corp.)	Determine the clearance between the sides of the connecting rods and the crankshaft, using feeler gauges. If clearance is below the minimum tolerance, the rod may be machined to provide adequate clearance. If clearance is excessive, substitute an unworn rod, and recheck. If clearance is still outside specifications, the crankshaft must be welded and reground, or replaced.
Inspect the timing chain:	Visually inspect the timing chain for broken or loose links, and replace the chain if any are found. If the chain will flex sideways, it must be replaced. Install the timing chain as specified. NOTE: *If the original timing chain is to be reused, install it in its original position.*

ENGINE AND ENGINE REBUILDING—B-1600 ONLY

Procedure	Method
Check timing gear backlash and runout: **Checking camshaft gear backlash** (© Chevrolet Div. G.M. Corp.) **Checking camshaft gear runout** (© Chevrolet Div. G.M. Corp.)	Mount a dial indicator with its stem resting on a tooth of the camshaft gear (as illustrated). Rotate the gear until all slack is removed, and zero the indicator. Rotate the gear in the opposite direction until slack is removed, and record gear backlash. Mount the indicator with its stem resting on the edge of the camshaft gear, parallel to the axis of the camshaft. Zero the indicator, and turn the camshaft gear one full turn, recording the runout. If either backlash or runout exceed specifications, replace the worn gear(s).

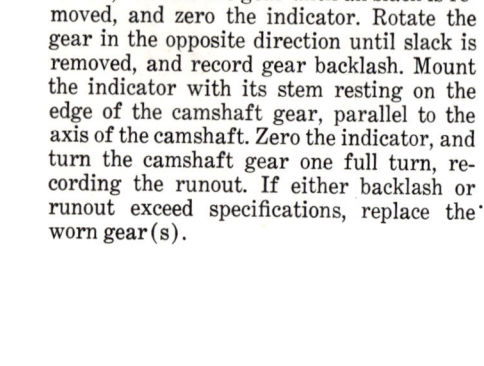

Completing the Rebuilding Process

Following the above procedures, complete the rebuilding process as follows:

Fill the oil pump with oil, to prevent cavitating (sucking air) on initial engine start up. Install the oil pump and the pickup tube on the engine. Coat the oil pan gasket as necessary, and install the gasket and the oil pan. Mount the flywheel and the crankshaft vibrational damper or pulley on the crankshaft. NOTE: *Always use new bolts when installing the flywheel.* Inspect the clutch shaft pilot bushing in the crankshaft. If the bushing is excessively worn, remove it with an expanding puller and a slide hammer, and tap a new bushing into place.

Position the engine, cylinder head side up. Lubricate the lifters, and install them into their bores. Install the cylinder head, and torque it as specified in the car section. Insert the pushrods (where applicable), and install the rocker shaft(s) (if so equipped) or position the rocker arms on the pushrods. If solid lifters are utilized, adjust the valves to the "cold" specifications.

Mount the intake and exhaust manifolds, the carburetor(s), the distributor and spark plugs. Adjust the point gap and the static ignition timing. Mount all accessories and install the engine in the car. Fill the radiator with coolant, and the crankcase with high quality engine oil.

Break-in Procedure

Start the engine, and allow it to run at low speed for a few minutes, while checking for leaks. Stop the engine, check the oil level, and fill as necessary. Restart the engine, and fill the cooling system to capacity. Check the point dwell angle and adjust the ignition timing and the valves. Run the engine at low to medium speed (800-2500 rpm) for approximately ½ hour, and retorque the cylinder head bolts. Road test the car, and check again for leaks.

Follow the manufacturer's recommended engine break-in procedure and maintenance schedule for new engines.

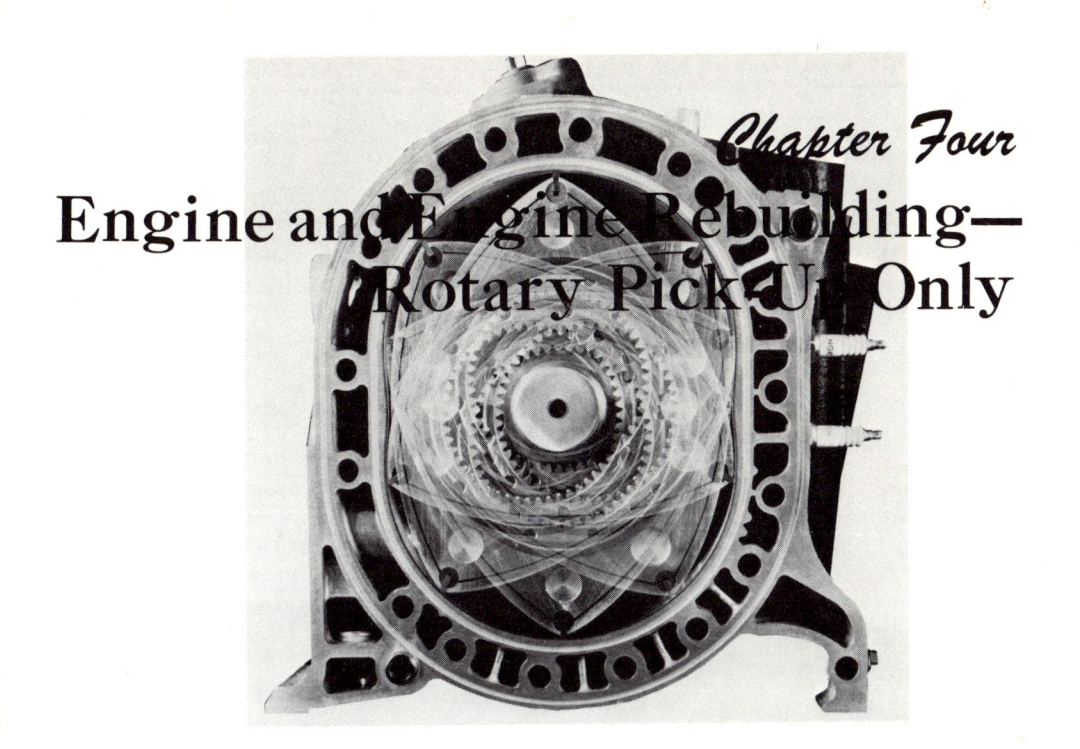

Chapter Four
Engine and Engine Rebuilding—Rotary Pick-Up Only

Engine Electrical

DISTRIBUTOR

The distributor is located on the right front side of the engine. In contrast to earlier rotary engines from Mazda, this uses only one distributor, not two.

Removal and Installation

1. Open the hood and locate the distributor.
2. Remove the distributor cap.
3. Disconnect the vacuum tube from the advance unit.
4. Disconnect the primary wires from the distributor.
5. Matchmark the distributor body in relation to the engine front housing.
6. Remove the distributor hold-down bolt.
7. Pull the distributor from the front cover.

To install the distributor:

8. Turn the eccentric shaft until the TDC mark on the drive pulley aligns with the indicator pin on the front cover.
9. Align the matchmarks on the distributor housing and drive gear.
10. Install the distributor so that the distributor lockbolt is located in the center of the slot. Engage the gears.
11. Rotate the distributor clockwise

Removing or installing the distributor—Rotary Pick-Up (© Toyo Kogyo Co., Ltd.)

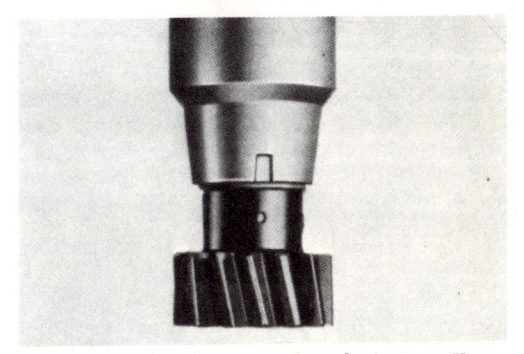

Aligning the distributor matchmarks (© Toyo Kogyo Co., Ltd.)

until the leading contact point set starts to separate, and tighten the distributor lockbolt.

12. Install the distributor cap and connect the primary wires.

77

13. Set the ignition timing.
14. Connect the vacuum tube to the vacuum unit on the distributor.

Firing Order

The firing order of the Rotary Pick-Up engine is alternate (1–2). The distributor cap terminals should be identified by T_1, L_1, T_2 and L_2 (Trailing No. 1 cylinder, Leading No. 1 cylinder, etc.). The top plug of each cylinder is the trailing plug and the bottom the leading. The rotors are numbered from front to rear.

ALTERNATOR

Alternator Precautions

Because of the nature of alternator design, special care must be taken when servicing the charging system.

1. Battery polarity should be checked before any connections, such as jumper cables or battery charger leads, are made. Reversed battery connections will damage the diode rectifiers.
2. The battery must never be disconnected while the alternator is running, because the regulator will be ruined.
3. Always disconnect the battery ground cable before replacing the alternator.
4. Do not attempt to polarize an alternator.
5. Do not short across or ground any alternator terminals.
6. Always disconnect the battery ground cable before removing the alternator output cable whether the engine is running or not.
7. If electric arc welding equipment is to be used on the car, first disconnect the battery and alternator cables. Never operate the car with the electric arc welding equipment attached.
8. If the battery is to be "quick charged," disconnect the positive cable from the battery.

Removal and Installation

1. Disconnect the battery ground cable at the negative (–) terminal.
2. Disconnect all of the leads from the alternator.
3. Remove the alternator adjusting link bolt. Do not remove the adjusting link.
4. Remove the alternator securing nuts and bolts. Withdraw the drive belt and remove the alternator.

Installation is performed in the reverse order of removal. Adjust the drive belt tension as detailed below.

BELT TENSION ADJUSTMENT

1. Check the drive belt tension by applying about 22 lbs of thumb pressure to the belt, midway between the eccentric shaft and alternator pulleys.
2. If belt deflection is not within specifications, loosen, but do not remove, the bolt on the adjusting link.
3. Push the alternator in the direction required to obtain proper belt deflection.
CAUTION: *Do not pry or pound on the alternator housing.*
4. Tighten the adjusting link bolt to 20 ft lbs.

REGULATOR

Removal and Installation

1. Disconnect the battery ground cable at the negative (–) battery terminal.
2. Disconnect the wiring from the regulator.
3. Remove the regulator mounting screws.
4. Remove the regulator.

Installation is performed in the reverse order of removal.

Voltage Adjustments

1. Remove the cover from the regulator.
2. Check the air gap, the point gap, and the back gap with a feeler gauge (see illustration).
3. If they do not fall within the specifications given in the "Alternator and Regulator" chart above, adjust the gaps by bending the stationary contact bracket.
4. Connect a voltmeter between the "A" and "E" terminals of the regulator.
NOTE: *Be sure that the car's battery is fully charged before proceeding with this test.*
5. Start the engine and run it at 2,000

ENGINE AND ENGINE REBUILDING—ROTARY ONLY

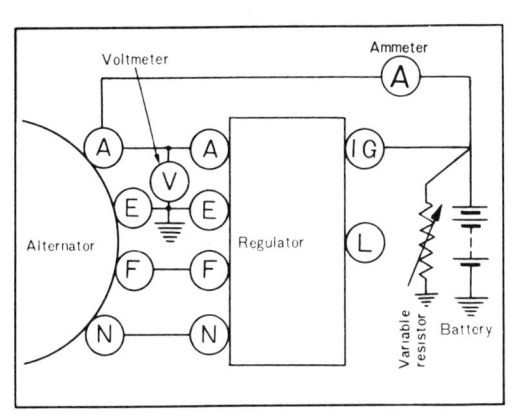

Checking the constant voltage relay (© Toyo Kogyo Co., Ltd.)

Adjusting the voltage regulator (© Toyo Kogyo Co., Ltd.)

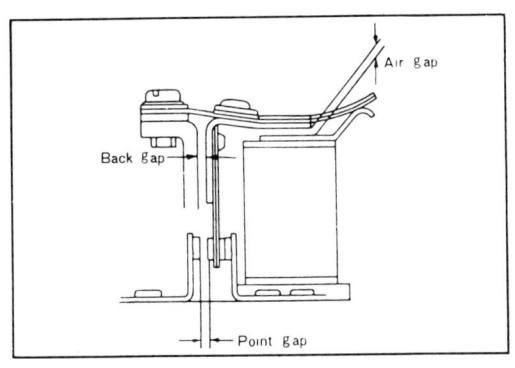

Regulator air gaps (© Toyo Kogyo Co., Ltd.)

rpm (4,000 alternator rpm). The voltmeter reading should be 13.5–14.5 V.

6. Stop the engine.
7. Bend the upper plate *down* to decrease the voltage setting, or *up* to increase the setting as required.
8. If the regulator cannot be brought within specifications, replace it.
9. When the test is completed, disconnect the voltmeter and replace the regulator cover.

Constant Voltage Relay

Air Gap	0.028–0.051 in.
Point Gap	0.012–0.018 in.
Back Gap	0.028–0.059 in.

STARTER

Removal and Installation

NOTE: *There are two possible locations for the starter motor; one is the lower right-hand side of the engine and the other is on the upper right-hand side.*

1. Remove the ground cable from the negative (−) battery terminal.
2. If the car is equipped with the lower mounted starter, remove the gravel shield from underneath the engine.
   CAUTION: *Be extremely careful not to contact the hot exhaust pipe, while working underneath the car.*
3. Remove the battery cable from the starter terminal.
4. Disconnect the solenoid leads from the solenoid terminals.
5. Remove the starter securing bolts and withdraw the starter assembly.
   Installation is the reverse of the above steps.

Starter Service

For repairs or service to the starter motor, see the appropriate section under the starter for the B-1600.

BATTERY

The battery is located in a compartment on the right-side of the cargo bed, just in front of the rear wheel.

Removal and Installation

1. Open the door and hold it open with the rubber snubber provided.

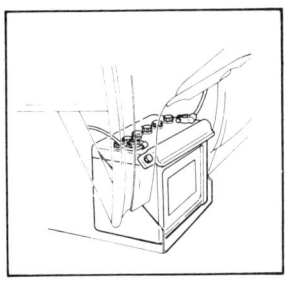

Battery location—Rotary Pick-Up (© Toyo Kogyo Co., Ltd.)

ENGINE AND ENGINE REBUILDING—ROTARY ONLY

Battery and Starter Specifications

Year	Engine Displacement cu in. (cc)	Battery Amp Hour Capacity	Volts	Ground	Lock Test Amps	Volts	Torque (ft lbs)	No Load Test Amps	Volts	RPM	Brush Spring Tension (oz)
1974-75	40 (654) x 2 rotors Rotary Pick-Up	70	12	Neg	1100 or less	5.0	17	100 or less	11.5	7800 or more	49-63

2. Pull the latch handle (on the outside of the battery box) upward to release the latch.
3. Swing the outside of the battery box downward and push the top strap upward.
4. Grab the metal tab at the bottom edge of the battery box and pull it outward, sliding the battery into the open.
5. Installation is the reverse of removal.

Engine Mechanical Rotary Pick-Up Only

DESIGN

The Mazda rotary engine replaces conventional pistons with three-cornered rotors which have rounded sides. The rotors are mounted on a shaft which has eccentrics rather than crank throws.

The chamber in which the rotor travels is roughly oval-shaped, but with the sides of the oval bowed in slightly. The technical name for this shape is a two-lobe epitrochoid.

As the rotor travels its path in the chamber, it performs the same four functions as the piston in a regular four-cycle engine:
1. Intake
2. Compression
3. Ignition
4. Exhaust

But all four functions in a rotary engine are happening concurrently, rather than in four separate stages.

Ignition of the compressed fuel/air mixture occurs each time a side of the rotor passes the spark plugs. Since the rotor has three sides there are three complete power impulses for each complete revolution of the rotor.

As it moves, the rotor exerts pressure on the cam of the eccentric shaft, causing the shaft to turn.

Because there are three power pulses for every revolution of the rotor, the eccentric shaft must make three complete revolutions for every one revolution of the rotor. To maintain this ratio, the rotor has an internal gear that meshes with a fixed gear in a three-to-one ratio. If it was not for this gear arrangement, the rotor would spin freely and timing would be lost.

The Mazda rotary engine has two rotors mounted 60 degrees out of phase. This produces six power impulses for each complete revolution of both rotors and two power inpulses for each revolution of the eccentric shaft.

Because of the number of power impulses for each revolution of the rotor and because all four functions are concurrent, the rotary engine is able to produce a much greater amount of power for its size and weight than a comparable reciprocating piston engine.

Instead of using valves to control the intake and exhaust operations, the rotor uncovers and covers ports on the wall of the chambers, as it turns. Thus, a complex valve train is unnecessary. The resulting elimination of parts further reduces the size and weight of the engine, as well as eliminating a major source of mechanical problems.

Spring-loaded carbon seals are used to prevent loss of compression around the rotor apexes and cast iron seals are used to prevent loss of compression around the side faces of the rotor. These seals are

ENGINE AND ENGINE REBUILDING—ROTARY ONLY

1. Intake. Fuel/air mixture is drawn into combustion chamber by revolving rotor through intake port (upper left). No valves or valve-operating mechanism needed.

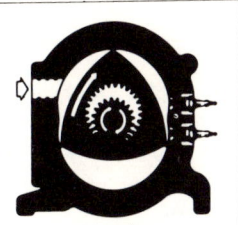

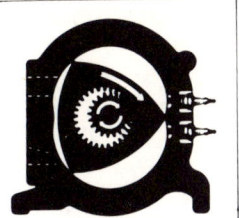

2. Compression. As rotor continues revolving, it reduces space in chamber containing fuel and air. This compresses mixture.

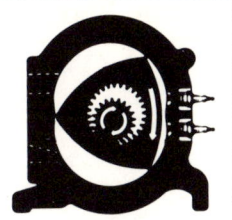

3. Ignition. Fuel/air mixture now fully compressed. Leading sparkplug fires. A split-second later, following plug fires to assure complete combustion.

4. Exhaust. Exploding mixture drives rotor, providing power. Rotor then expels gases through exhaust port.

How your piston engine works.

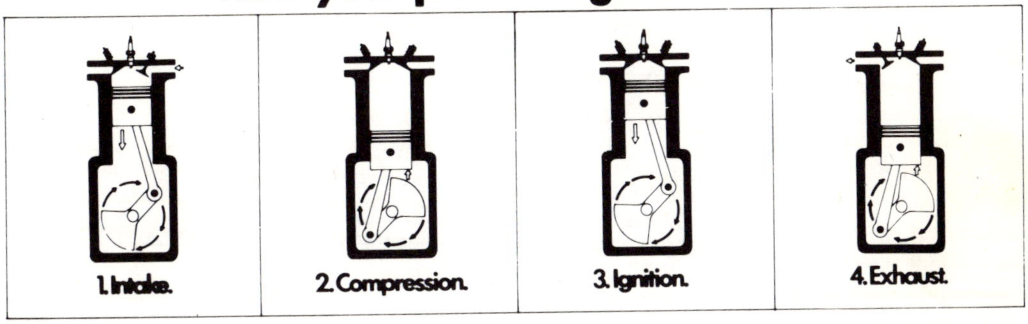

1. Intake.

2. Compression.

3. Ignition.

4. Exhaust.

equivalent to compression rings on a conventional piston, but must be more durable because of the high rotor rpm to which they are exposed.

Oil is controlled by means of circular seals mounted in two grooves on the side face of the rotor. These oil seals function to keep oil out of the combustion chamber and gasoline out of the crankcase, in a similar manner to the oil control ring on a piston.

The rotor housing is made of aluminum and the surfaces of the chamber are chrome-plated.

General Engine Specifications

Model	Engine Displacement (cu in./cc)	Carburetor Type	Net Horsepower @ rpm	Net Torque @ rpm	Rotor Displacement (cu in.)	Compression Ratio	Oil Pressure @ rpm (psi)
Rotary Pick-Up	40 (654) x 2 rotors	4-bbl	90 @ 6000	96 @ 4000	40	9.2 : 1	71.1 @ 3000

Eccentric Shaft Specifications (in.)

Model	Journal Diameter Main Bearing	Journal Diameter Rotor Bearing	Oil Clearance Main Bearing	Oil Clearance Rotor Bearing	Shaft End-Play Normal	Shaft End-Play Limit	Maximum Permissible Shaft Run-out
Rotary Pick-Up	1.6929	2.9134	0.0016–0.0028	0.0016–0.0031	0.0016–0.0028	0.00035	0.0024

Rotor and Housing Specifications (in.)

Model	Rotor Side Clearance	Rotor Standard Protrusion of Land	Rotor Limit of Protrusion of Land	Housings Front and Rear Distortion Limit	Housings Front and Rear Wear Limit	Rotor Width	Rotor Distortion Limit	Intermediate Distortion Limit	Intermediate Wear Limit
Rotary Pick-Up	0.0047–0.0083	0.004–0.006	0.003	0.002	0.004	3.1438	0.002	0.002	0.004

Seal Clearances (in.)

Model	Apex Seals To Side Housing Normal	Limit	Apex Seals To Rotor Groove Normal	Limit	Corner Seal to Rotor Groove Normal	Limit	Side Seal To Rotor Groove Normal	Limit	Side Seal To Corner Seal Normal	Limit
Rotary Pick-Up	0.0051–0.0067	0.012	0.0020–0.0035	0.006	0.0018–0.0019	0.0031	0.0016–0.0028	0.004	0.0020–0.0059	0.016

Seal Specifications (in.)

Model	Apex Seal Normal Height	Apex Seal Height Limit	Corner Seal OD	Side Seal Thickness	Side Seal Width	Oil Seal Contact Width of Lip Normal	Oil Seal Contact Width of Lip Limit
Rotary Pick-Up	0.335	0.276	0.4331	0.039	0.138	0.008	0.031

Rotary Pick-Up Torque Specifications

(All figures given in ft lbs)

Side plate-to-control valve body	2–3
Reamer bolt of control valve body	4–5
Oil strainer	2–3
Governor valve body-to-oil distributor	4–5
Oil pump cover	4–6
Inhibitor switch	4–5
Manual shaft locknut	22–29
Oil cooler pipe set bolt	17–26
Oil pressure test plug	4–7
Actuator for parking rod-to-extension housing	5–8

NOTE: When adjusting the band brake, tighten the piston stem to a torque of 9–11 ft lbs, and then loosen it by two turns.

Driveshaft

Yoke-to-rear axle companion flange	40–47
Yoke-to-front driveshaft	116–130
Center bearing support	14–21

Rear axle

Ring gear	40–47
Differential side bearing caps	47–56
Companion flange-to-pinion	145–253

Steering

Steering wheel nut	22–29
Steering gear housing-to-frame	33–41
Pitman arm-to-sector shaft	108–130
Idler arm bracket-to-frame	33–41
Idler arm-to-bracket	33–47
Idler arm-to-center link	33–47
Pitman arm-to-center link	33–47
Tie-rod-to-center link	18–25
Tie-rod-to-knuckle arm	33–47
Tie-rod locknut	13–18

Wheels

Wheel nuts	58–65

Suspension

Ball joints-to-knuckle	51–65
Ball joint-to-lower suspension arm	60–70
Upper suspension arm shaft-to-frame	61–76
Lower suspension arm shaft-to-frame	61–76
U-bolts	46–58
Spring pin nuts	61–76
Spring pin-to-frame bracket	14–18
Shackle pin nuts	46–58

Unless otherwise specified

	6T	8T
6 mm bolt/nut	5–7	6–9
8 mm bolt/nut	12–17	13–20
10 mm bolt/nut	23–34	27–40
12 mm bolt/nut	41–59	46–69
14 mm bolt/nut	56–76	75–101

ENGINE AND ENGINE REBUILDING—ROTARY ONLY

Removal and Installation

1. Scribe matchmarks on the hood and hinges. Remove the hood from the hinges.
2. Working from underneath the car, remove the gravel shield then drain the cooling system and the engine oil.
3. Disconnect the cable from the negative (−) battery terminal.
4. Remove the air cleaner, bracket, and hoses.
5. Detach the accelerator cable, choke cable, and fuel lines from the carburetor.
6. Remove the nuts which secure the thermostat housing. Disconnect the ground cable from the housing and install the housing again after the cable is removed.
7. Disconnect the power brake vacuum line from the intake manifold.
8. Remove the fan shroud securing bolts and then the shroud itself.
9. Remove the bolts which secure the fan clutch to the eccentric shaft pulley. Withdraw the fan and clutch as a single unit.

CAUTION: *Keep the fan clutch in an upright position so that its fluid does not leak out.*

10. Unfasten the clamps and remove both radiator hoses.
11. Note their respective positions and remove the spark plug cables. Disconnect the primary leads from the distributor and the distributor cap.
12. Detach all of the leads from the alternator, the water temperature sender, the oil pressure sender, and the starter motor.
13. Disconnect all of the wiring from the emission control system components.
14. Detach the heater hoses at the engine.
15. Detach the oil lines from the front and the rear of the engine.
16. Disconnect the battery cable from the positive (+) battery terminal and from the engine.
17. Unfasten the clutch slave cylinder retaining nuts from the clutch housing and tie the cylinder up and out of the way.

NOTE: *Do not remove the hydraulic line from the slave cylinder.*

18. Remove the exhaust pipe and the thermal reactor.

CAUTION: *Be sure that the thermal reactor has completely cooled; severe burns could result if it has not.*

19. Remove the nuts and bolts, evenly and in two or three stages, which secure the clutch housing to the engine.
20. Support the transmission with a jack.
21. Remove the nuts from each of the engine mounts.
22. Attach a lifting sling to the lifting bracket on the rear of the engine housing.
23. Use a hoist to take up the slack on the sling.
24. Pull the engine forward until it clears the transmission input shaft. Lift the engine straight up and out of the car.
25. Remove the heat stove from the exhaust manifold.
26. Remove the thermal reactor.
27. Mount the engine on a workstand.

Engine installation is performed in the reverse order of removal. Remember to refill all fluids according to specifications and to adjust the ignition after installation.

ENGINE DISASSEMBLY

NOTE: *Because of the design of the rotary engine, it is not practical to attempt component removal and installation. It is best to disassemble and assemble the entire engine, or, go as far as necessary with the disassembly procedure.*

1. Mount the engine on a stand.
2. Remove the oil hose support bracket from the front housing.
3. Disconnect the vacuum hoses, air hoses and remove the decel valve.
4. Remove the air pump and drive belt. Remove the air pump adjusting bar.
5. Remove the alternator and drive belt.
6. Disconnect the metering oil pump connecting rod, oil tubes and vacuum sensing tube from the carburetor.
7. Remove the carburetor and intake manifold as an assembly.
8. Remove the gasket and two rubber rings.
9. Remove the thermal reactor and gaskets.

ENGINE AND ENGINE REBUILDING—ROTARY ONLY

Removing the intake manifold (© Toyo Kogyo Co., Ltd.)

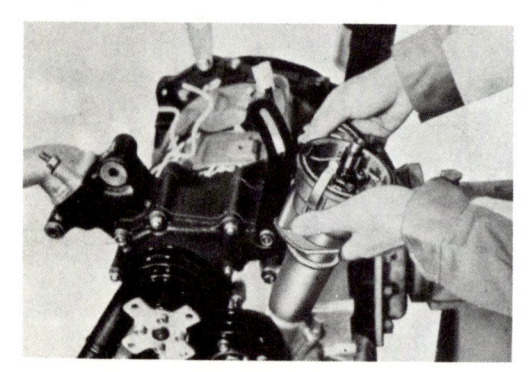

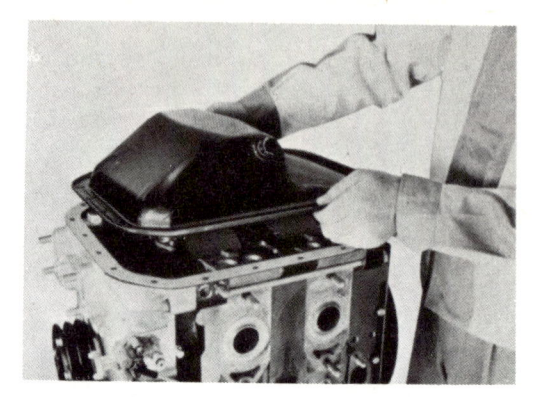

Removing the oil pan (© Toyo Kogyo Co., Ltd.)

Removing the distributor (© Toyo Kogyo Co., Ltd.)

Removing the oil pump strainer (© Toyo Kogyo Co., Ltd.)

10. Remove the distributor from the front cover.
11. Remove the water pump and gasket.

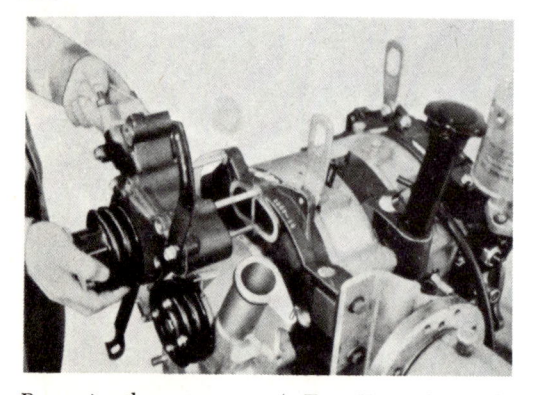

Removing the water pump (© Toyo Kogyo Co., Ltd.)

Identify the front and rear rotor housings (© Toyo Kogyo Co., Ltd.)

12. Invert the engine on the stand.
13. Remove the oil pan and gasket.
14. Remove the oil pump screen and gasket.
15. Identify the front and rear rotor housing with a felt tip pen. These are common parts and must be identified to be reassembled in their respective locations.

Remove the eccentric shaft pulley (© Toyo Kogyo Co., Ltd.)

ENGINE AND ENGINE REBUILDING—ROTARY ONLY

16. Turn the engine on the stand so that the top of the engine is up.
17. Remove the engine mounting bracket from the front cover.
18. Hold the flywheel with a flywheel holder and remove the eccentric shaft pulley.
19. Turn the engine on a stand so that the front end of the engine is up.
20. Remove the front cover and gasket.

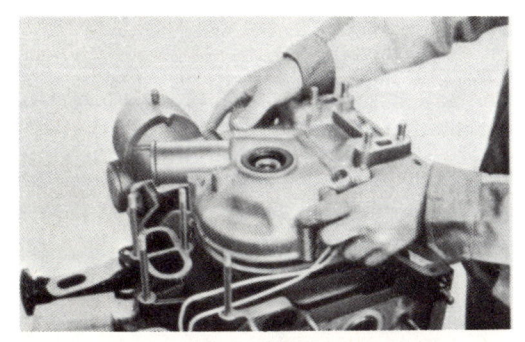

Remove the front cover (© Toyo Kogyo Co., Ltd.)

21. Remove the O-ring from the oil passage on the front housing.
22. Remove the oil slinger and distributor drive gear from the shaft.

Remove the chain adjuster (© Toyo Kogyo Co., Ltd.)

23. Unbolt and remove the chain adjuster.
24. Remove the locknut and washer from the oil pump driven sprocket.
25. Slide the oil pump drive sprocket and driven sprocket together with the drive chain off the eccentric shaft and oil pump simultaneously.
26. Remove the keys from the eccentric and oil pump shafts.
27. Slide the balance weight, thrust washer and needle bearing from the shaft.
28. Unbolt the bearing housing and

Removing the chain and sprockets (© Toyo Kogyo Co., Ltd.)

slide the bearing housing, needle bearing, spacer and thrust plate off the shaft.
29. Turn the engine on the stand so that the top of the engine is up.
30. If equipped with a manual transmission, remove the clutch pressure plate and clutch disc. Loosen the pressure plate bolts evenly in small stages to prevent distortion and possible injury from the pressure plate flying off. Straighten the tab of the lockwasher and remove the flywheel nut. Remove the flywheel with a puller.
31. If equipped with an automatic transmission, remove the drive plate. Straighten the tab on the lockwasher and remove the counterweight nut, while holding the flywheel with a flywheel holder. Remove the counterweight using a puller.
32. Working at the rear of the engine, loosen the tension bolts in the sequence shown, and remove the tension bolts.

NOTE: *Do not loosen the tension bolts one at a time. Loosen the bolts*

Loosen the tension bolts in the order shown (© Toyo Kogyo Co., Ltd.)

Removing the rear housing (© Toyo Kogyo Co., Ltd.)

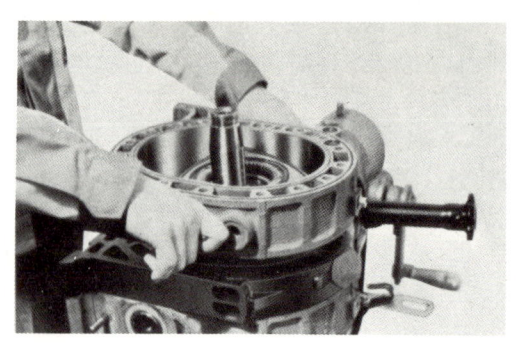

Removing the rear rotor housing (© Toyo Kogyo Co., Ltd.)

evenly in small stages to prevent distortion.

33. Lift the rear housing off the shaft.
34. Remove any seals that are stuck to the rotor sliding surface of the rear housing and reinstall them in their original locations.

Removing the seals (© Toyo Kogyo Co., Ltd.)

35. Remove all the corner seals, corner seal springs, side seal and side seal springs from the rear side of the rotor. Mazda has a special tray which holds all the seals and keeps them segregated to prevent mistakes during reassembly. Each seal groove is marked to prevent confusion.
36. Remove the two rubber seals and two O-rings from the rear rotor housing.
37. Remove the dowels from the rear rotor housing.
38. Lift the rear rotor housing away from the rear rotor, being very careful not to drop the apex seals on the rear rotor.
39. Remove each apex seal, side piece and spring from the rear rotor and segregate them.
40. Remove the rear rotor from the eccentric shaft and place it upside down on a clean rag.
41. Remove each seal and spring from the other side of the rotor and segregate these.

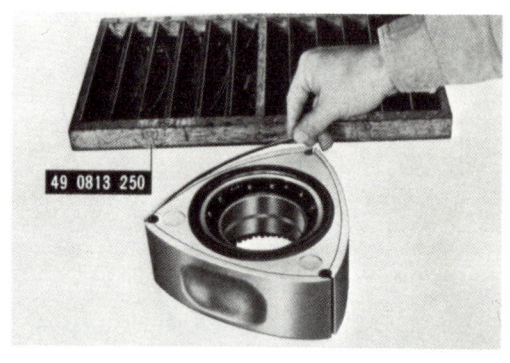

Removing the seals from the rotor (© Toyo Kogyo Co., Ltd.)

42. If some of the seals fall from the rotor, be careful not to change the original position of each seal.
43. Identify the rear rotor with a felt tip pen.
44. Remove the oil seals and the springs. Do not exert heavy pressure at only one place on the seal, since it could

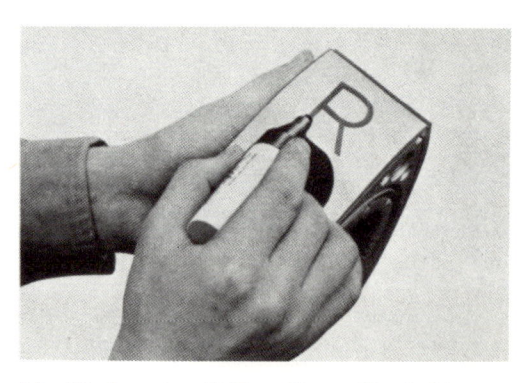

Identify the rotors (© Toyo Kogyo Co., Ltd.)

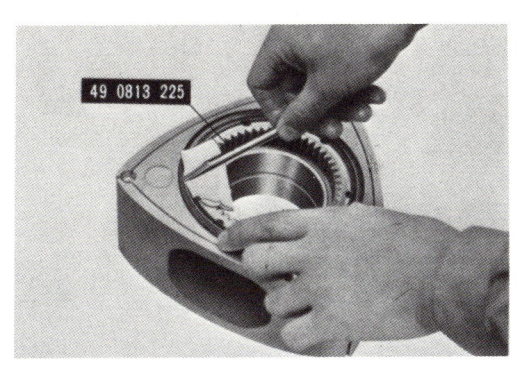

ENGINE AND ENGINE REBUILDING—ROTARY ONLY

Removing the oil seals from the rotor (© Toyo Kogyo Co., Ltd.)

be deformed. Replace the O-rings in the oil seal when the engine is overhauled.

45. Hold the intermediate housing down and remove the dowels from it.

46. Lift off the intermediate housing being careful not to damage the eccentric shaft. It should be removed by sliding it beyond the rear rotor journal on the eccentric shaft while holding the intermediate housing up and, at the same time, pushing the eccentric shaft up.

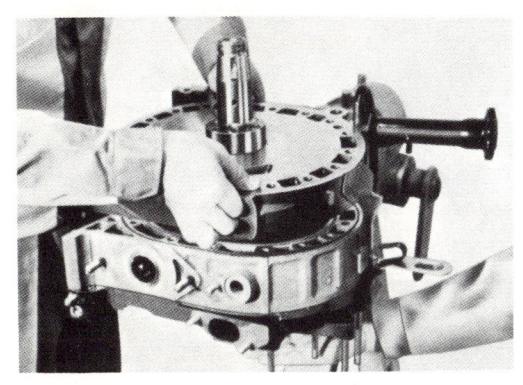

Removing the intermediate housing (© Toyo Kogyo Co., Ltd.)

47. Lift out the eccentric shaft.
48. Repeat the above procedures to remove the front rotor housing and front rotor.

INSPECTION

Front Housing

1. Check the housing for signs of gas or water leakage.
2. Remove the carbon deposits from the front housing with an extra fine emery cloth.

NOTE: *If a carbon scraper must be used, be careful not to damage the mating surfaces of the housing.*

3. Remove any old sealer which is adhering to the housing using a brush or a cloth soaked in ketone.
4. Check for distortion by placing a straightedge on the surface of the housing. Measure the clearance between the straightedge and the housing with a feeler gauge. If the clearance is greater than 0.002 in. at any point, replace the housing.
5. Use a dial indicator to check for wear on the rotor contact surfaces of the housing. If the wear is greater than 0.004 in., replace the housing.

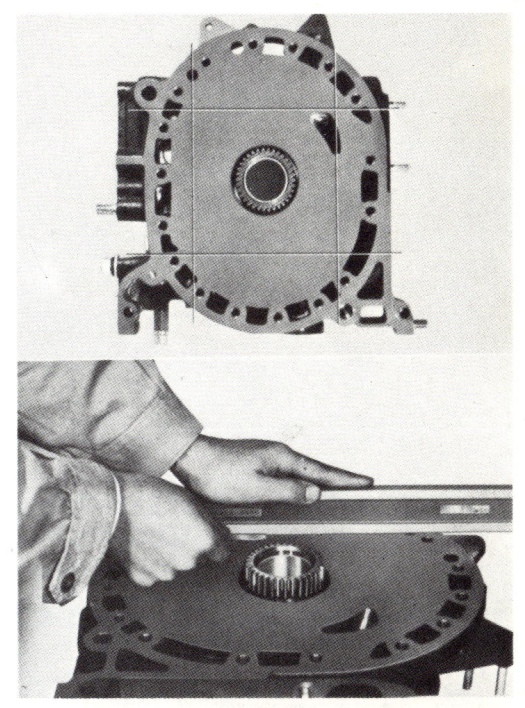

Check the housings for distortion along the lines shown (© Toyo Kogyo Co., Ltd.)

Position of normal wear pattern (© Toyo Kogyo Co., Ltd.)

ENGINE AND ENGINE REBUILDING—ROTARY ONLY

Checking the housing for wear with a dial indicator (© Toyo Kogyo Co., Ltd.)

Removing the stationary gear (© Toyo Kogyo Co., Ltd.)

NOTE: *The wear at either end of the minor axis is greater than at any other point on the housing. However, this is normal and should be no cause for concern.*

Front Stationary Gear and Main Bearing

1. Examine the teeth of the stationary gear for wear or damage.
2. Be sure that the main bearing shows no signs of excessive wear, scoring, or flaking.
3. Check the main bearing-to-eccentric journal clearance by measuring the journal with a vernier caliper and the bearing with a pair of inside calipers. The clearance should be between 0.0018–0.0028 in., and the wear limit is 0.0039 in. Replace either the main bearing or the eccentric shaft if it is greater than this. If the main bearing is to be replaced, proceed as detailed in the following section.

Checking the main bearing oil clearance (© Toyo Kogyo Co., Ltd.)

MAIN BEARING REPLACEMENT

1. Unfasten the securing bolts, if used. Drive the stationary gear and main bearing assembly out of the housing with a brass drift.
2. Press the main bearing out of the stationary gear.
3. Press a new main bearing into the stationary gear so that it is in the same position as the old bearing before it was removed.
4. Align the slot in the stationary gear flange with the dowel pin in the housing and press the gear into place. Install the securing bolts, if required.

NOTE: *To aid in stationary gear and main bearing removal and installation, Mazda supplies a special tool, part number 49 0813 235.*

Intermediate and Rear Housings

Inspection of the intermediate and rear housings is carried out in the same manner as detailed for the front housing above. Replacement of the rear main bearing and stationary gear (mounted on the rear housing) is given below.

Rear Stationary Gear and Main Bearing

Inspect the rear stationary gear and main bearing in a similar manner to the front. In addition, examine the O-ring, which is located in the stationary gear, for signs of wear or damage. Replace the O-ring, if necessary.

If required, replace the stationary gear in the following manner:
1. Remove the rear stationary gear securing bolts.
2. Drive the stationary gear out of the rear housing with a brass drift.
3. Apply a light coating of grease on a new O-ring and fit it into the groove on the stationary gear.

ENGINE AND ENGINE REBUILDING—ROTARY ONLY

Installing the stationary gear in the rear housing (© Toyo Kogyo Co., Ltd.)

4. Apply sealer to the flange of the stationary gear.
5. Install the stationary gear on the housing so that the slot on its flange aligns with the pin on the rear housing.
   CAUTION: *Use care not to damage the O-ring during installation.*
6. Tighten the stationary gear bolts evenly, and in several stages, to 15 ft lbs.

Rotor Housings

1. Examine the inner margin of both housings for signs of gas or water leakage.
2. Wipe the inner surface of each housing with a clean cloth to remove the carbon deposits.
   NOTE: *If the carbon deposits are stubborn, soak the cloth in a solution of ketone. Do not scrape or sand the chrome plated surfaces of the rotor chamber.*
3. Clean all of the rust deposits out of the cooling passages of each rotor housing.
4. Remove the old sealer with a cloth soaked in ketone.
5. Examine the chromium plated inner surfaces for scoring, flaking, or other signs of damage. If any are present, the housing must be replaced.
6. Check the rotor housings for distortion by placing a straightedge on the areas illustrated.
7. Measure the clearance between the straightedge and the housing with a feeler gauge. If the gap exceeds 0.002 in., replace the rotor housing.
8. Check the widths of both rotor housings, at a minimum of eight points near the trochoid surfaces of each housing, with a vernier caliper.
   If the difference between the max-

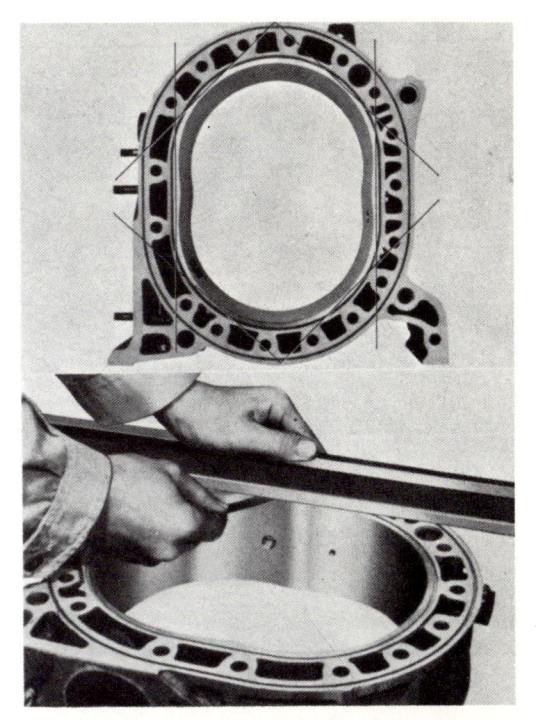

Check the rotor housing for distortion along the lines shown (© Toyo Kogyo Co., Ltd.)

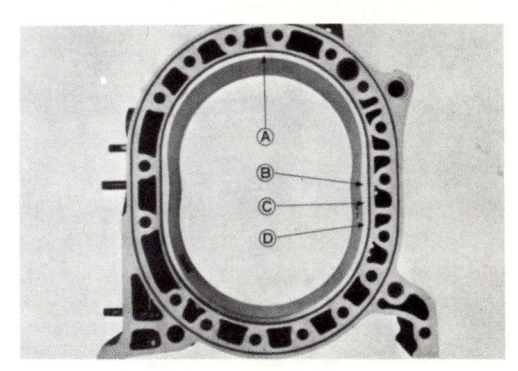

Check the rotor housing width at points A, B, C, and D (© Toyo Kogyo Co., Ltd.)

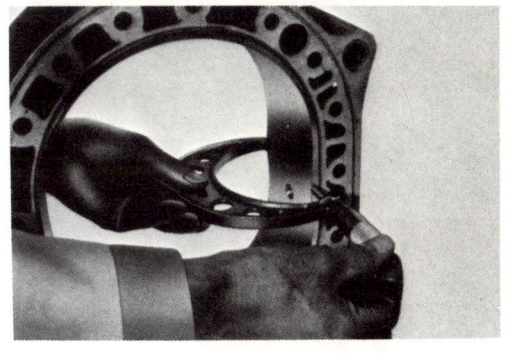

Checking the rotor housing width (© Toyo Kogyo Co., Ltd.)

imum and minimum values obtained is greater than 0.0024 in., replace the housing. A housing in this condition will be prone to gas and coolant leakage.

NOTE: *Standard rotor housing width is 2.7559 in.*

Rotors

1. Check the rotor for signs of blow-by around the side and corner seal areas.
2. The color of the carbon deposits on the rotor should be brown, just as in a piston engine.

NOTE: *Usually the carbon on the leading side of the rotor is brown, while carbon on the trailing side tends toward black, as viewed from the direction of rotation.*

3. Remove the carbon on the rotor with a scraper or extra fine emery paper. Use the scraper carefully when doing the seal grooves, so that no damage is done to them.
4. Wash the rotor in solvent and blow it dry with compressed air after removing the carbon.
5. Examine the internal gear for cracks or damaged teeth.

NOTE: *If the internal gear is damaged, the rotor and gear must be replaced as a single assembly.*

6. With the oil seal removed, check the land protrusions by placing a straightedge over the lands. Measure the gap between the rotor surface and the straightedge with a feeler gauge. The standard specification is 0.004–0.008 in.; if it is less than this, the rotor must be replaced.
7. Check the gaps between the housings and the rotor on both sides:
    a. Measure the rotor width with a vernier caliper. The standard rotor width is 2.7500 in.
    b. Compare the rotor width with the width of the rotor housing measured above. The standard rotor housing width is 2.7559 in.
    c. Replace the rotor if the difference between the two measurements is not within 0.0051–0.0067 in.
8. Check the rotor bearing for flaking, wearing, or scoring and proceed as indicated in the next section, if any of these are present.

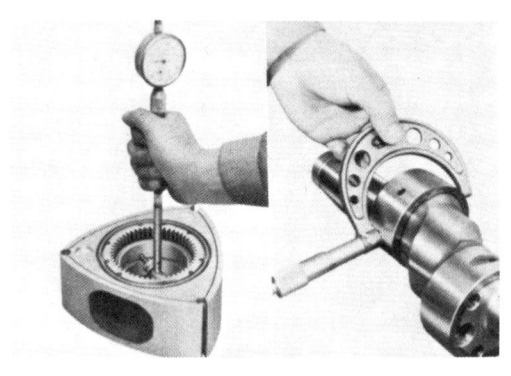

Checking the rotor bearing oil clearance (© Toyo Kogyo Co., Ltd.)

The rotors are classified into five lettered grades, according to their weight. A letter between A and E is stamped on the internal gear side of the rotor. If it becomes necessary to replace a rotor, use one marked with a "C" because this is the standard replacement rotor.

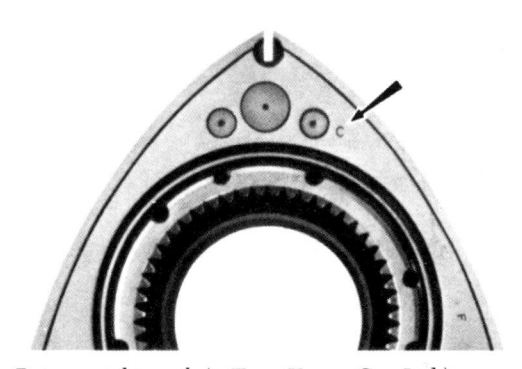

Rotor weight mark (© Toyo Kogyo Co., Ltd.)

ROTOR BEARING REPLACEMENT

Special service tools are required to replace a rotor bearing. Replacement is also a tricky procedure which, if done improperly, could result in serious damage to the rotor and could even make replacement of the entire rotor necessary. Therefore, this service procedure is best

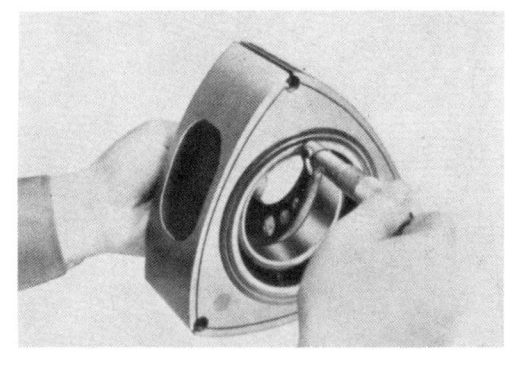

Checking the rotor width (© Toyo Kogyo Co., Ltd.)

ENGINE AND ENGINE REBUILDING—ROTARY ONLY

left to an authorized service facility or a qualified machine shop.

Oil Seal Inspection

NOTE: *Inspect the oil seal while it is mounted in the rotor.*

1. Examine the oil seal for signs of wear or damage.
2. Measure the width of the oil seal lip. If it is greater than 0.031 in., replace the oil seal.

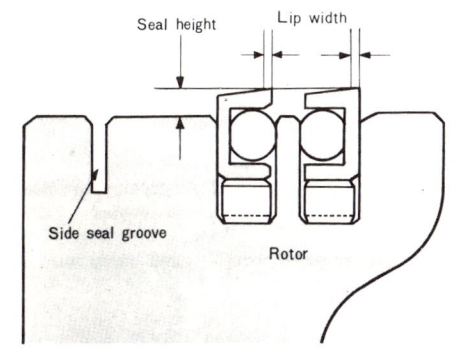

Checking the oil seal (© Toyo Kogyo Co., Ltd.)

3. Measure the protrusion of the oil seal, it should be greater than 0.020 in. Replace the seal, as detailed below, if it is not.

OIL SEAL REPLACEMENT

NOTE: *Replace the rubber O-ring in the oil seal as a normal part of engine overhaul.*

1. Pry the seal out gently by inserting a screwdriver in the slots on the rotor. Do not remove the seal by prying it at only one point as seal deformation will result.

CAUTION: *Be careful not to deform the lip of the oil seal if it is to be reinstalled.*

2. Fit both of the oil seal springs into their respective grooves, so that their ends are facing upward and their gaps are opposite each other on the rotor.
3. Insert a new rubber O-ring into each of the oil seals.

NOTE: *Before installing the O-rings into the oil seals, fit each of the seals into its proper groove on the rotor. Check to see that all of the seals move smoothly and freely.*

4. Coat the oil seal groove and the oil seal with engine oil.
5. Gently press the oil seal into the groove with your fingers. Be careful not to distort the seal.

NOTE: *Be sure that the white mark is on the bottom side of each seal when it is installed.*

6. Repeat the installation procedure for the oil seals on both sides of each rotor.

Apex Seals

CAUTION: *Although the apex seals are extremely durable when in service, they are easily broken when they are being handled. Be careful not to drop them.*

1. Remove the carbon deposits from the apex seals and their springs. Do not use emery cloth on the seals as it will damage their finish.
2. Wash the seals and the springs in cleaning solution.
3. Check the apex seals for cracks and other signs of wear or damage.
4. Test the seal springs for weakness.
5. Use a micrometer to check the seal height. Replace any seal if its height is less than 0.275 in.

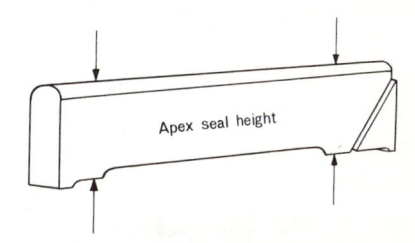

Checking the apex seal height (© Toyo Kogyo Co., Ltd.)

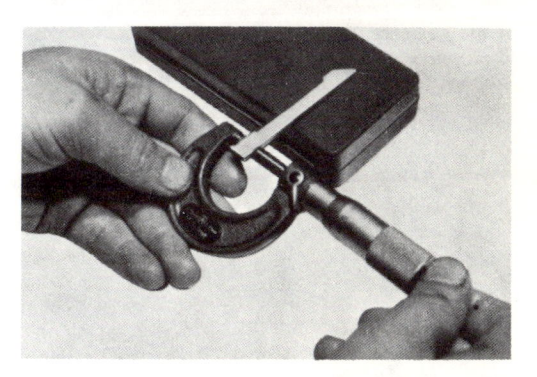

Checking the apex seal (© Toyo Kogyo Co., Ltd.)

6. With a feeler gauge, check the side clearance between the apex seal and the groove in the rotor. Insert the gauge until its tip contacts the bottom of the

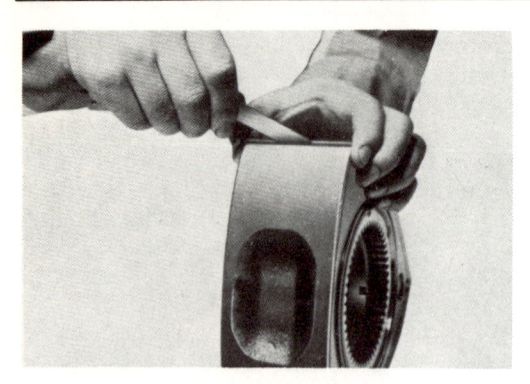

ENGINE AND ENGINE REBUILDING—ROTARY ONLY

Checking the gap between the apex seal and the groove (© Toyo Kogyo Co., Ltd.)

groove. If the gap is greater than 0.006 in., replace the seal.

7. Check the gap between the apex seals and the side housing, in the following manner:

    a. Use a vernier caliper to measure the length of each apex seal.

    b. Compare this measurement to the *minimum* figure obtained when rotor housing width was being measured.

    c. If the difference is more than 0.0118 in., replace the seal. The standard gap is 0.0051–0.0067 in.

    d. If, on the other hand, the seal is too long, sand the ends of the seal with emery cloth until the proper length is reached.

CAUTION: *Do not use the emery cloth on the faces of the seal.*

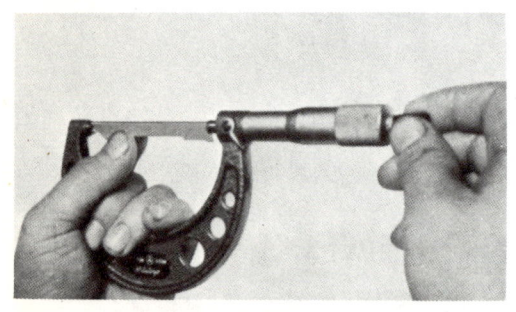

Side Seals

1. Remove the carbon deposits from the side seals and their springs with a carbon scraper.

2. Check the protrusion of the side seals. It should be 0.02 in. or more.

3. Check the side seals for cracks or wear. Replace any of the seals found to be defective.

Checking the side seal gap (© Toyo Kogyo Co., Ltd.)

Measure the apex seal length (© Toyo Kogyo Co., Ltd.)

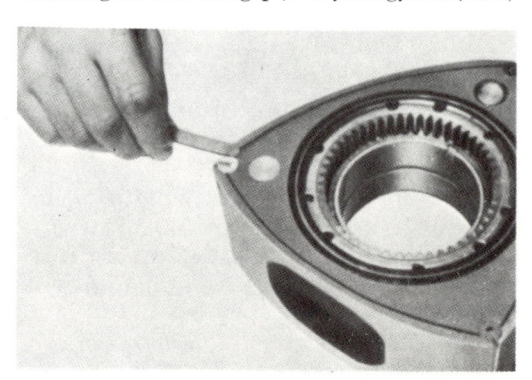

Checking the side seal and corner seal gap (© Toyo Kogyo Co., Ltd.)

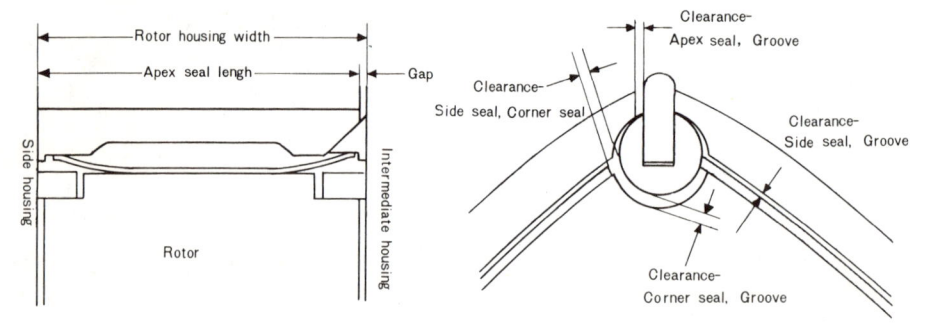

Seal clearance (© Toyo Kogyo Co., Ltd.)

ENGINE AND ENGINE REBUILDING—ROTARY ONLY

4. Check the clearance between the side seals and their grooves with a feeler gauge. Replace any side seals if they have a clearance of more than 0.0039 in. The standard clearance is 0.002–0.003 in.

5. Check the clearance between the side seals and the corner seals with both of them installed in the rotor.

   a. Insert a feeler gauge between the end of the side seal and the corner seal.

NOTE: *Insert the gauge against the direction of the rotor's rotation.*

   b. Replace the side seal if the clearance is greater than 0.016 in.

6. If the side seal is replaced, adjust the clearance between it and the corner seal as follows:

   a. File the side seal on its reverse side, in the same rotational direction of the rotor, along the outline made by the corner seal.

   b. The clearance obtained should be 0.002–0.006 in. If it exceeds this, the performance of the seals will deteriorate.

CAUTION: *There are four different types of side seals, depending upon their location. Do not mix the seals up and be sure to use the proper type of seal for replacement.*

Corner Seals

1. Clean the carbon deposits from the corner seals.

2. Examine each of the seals for wear or damage.

3. Check the corner seal protrusion from the rotor surface. It should be free to move under finger pressure and protrude 0.02 in. or more.

4. Measure the clearance between the corner seal and its groove. The clearance should be 0.0008–0.0019 in. The wear limit of the gap is 0.0031 in.

5. If the wear between the corner seal and the groove is uneven, check the clearance with the special "bar limit gauge" (Mazda part number 49 0839 165). The gauge has a "go" end and a "no go" end. Use the gauge in the following manner:

   a. If neither end of the gauge goes into the groove, the clearance is within specifications.

   b. If the "go" end of the gauge fits into the groove, but the "no go" end does not, replace the corner seal with one that is 0.0012 in. oversize.

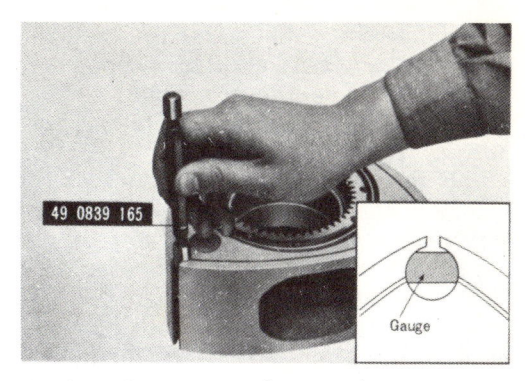

   c. If both ends of the gauge fit into the groove, then the groove must be reamed out as detailed below. Replace the corner seal with one which is 0.0072 in. oversize, after completing reaming.

NOTE: *Take the measurement of the groove in the direction of maximum wear, i.e., that of rotation.*

Corner Seal Groove Reaming

NOTE: *This procedure requires the use of special tools; if attempted without them, damage to the rotor could result.*

1. Carefully remove all of the deposits which remain in the groove.

2. Fit the jig (Mazda part number 49 2113 030) over the rotor. Tighten its adjusting bar, being careful not to damage the rotor bearing or the apex seal grooves.

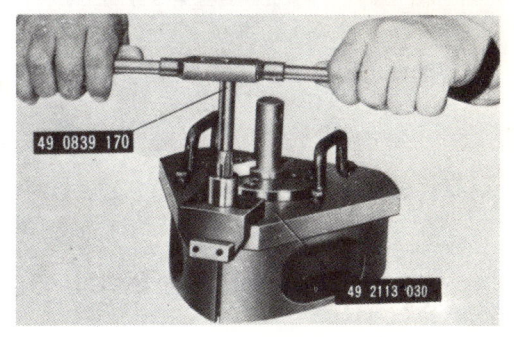

Checking the corner seal groove (© Toyo Kogyo Co., Ltd.)

Reaming the corner seal groove (© Toyo Kogyo Co., Ltd.)

3. Use the corner seal groove reamer (Mazda part number 49 0839 170) to ream the groove.

ENGINE AND ENGINE REBUILDING—ROTARY ONLY

4. Rotate the reamer at least 20 times while applying engine oil as a coolant.
   NOTE: *If engine oil is not used, it will be impossible to obtain the proper groove surfacing.*
5. Remove the reamer and the jig.
6. Repeat Steps 1–5 for each of the corner seal grooves.
7. Clean the rotor completely and check it for any signs of damage.
8. Fit a 0.0079 in. oversize corner seal into the groove and check its clearance. Clearance should be 0.0008–0.0019 in.

Seal Springs

Check the seal springs for damage or weakness. Be exceptionally careful when checking the spring areas which contact either the rotor or the seal.

Eccentric Shaft

1. Wash the eccentric shaft in solvent and blow its oil passages dry with compressed air.
2. Check the shaft for wear, cracks, or other signs of damage. Make sure that none of the oil passages are clogged.
3. Measure the shaft journals with a vernier caliper. The standard specifications are:
   Main journals—1.6929 in.
   Rotor journals—2.9134 in.

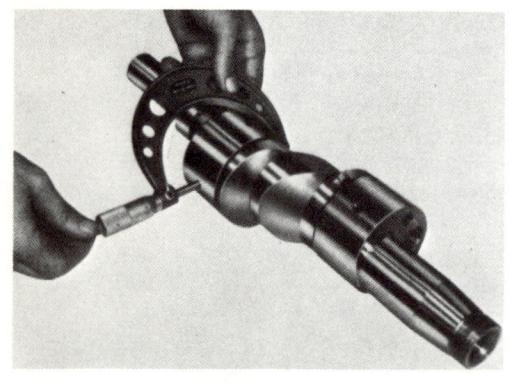

Measure the eccentric shaft rotor journal diameter (© Toyo Kogyo Co., Ltd.)

Replace the shaft if any of its journals show excessive wear.

4. Check eccentric shaft run-out by placing the shaft on V-blocks and using a dial indicator as shown. Rotate the shaft slowly and note the dial indicator reading. If run-out is more than 0.0024 in., replace the eccentric shaft.

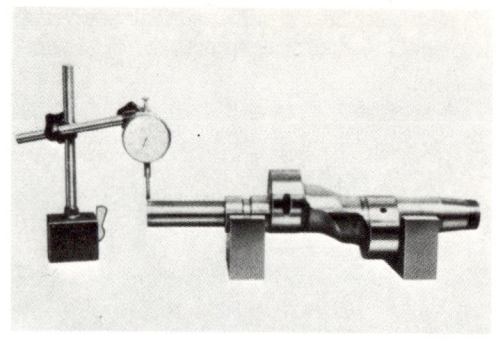

Checking the eccentric shaft run-out (© Toyo Kogyo Co., Ltd.)

5. Check the blind plug at the end of the shaft. If it is loose or leaking, remove it with an allen wrench and replace the O-ring.

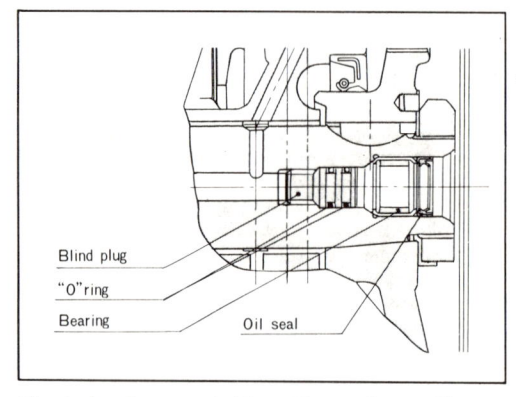

Blind plug location (© Toyo Kogyo Co., Ltd.)

6. Check the operation of the needle roller bearing for smoothness by inserting a mainshaft into the bearing and rotating it. Examine the bearing for signs of wear or damage.

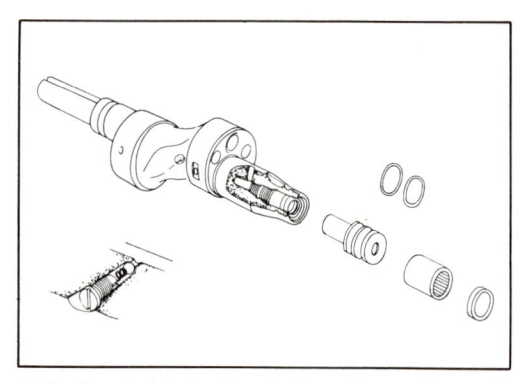

Roller bearing and oil jet (© Toyo Kogyo Co., Ltd.)

7. Replace the bearing, if necessary, with the special tool (Mazda part number 49 0823 073 and 49 0823 072).

ENGINE AND ENGINE REBUILDING—ROTARY ONLY

ENGINE ASSEMBLY

1. Place the rotor on a rubber pad or cloth.
2. Install the oil seal rings in their respective grooves in the rotors with the edge of the spring in the stopper hole. The oil springs are painted cream or blue in color. The cream colored springs must be installed on the front faces of both rotors. The blue colored springs must be installed on the rear faces of both rotors. When installing each oil seal spring, the painted side (square side) of the spring must face upward (toward the oil seal).

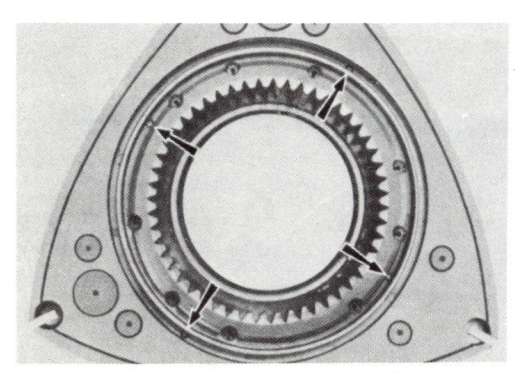

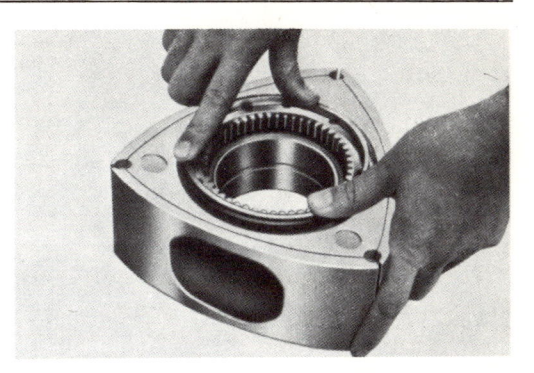

Installing the oil seal (© Toyo Kogyo Co., Ltd.)

Stopper hole (arrow) of the oil seal spring (© Toyo Kogyo Co., Ltd.)

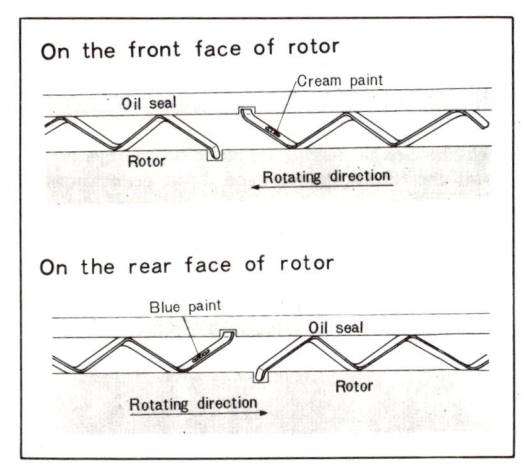

Installation of the oil seal spring (© Toyo Kogyo Co., Ltd.)

3. Install a new O-ring in each groove. Place each oil seal in the groove so that the square edge of the spring fits in the stopper hole of the oil seal. Push the head of the oil seal slowly with the fingers, being careful that the seal is not deformed. Be sure that the oil seal moves smoothly in the groove before installing the O-ring.
4. Lubricate each oil seal and groove with engine oil and check the movement of the seal. It should move freely when the head of the seal is pressed.
5. Check the oil seal protrusion and install the seals on the other side of each rotor.
6. Install the apex seals without springs and side pieces into their respective grooves so that each side piece positions on the side of each rotor.
7. Install the corner seal springs and corner seals into their respective grooves.
8. Install the side seal springs and side seals into their respective grooves.

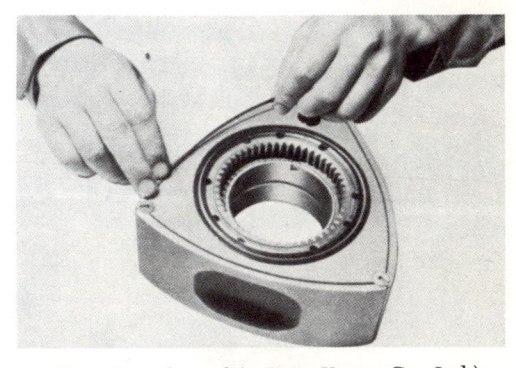

Installing the side seal (© Toyo Kogyo Co., Ltd.)

9. Apply engine oil to to each spring and check each spring for smooth movement.
10. Check each seal protrusion.
11. Invert the rotor being careful that the seals do not fall out, and install the oil seals on the other side in the same manner.
12. Mount the front housing on a workstand so that the top of the housing is up.

96 ENGINE AND ENGINE REBUILDING—ROTARY ONLY

13. Lubricate the internal gear of the rotor with engine oil.

14. Hold the apex seals with used O-rings to keep the apex seals installed and place the rotor on the front housing. Be careful that you do not drop the seals. Turn the front housing so that the sliding surfaces faces upward.

15. Mesh the internal and stationary gears so that the one of the rotor apexes is at any one of the four places shown and remove the old O-ring which is holding the apex seals in position.

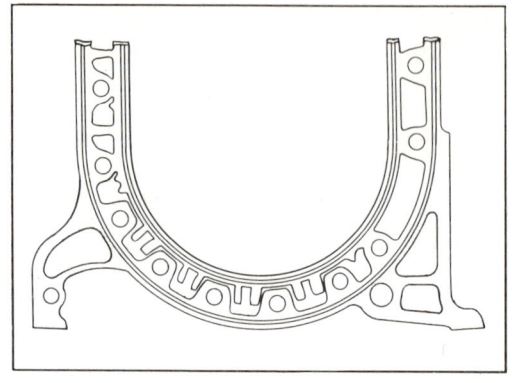

Apply sealer to the shaded areas (© Toyo Kogyo Co., Ltd.)

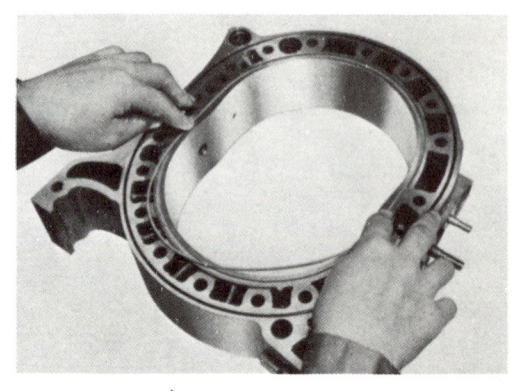

Positioning the front rotor (© Toyo Kogyo Co., Ltd.)

16. Lubricate the front rotor journal of the eccentric shaft with engine oil and lubricate the eccentric shaft main journal.

17. Insert the eccentric shaft. Be careful that you do not damage the rotor bearing and main bearing.

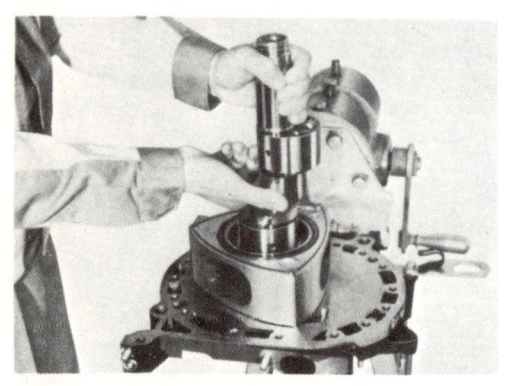

Install the rubber seal (© Toyo Kogyo Co., Ltd.)

install the O-rings and rubber seals on the front side of the rotor housing.

NOTE: *The inner rubber seal is of the square type. The wider white line of the rubber seal should face the combustion chamber and the seam of the rubber seal should be positioned as shown. Do not stretch the rubber seal.*

20. If the engine is being overhauled, install the seal protector to only the inner rubber seal to improve durability.

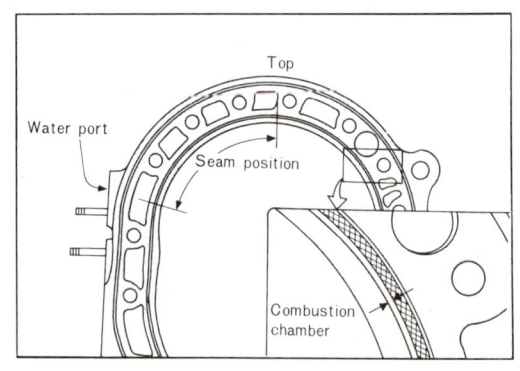

Installing the eccentric shaft (© Toyo Kogyo Co., Ltd.)

18. Apply sealing agent to the front side of the front rotor housing.

19. Apply a light coat of petroleum jelly onto new O-rings and rubber seals (to prevent them from coming off) and

Positioning the inner rubber seal (© Toyo Kogyo Co., Ltd.)

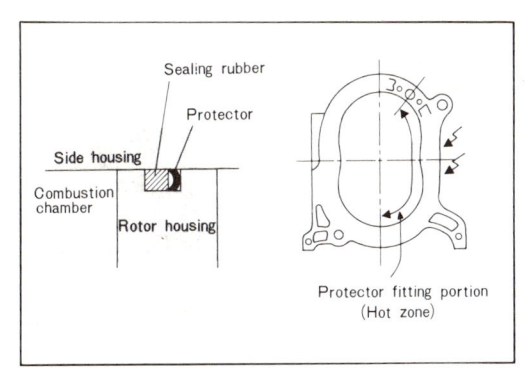

ENGINE AND ENGINE REBUILDING—ROTARY ONLY

Installation of the rubber seal protector (© Toyo Kogyo Co., Ltd.)

21. Invert the front rotor housing, being careful not to let the rubber seals and O-rings fall from their grooves, and mount it on the front housing.
22. Lubricate the dowels with engine oil and insert them through the front rotor housing holes and into the front housing.
23. Apply sealer to the front side of the rotor housing.
24. Install new O-rings and rubber seals on the front rotor housing in the same manner as for the other side.
25. Insert each apex spring seal, making sure that the seal is installed in the proper direction.
26. Install each side piece in its original position and be sure that the springs seat on the side piece.

Install the side piece and spring (© Toyo Kogyo Co., Ltd.)

27. Lubricate the side pieces with engine oil. Make sure that the front rotor housing is free of foreign matter and lubricate the sliding surface of the front housing with engine oil.
28. Turn the front housing assembly with the rotor, so that the top of the housing is up. Pull the eccentric shaft about 1 in.
29. Position the eccentric portion of the eccentric shaft diagonally, to the upper right.
30. Install the intermediate housing over the eccentric shaft onto the front rotor housing. Turn the engine so that the rear of the engine is up.

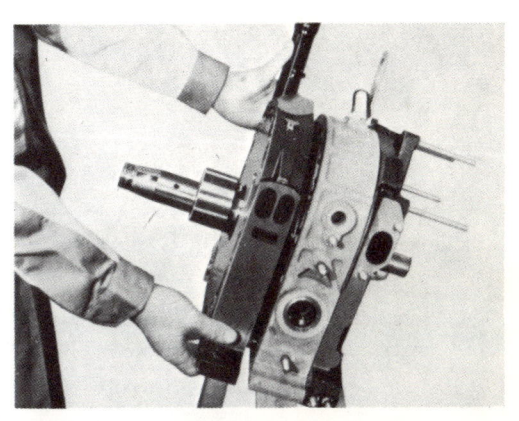

Install the intermediate housing (© Toyo Kogyo Co., Ltd.)

31. Install the rear rotor and rear rotor housing following the same steps as for the front rotor and the front housing.

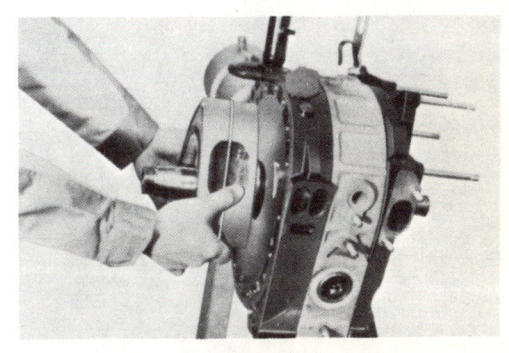

Install the rear rotor (© Toyo Kogyo Co., Ltd.)

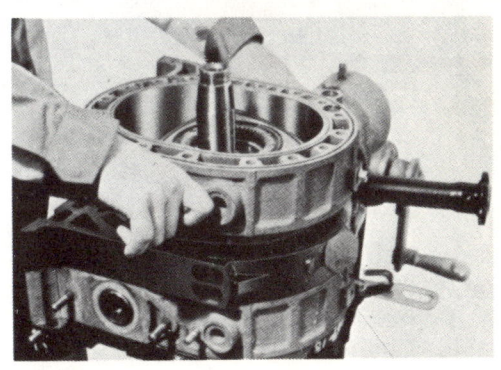

Install the rear rotor housing (© Toyo Kogyo Co., Ltd.)

ENGINE AND ENGINE REBUILDING—ROTARY ONLY

32. Turn the engine so that the rear of the engine is up.
33. Lubricate the stationary gear and main bearing.
34. Install the rear housing onto the rear rotor housing. If necessary, turn the rear rotor slightly to mesh the rear housing stationary gear with the rear rotor internal gear.

Install the rear engine housing (© Toyo Kogyo Co., Ltd.)

35. Install a new washer on each tension bolt, and lubricate each bolt with engine oil.
36. Install the tension bolts and tighten them evenly, in several stages following the sequence shown. The specified torque is 23–27 ft lbs.

Tension bolt tightening sequence (© Toyo Kogyo Co., Ltd.)

37. After tightening the bolts, turn the eccentric shaft to be sure that the shaft and rotors turn smoothly and easily.
38. Lubricate the oil seal in the rear housing.
39. On trucks with manual transmission, install the flywheel on the rear of the eccentric shaft so that the keyway of the flywheel fits the key on the shaft.
40. Apply sealer to both sides of the flywheel lockwasher and install the lockwasher.
41. Install the flywheel locknut. Hold the flywheel SECURELY and tighten the nut to THREE HUNDRED AND FIFTY FT LBS (350 ft lbs) of torque.

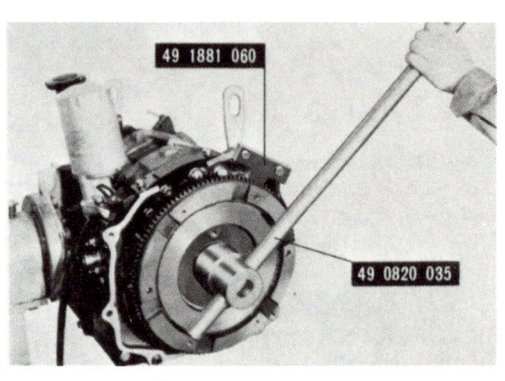

Tighten the flywheel nut (© Toyo Kogyo Co., Ltd.)

NOTE: *350 ft lbs is a great deal of torque. In actual practice, it is practically impossible to accurately measure that much torque on the nut. At least a 3 ft bar will be required to generate sufficient torque. Tighten it as tight as possible, with no longer than 3 ft of leverage. Be sure the engine is held SECURELY.*

42. On trucks with automatic transmission, install the key, counterweight, lockwasher and nut. Tighten the nut to 350 ft lbs. SEE STEP 41 AND THE NOTE FOLLOWING STEP 41.
Install the drive plate on the counterweight and tighten the attaching nuts.
43. Turn the engine so that the front faces up.

Install the thrust plate (© Toyo Kogyo Co., Ltd.)

ENGINE AND ENGINE REBUILDING—ROTARY ONLY

44. Install the thrust plate with the tapered face down, and install the needle bearing on the eccentric shaft. Lubricate with engine oil.

45. Install the bearing housing on the front housing. Tighten the bolts and bend up the lockwasher tabs.

The spacer should be installed so that the center of the needle bearing comes to the center of the eccentric shaft and the spacer should be seated on the thrust plate.

46. Install the needle bearing on the shaft and lubricate it with engine oil.

47. Install the balancer and thrust washer on the eccentric shaft.

Install the oil pump chain and sprockets (© Toyo Kogyo Co., Ltd.)

48. Install the oil pump drive chain over both of the sprockets. Install the sprocket and chain assembly over the eccentric shaft and oil pump shafts simultaneously. Install the key on the eccentric shaft.

NOTE: *Be sure that both of the sprockets are engaged with the chain before installing them over the shafts.*

49. Install the distributor drive gear onto the eccentric shaft with the "F" mark on the gear facing the front of the engine. Slide the spacer and oil slinger onto the eccentric shaft.

50. Align the keyway and install the eccentric shaft pulley. Tighten the pulley bolt to 60 ft lbs.

51. Turn the engine so that the top of the engine faces up.

52. Check eccentric shaft end-play in the following manner:

   a. Attach a dial indicator to the flywheel. Move the flywheel forward and backward.

Checking eccentric shaft end-play (© Toyo Kogyo Co., Ltd.)

   b. Note the reading on the dial indicator; it should be 0.0016–0.0028 in.

   c. If the end-play is not within specifications, adjust it by replacing the front spacer. Spacers come in four sizes, ranging from 0.3150–0.3181 in. If necessary, a spacer can be ground on a surface plate with emery paper.

   d. Check the end-play again and, if it is now within specifications, proceed with the next step.

Eccentric Shaft Spacer Thickness Chart

Identification Mark	Thickness
X	8.08 ± 0.01 mm (0.3181 ± 0.0004 in.)
Y	8.04 ± 0.01 mm (0.3165 ± 0.0004 in.)
V	8.02 ± 0.01 mm (0.3158 ± 0.0004 in.)
Z	8.00 ± 0.01 mm (0.3150 ± 0.0004 in.)

53. Remove the pulley from the front of the eccentric shaft. Tighten the oil pump drive sprocket nut and bend the locktabs on the lockwasher.

54. Fit a new O-ring over the front cover oil passage.

Install a new O-ring in the front cover oil passage (© Toyo Kogyo Co., Ltd.)

ENGINE AND ENGINE REBUILDING—ROTARY ONLY

55. Install the chain tensioner and tighten its securing bolts.

56. Position the front cover gasket and the front cover on the front housing, then secure the front cover with its attachment bolts.

57. Install the eccentric shaft pulley again. Tighten its bolt to 60 ft lbs.

58. Turn the engine so that the bottom faces up.

59. Cut off the excess gasket on the front cover along the mounting surface of the oil pan.

60. Install the oil strainer gasket and strainer on the front housing and tighten the attaching bolts.

Install the oil strainer (© Toyo Kogyo Co., Ltd.)

61. Apply sealer to the joint surfaces of each housing.

62. Install the gasket and oil pan. Tighten the bolts evenly in two stages to 3.5 ft lbs.

63. Turn the engine so that the top is up.

64. Install the water pump and gasket on the front housing. Tighten the attaching bolts.

65. Rotate the eccentric shaft until the yellow mark (leading side mark) aligns with the pointer on the front cover.

66. Align the marks on the distributor gear and housing and install the distributor so that the lockbolt is in the center of the slot.

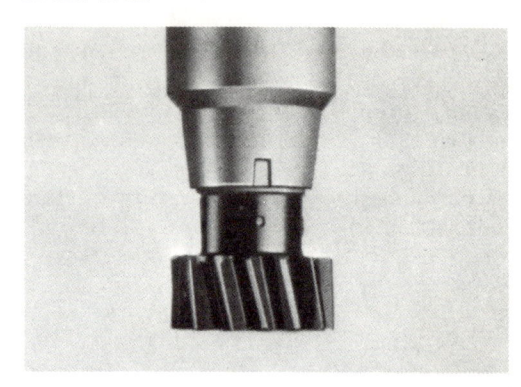

Align the distributor matchmarks (© Toyo Kogyo Co., Ltd.)

Install the distributor so that the lockbolt (arrow) is centered in the slot (© Toyo Kogyo Co., Ltd.)

67. Rotate the distributor until the leading points start to separate and tighten the distributor locknut.

68. Install the gaskets and thermal reactor and tighten the attaching nuts.

69. Install the hot air duct.

Install the water pump (© Toyo Kogyo Co., Ltd.)

Install the intake manifold (© Toyo Kogyo Co., Ltd.)

ENGINE AND ENGINE REBUILDING—ROTARY ONLY

70. Install the carburetor and intake manifold assembly with a new gasket. Tighten the attaching nuts.

71. Connect the oil tubes, vacuum tube and metering oil pump connecting rod to the carburetor.

72. Install the decel valve and connect the vacuum lines, air hoses and wires.

73. Install the alternator bracket, alternator and bolt and check the clearance. If the clearance is more than 0.006 in., adjust the clearance using a shim. Shims are available in three sizes: 0.0059 in., 0.0118 in., and 0.0197 in.

Adjust the alternator bracket clearance (A, arrow) (© Toyo Kogyo Co., Ltd.)

74. Install the alternator drive belt. Attach the alternator to the adjusting brace and adjust the belt tension to specification.

75. Install the air pump with the adjusting brace and install the air pump drive belt. Adjust the air pump drive belt to specifications.

76. Install the engine hanger bracket to the front cover.

77. Remove the engine from the stand.

78. Install the engine in the truck.

79. Fill the engine with fresh engine oil and install a new filter. Fill the engine with coolant. Start the engine, check the oil pressure, and warm it to normal operating temperature. Adjust the idle speed, timing and dwell. Recheck all capacities and refill if necessary. Check for leaks.

INTAKE MANIFOLD

Removal and Installation

To remove the intake manifold and carburetor assembly, with the engine remaining in the automobile, proceed in the following manner:

1. Perform Steps 2, 3, 4, 5, 7, and 13 of "Engine Removal and Installation," above. Do not remove the engine. Do not drain the engine oil; merely remove the metering oil pump hose from the carburetor.

2. Perform Steps 2, 3, and 4 of "Engine Disassembly," above.

Install the intake manifold and carburetor assembly in the reverse order of removal. Tighten the manifold securing nuts working from the inside out, and in two or three stages, to the specifications in the "Torque Chart." Refill the cooling system.

THERMAL REACTOR

Removal and Installation

CAUTION: *The thermal reactor operates at extremely high temperatures. Allow the engine to cool completely before attempting its removal.*

To remove the thermal reactor, which replaces the exhaust manifold, proceed in the following manner:

1. Remove the air cleaner assembly from the carburetor.

2. Unbolt and remove the air injection pump, as outlined in "Emission Controls."

3. Remove the intake manifold assembly, complete with the carburetor.

4. Remove the heat stove from the thermal reactor.

5. Unfasten the thermal reactor securing nuts.

NOTE: *The bottom nut is difficult to reach. Mazda makes a special wrench (part number 49 213 001) to remove it. If the wrench is unavailable, a flexible drive metric socket wrench can be substituted*

6. Lift the thermal reactor away from the engine.

7. Installation is the reverse of removal.

Engine Lubrication

A conventional oil pump, which is either gear (1971) or chain (1972–73)

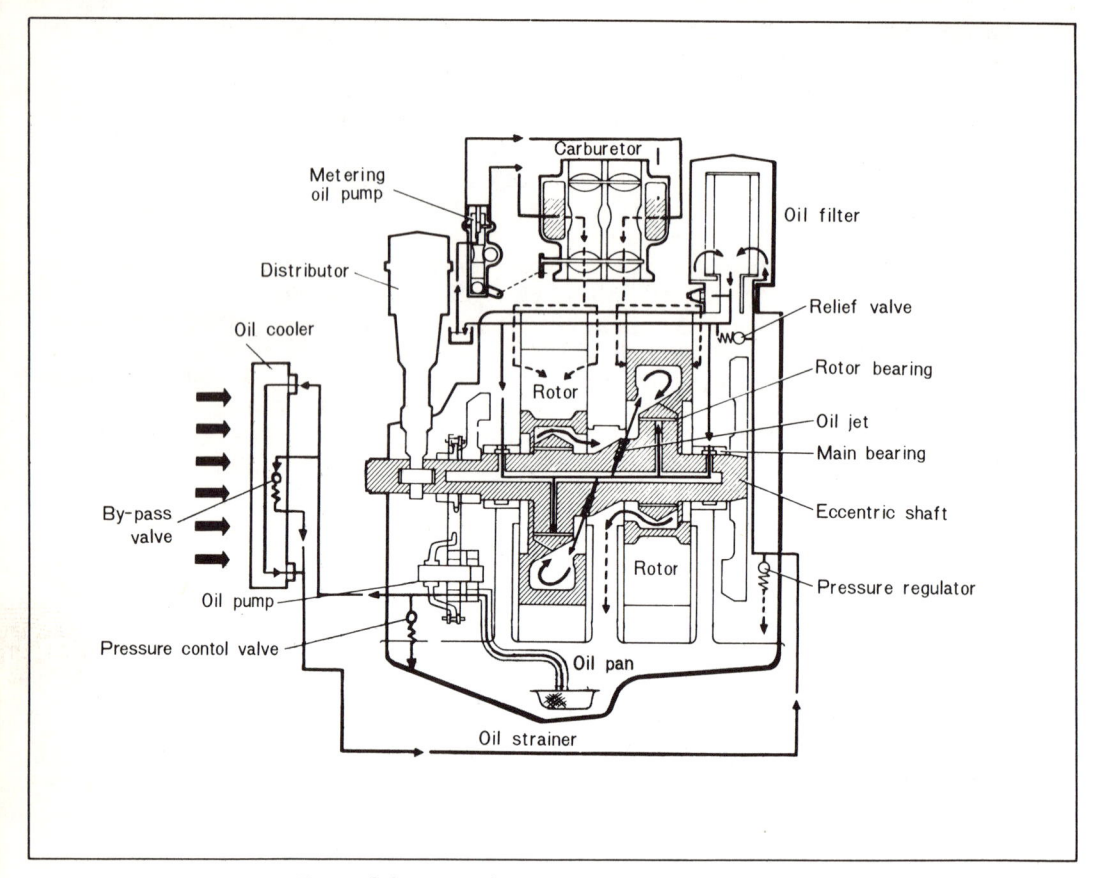

Engine lubrication diagram (© Toyo Kogyo Co., Ltd.)

driven, circulates oil through the rotary engine. A full-flow filter is mounted on the top of the rear housing and an oil cooler is used to reduce the temperature of the engine oil.

An unusual feature of the rotary engine lubrication system is a metering oil pump which injects oil into the float chamber of the carburetor. Once there, it is mixed with the fuel which is to be burned, thus providing extra lubrication for the seals. The metering oil pump is designed to work only when the engine is operating under a load.

OIL PAN

Removal and Installation

1. Raise the front of the car and support it with jackstands.
2. Remove the drain plug and drain the engine oil.
3. Remove the nuts and bolts which secure the gravel shield and withdraw it from underneath the car.
4. Unfasten the retaining bolts and remove the oil pan with its gasket.

Oil pan installation is performed in the reverse order of removal. Coat both the oil pan flange and its mounting flange with sealer, prior to assembly.

OIL PUMP

Removal and Installation

Oil pump removal and installation is contained in the "Engine Overhaul" section above. Perform only those steps needed in order to remove the oil pump.

METERING OIL PUMP

Operation

A metering oil pump, mounted on the top of the engine, is used to provide additional lubrication to the engine when it is operating under a load. The pump

ENGINE AND ENGINE REBUILDING—ROTARY ONLY

provides oil to the carburetor, where it is mixed in the float chamber with the fuel which is to be burned.

The metering pump is a plunger type and is controlled by throttle opening. A cam arrangement, connected to the carburetor throttle lever, operates a plunger. The plunger in turn, acts on a differential plunger, the stroke of which determines the amount of oil flow.

When the throttle opening is small, the amount of the plunger stroke is small; as the throttle opening increases, so does the amount of the plunger stroke.

Testing

1. Disconnect the oil lines which run from the metering oil pump to the carburetor, at the carburetor end.
2. Use a container which has a scale calibrated in cubic centimeters (cc) to catch the pump discharge from the oil lines.

NOTE: *Such a container is available from a scientific equipment supply house.*

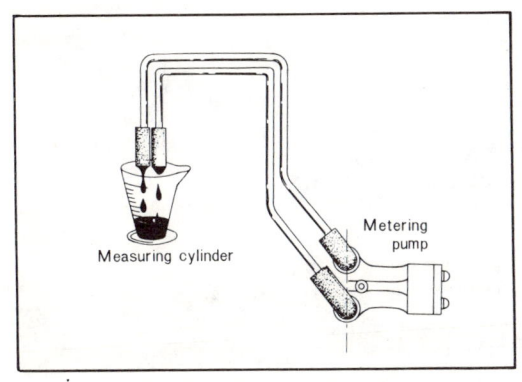

Checking the oil discharge rate of the metering oil pump (© Toyo Kogyo Co., Ltd.)

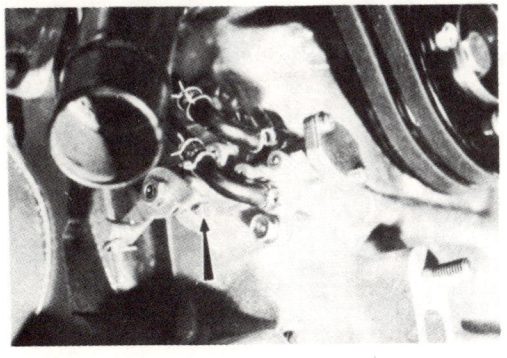

Metering oil pump adjusting screw (© Toyo Kogyo Co., Ltd.)

3. Run the engine at 2,000 rpm for six minutes.
4. At the end of this time, 2.2 cc of oil should be collected in the container. If not, adjust the pump as explained below.

Adjustments

Rotate the adjusting screw on the metering oil pump to obtain the proper oil flow. Clockwise rotation of the screw *increases* the flow; counterclockwise rotation *decreases* the oil flow.

If necessary, the oil discharge rate may further be adjusted by changing the position of the cam in the pump connecting rod. The shorter the rod throw the more oil will be pumped. Adjust the throw by means of three holes provided.

NOTE: *After adjusting the metering oil pump, check the discharge rate again.*

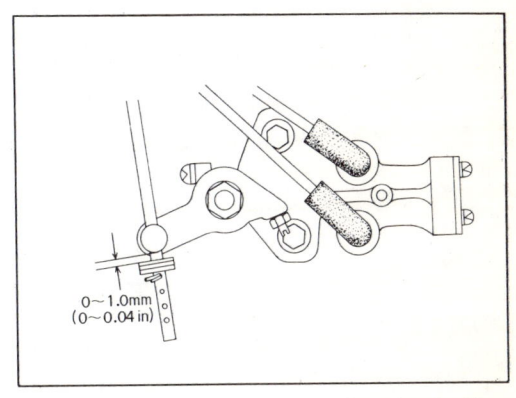

Metering oil pump connecting rod setting (© Toyo Kogyo Co., Ltd.)

OIL COOLER

Removal and Installation

1. Raise the car and support it with jackstands.
2. Drain the engine oil.
3. Unfasten the screws which retain the gravel shield and remove the shield.
4. Remove the oil lines from the oil cooler.
5. Unfasten the nuts which secure the oil cooler to the radiator.
6. Remove the oil cooler.

Examine the oil cooler for signs of leakage. Solder any leaks found. Blow the fins of the cooler clean with compressed air.

Installation is the reverse of removal.

ENGINE AND ENGINE REBUILDING—ROTARY ONLY

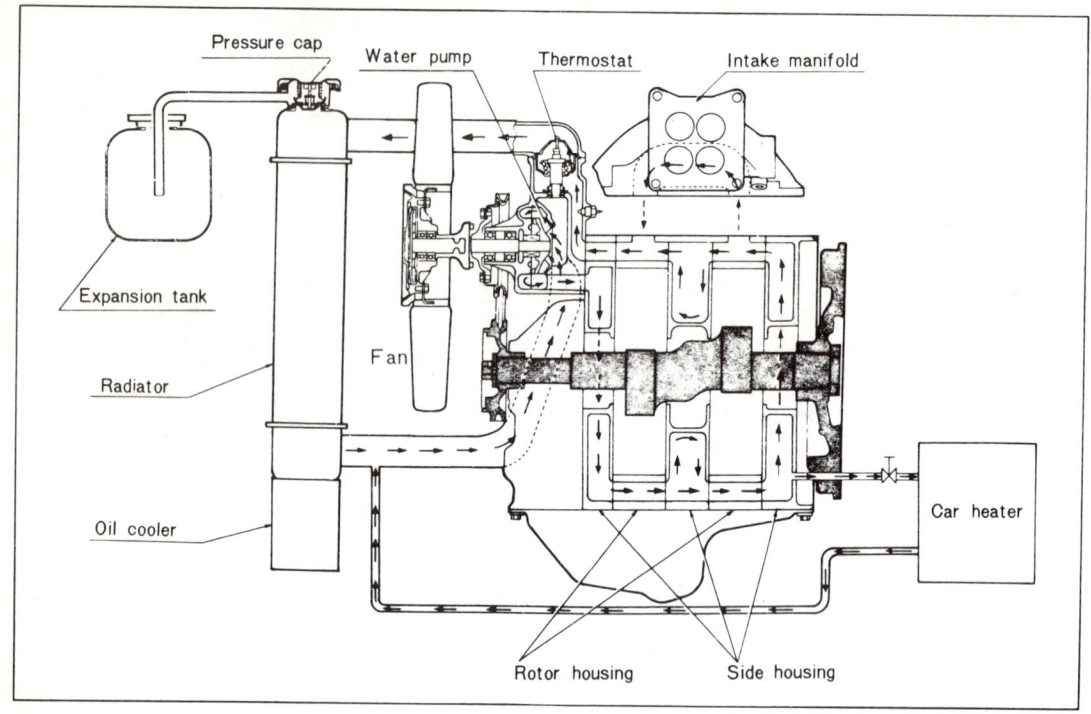

Engine cooling diagram (© Toyo Kogyo Co., Ltd.)

Engine Cooling

RADIATOR

Removal and Installation

CAUTION: *Perform this operation when the engine has cooled completely.*

1. Drain the engine coolant into a large, clean container so that it may be reused.
2. Remove the nuts and bolts which attach the shroud to the radiator.
3. Remove the upper, lower, and expansion tank hoses from the radiator.
4. Unfasten the bolts which attach the radiator to its mounting bracket. Remove the oil cooler nuts and bolts.
5. Withdraw the radiator from the car.

Install the radiator in the reverse order of removal.

WATER PUMP

Removal and Installation

1. Drain the cooling system.
2. Remove the air cleaner.

Water pump attaching bolts (arrows) (© Toyo Kogyo Co., Ltd.)

3. Remove the bolts attaching the rear of the fan drive and remove the fan drive.
4. If necessary to disassemble the water pump, loosen the bolts attaching the water pump pulley to the water pump boss.
5. Remove the air pump and drive belt.
6. Remove the alternator and disconnect the drive belt.
7. If necessary, remove the water pump pulley and bolts.

ENGINE AND ENGINE REBUILDING—ROTARY ONLY

8. Unbolt and remove the water pump.

9. Installation is the reverse of removal.

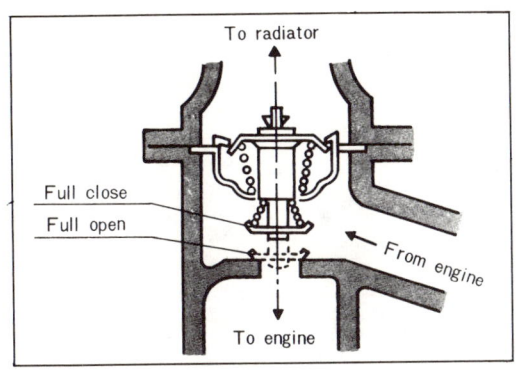

Thermostat operation (© Toyo Kogyo Co., Ltd.)

THERMOSTAT

Removal and Installation

1. Drain the engine coolant into a large, clean container for reuse.
2. Remove the nuts which secure the thermostat housing to the water pump.
3. Lift the thermostat out.

Thermostat installation is performed in the reverse order of removal.

CAUTION: *The thermostat is equipped with a plunger which covers and uncovers a by-pass hole at its bottom. Because of its unusual construction, only the specified Mazda thermostat should be used for replacement. Use of a standard thermostat will cause the engine to overheat.*

Path of the rotor in the Mazda rotary engine (© Toyo Kogyo Co., Ltd.)

Chapter Five
Emission Controls and Fuel System

Emission Controls—B-1600

The Mazda B-1600 uses three emission control systems: a throttle positioner system, a positive crankcase ventilation system and evaporative emission control system.

THROTTLE POSITIONER

The throttle positioner system consists of a servo diaphragm connected to the throttle lever and a vacuum control valve which controls intake manifold vacuum through the servo diaphragm.

Testing the System

SERVO DIAPHRAGM

1. Start the engine and set the idle speed to 800 rpm. Stop the engine.
2. Disconnect the vacuum sensing tube between the servo diaphragm and the vacuum control valve at the servo diaphragm.
3. Remove the intake manifold suction hole plug.
4. Connect the intake manifold and the servo diaphragm with a tube so that the intake manifold vacuum goes directly to the servo diaphragm.
5. Connect a tachometer and remove the vacuum sensing tube between the carburetor and distributor.

Servo diaphragm—B-1600 (© Toyo Kogyo Co., Ltd.)

6. Start the engine and read the speed. If the engine is running between 1,300–1,500 rpm, the servo diaphragm is operating normally. If the engine speed is 800–1,500 rpm, adjust the speed with the throttle opening screw. If the engine speed remains normal, about 800 rpm, the servo diaphragm is defective and should be replaced.
7. Remove the test equipment and reconnect all the lines.

Service

SERVO DIAPHRAGM

Removal and Installation

1. Remove the air cleaner.
2. Disconnect the vacuum sensing tube from the servo diaphragm.

EMISSION CONTROLS AND FUEL SYSTEM

3. Remove the cotter pin and link.
4. Loosen the locknut and remove the servo diaphragm.
5. Installation is the reverse of removal. Adjust the servo diaphragm.

Vacuum Control Valve

Removal and Installation

1. Remove the air cleaner.
2. Disconnect the vacuum sensing tubes from the vacuum control valve.

Vacuum control valve—B-1600 (© Toyo Kogyo Co., Ltd.)

3. Unbolt and remove the vacuum control valve.
4. Installation is the reverse of removal.

Adjustments

Throttle Opener

1. Install a tachometer on the engine.
2. Start the engine and set the idle speed.
3. Stop the engine.
4. Disconnect the vacuum sensing tube between the servo diaphragm and

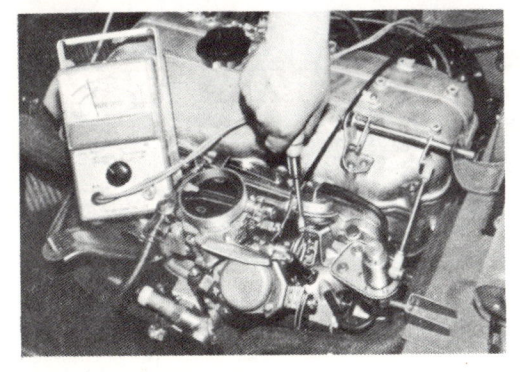

Adjusting the throttle position—B-1600 (© Toyo Kogyo Co., Ltd.)

Intake manifold suction hole plug—B-1600 (© Toyo Kogyo Co., Ltd.)

the vacuum control valve from the servo diaphragm.
5. Remove the plug from the intake manifold suction hole.
6. Attach a test tube between the intake manifold and the servo diaphragm to route intake manifold vacuum directly to the servo diaphragm.
7. Start the engine and note the speed.
8. Set the engine speed to 1,400 rpm using the throttle opener screw. Turning the adjusting screw clockwise increases engine speed.
9. Stop the engine and disconnect the tachometer. Reconnect all lines.

POSITIVE CRANKCASE VENTILATION (PCV) SYSTEM

The function of the PCV valve is to divert blow-by gases from the crankcase to the intake manifold to be burned in the cylinders. The system consists of a PCV valve, an oil separator and the hoses necessary to connect the components.

Ventilating air is routed into the rocker cover from the air cleaner. The air

PCV valve—typical (© Toyo Kogyo Co., Ltd.)

EMISSION CONTROLS AND FUEL SYSTEM

is then moved to the oil separator and from the separator to the PCV valve. The PCV valve is operated by differences in air pressure between the intake manifold and the rocker cover.

Testing the System

PCV Valve

Standard Test

1. Remove the hose from the PCV valve.
2. Start the engine and run it at approximately 700–1,000 rpm.
3. Cover the end of the PCV valve with a finger. A distinct vacuum should be felt. If no vacuum is felt, replace the valve.

Alternate Test

Remove the valve from its fitting. Shake the valve. If a rattle is heard, the valve is probably functioning normally. If no rattle is heard, the valve is probably stuck (open or shut) and should be replaced.

Service

PCV Valve Removal and Installation

1. Remove the air cleaner.
2. Disconnect the hose from the PCV valve.
3. Remove the valve from the intake manifold fitting.

To install the valve:

4. Install the valve in the fitting.
5. Connect the hose to the valve.
6. Install the air cleaner.

EVAPORATIVE EMISSION CONTROL SYSTEM

The evaporative emission control system is designed to control the emission of gasoline vapors into the atmosphere. The system consists of a fuel tank, a condenser tank and a check valve.

When the engine is not running, fuel vapors are channeled to the condenser tank. The fuel returns to the fuel tank as the vapors condense. During periods of engine operation, fuel vapor that has not condensed in the condenser tank moves to the carbon canister. The stored vapors are removed from the charcoal by fresh air moving through the inlet hole in the bottom of the canister.

Service

Condenser Tank Removal and Installation

1. Raise and support the rear of the truck.
2. Disconnect the hoses from the condenser tank.

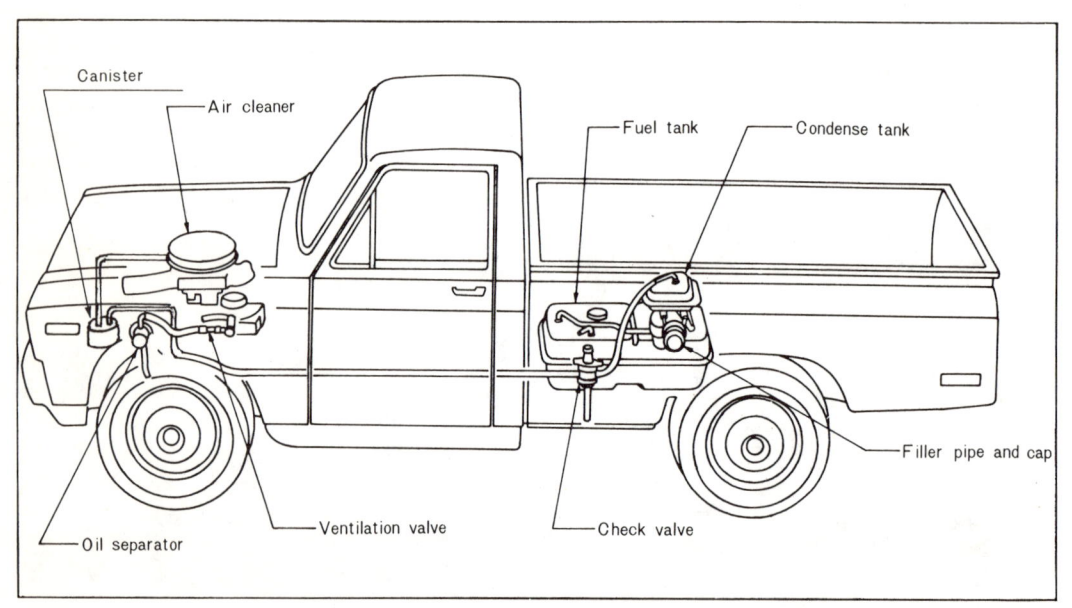

Evaporative emission control system (© Toyo Kogyo Co., Ltd.)

EMISSION CONTROLS AND FUEL SYSTEM

3. Unbolt and remove the condenser tank.

To install the tank:

4. Install the tank and tighten the bolts.
5. Connect the hoses to the tank.
6. Lower the truck.

Check Valve Removal and Installation

1. Disconnect the hoses from the check valve.
2. Unscrew and remove the valve.

To install the check valve:

3. Position a new valve on the crossmember. Tighten the attaching screws.
4. Connect all hoses to the valve.

Emission Controls— Rotary Pick-Up 1974–75

POSITIVE CRANKCASE VENTILATION (PCV) SYSTEM

The positive crankcase ventilation (PCV) valve is located on the intake manifold below the carburetor. In this case, the word "crankcase" is not quite correct, as the Mazda rotary engine has no crankcase in the normal sense of the term. Rather, the valve, which is operated by intake manifold vacuum, is used to meter the flow of fuel and air vapors through the rotor housings.

Testing and Replacement

The procedures for PCV valve testing and replacement may be found under "Routine Maintenance," in Chapter 1.

AIR INJECTION SYSTEM

The air injection system used on the Mazda rotary engine differs from the type used on a conventional piston engine in two respects:

1. Air is not only supplied to burn the gases in the exhaust ports, but it is also used to cool the thermal reactor.
2. A three-way air control valve is used in place of the conventional antibackfire and diverter valves. It contains an air cut-out valve, a relief valve, and a safety valve.

Air is supplied to the system by a normal vane type air pump. The air flows from the pump to the air control valve, where it is routed to the air injection nozzles to cool the thermal reactor or, in the case of a system malfunction, to the air cleaner. A check valve, located beneath the air control valve seat, prevents the back-flow of hot exhaust gases into the air injection system in case of air pressure loss.

Air injection nozzles are used to feed air into the exhaust ports, just as in a conventional piston engine.

Component Testing

AIR PUMP

1. Check the air pump drive belt tension by applying 22 lbs of pressure halfway between the water pump and air pump pulleys. The belt should deflect 0.28–0.35 in. Adjust the belt if necessary, or replace it if it is cracked or worn.

2. Turn the pump by hand. If it has seized, the drive belt will slip, producing noise

NOTE: *Disregard any chirping, squealing, or rolling sounds coming from inside the pump; these are normal when it is being turned by hand.*

3. Check the hoses and connections for leaks. Hissing or a blast of air is indicative of a leak. Soapy water, applied around the area in question, is a good method of detecting leaks.

4. Connect a pressure gauge between the air pump and the air control valve with a T-fitting.

5. Plug the other hose connections (outlets) on the air control valve, as illustrated.

CAUTION: *Be careful not to touch the thermal reactor; severe burns will result.*

6. With the engine at normal idle speed, the pressure gauge should read 0.48–0.68 psi. Replace the air pump if it is less than this.

7. If the air pump is not defective, leave the pressure gauge connected but unplug the connections at the air control valve and proceed with the next test.

EMISSION CONTROLS AND FUEL SYSTEM

Air Injection System Diagnosis Chart

Problem	Cause	Cure
1. Noisy drive belt	1a. Loose belt	1a. Tighten belt
	1b. Seized pump	1b. Replace
2. Noisy pump	2a. Leaking hose	2a. Trace and fix leak
	2b. Loose hose	2b. Tighten hose clamp
	2c. Hose contacting other parts	2c. Reposition hose
	2d. Air control or check valve failure	2d. Replace
	2e. Pump mounting loose	2e. Tighten securing bolts
	2g. Defective pump	2g. Replace
3. No air supply	3a. Loose belt	3a. Tighten belt
	3b. Leak in hose or at fitting	3b. Trace and fix leak
	3c. Defective air control valve	3c. Replace
	3d. Defective check valve	3d. Replace
	3e. Defective pump	3e. Replace
4. Exhaust backfire	4a. Vacuum or air leaks	4a. Trace and fix leak
	4b. Defective air control valve	4b. Replace
	4c. Sticking choke	4c. Service choke
	4d. Choke setting rich	4d. Adjust choke

AIR CONTROL VALVE

CAUTION: *When testing the air control valve, avoid touching the thermal reactor as severe burns will result.*

1. Test the air control valve solenoid as follows:

   a. Turn the ignition switch off and on. A click should be heard coming from the solenoid. If no sound is audible, check the solenoid wiring.

   b. If no defect is found in the solenoid wiring, connect the solenoid directly to the car's battery. If the solenoid still does not click, it is defective and must be replaced. If the solenoid works, then check the components of the air flow control system. See below.

2. Start the engine and run it at idle speed. The pressure gauge should still read 0.37–0.75 psi. No air should leak from the two outlets which were unplugged.

3. Increase the engine speed to 3,500 rpm (3,000 rpm—automatic transmission). The pressure gauge should now read 1.2–2.8 psi and the two outlets still should not be leaking air.

4. Return the engine to idle.

5. Disconnect the solenoid wiring. Air should now flow from the outlet marked (A) in the illustration, but not from the outlet marked (B). The pressure gauge reading should remain the same as in Step 2.

6. Reconnect the solenoid.

7. If the relief valve is faulty, air sent from the air pump will flow into the cooling passages of the thermal reactor when the engine is at idle speed.

8. If the safety valve is faulty, air will flow into the air cleaner when the engine is idling.

9. Replace the air control valve if it fails to pass any one of the above tests. Remember to disconnect the pressure gauge.

CHECK VALVE

1. Remove the check valve, as detailed below.

2. Depress the valve plate to see if it will seat properly.

3. Measure the free length of the valve spring; it should be 1.22 in.

NOTE: *The spring free length should be 0.75 in. on automatic transmission equipped models.*

4. Measure the installed length of the spring: it should be 0.68 in.

Replace the check valve if it is not up to specifications.

Component Removal and Installation

AIR PUMP

1. Remove the air cleaner assembly from the carburetor.

2. Loosen, but do not remove, the adjusting link bolt.

3. Push the pump toward the engine to slacken belt tension and remove the drive belt.

EMISSION CONTROLS AND FUEL SYSTEM

4. Disconnect the air supply hoses from the pump.
5. Unfasten the pump securing bolts and remove the pump.
CAUTION: *Do not pry on the air pump housing during removal and do not clamp the housing in a vise once the pump has been removed. Any type of heavy pressure applied to the housing will distort it.*
Installation is performed in the reverse order of removal. Adjust the belt tension by moving the air pump to the specification given in the "Testing" section, above.

AIR CONTROL VALVE

CAUTION: *Remove the air control valve only after the thermal reactor has cooled sufficiently to prevent the danger of a serious burn.*
1. Remove the air cleaner assembly.
2. Unfasten the leads from the air control valve solenoid.
3. Disconnect the air hoses from the valve.
4. Loosen the screws which secure the air control valve and remove the valve.
Valve installation is performed in the reverse order of removal.

CHECK VALVE

1. Perform the air control valve removal procedure, detailed above. Be sure to pay attention to the CAUTION.
2. Remove the check valve seat.
3. Withdraw the valve plate and spring.
Install the check valve in the reverse order of removal.

AIR INJECTION NOZZLE

1. Remove the gravel shield from underneath the car.
2. Perform the oil pan removal procedure as detailed in "Engine Lubrication," above.
3. Unbolt the air injection nozzles from both of the rotor housings.
Nozzle installation is performed in the reverse order of removal.

THERMAL REACTOR

A thermal reactor is used in place of a conventional exhaust manifold. It is used to oxidize unburned hydrocarbons and carbon monoxide before they can be released into the atmosphere.
If the engine speed exceeds 4,000 rpm, or if the car is decelerating, the air control valve diverts air into passages in the thermal reactor housing in order to cool the reactor.
A one-way valve prevents hot exhaust gases from flowing back into the air injection system. The valve is located at the reactor air intake

Inspection

CAUTION: *Perform thermal reactor inspection only after the reactor has cooled sufficiently to prevent the danger of being severely burned.*
1. Examine the reactor housing for cracks or other signs of damage.
2. Remove the air supply hose from the one-way valve. Insert a screwdriver into the valve and test the butterfly for smooth operation. Replace the valve if necessary.
3. If the valve is functioning properly, connect the hose to it.
NOTE: *Remember to check the components of the air injection system which are related to the thermal reactor.*

Removal and Installation

Thermal reactor removal and installation are given in the "Engine Mechanical" section of Chapter 4.

AIRFLOW CONTROL SYSTEM

The airflow control system consists of a thermosensor, thermodetector, vacuum switch, and a control box.
The system determines when the trailing distributor should be used, depending upon engine temperature and speed (rpm).
The airflow control system also operates the solenoid on the airflow control valve.
When the engine is cold, the thermosensor sends a signal to the control box which, in turn, activates the distributor. The thermodetector is used to keep the thermosensor from being influenced by ambient temperatures. This ensures easier cold starting and better driveability. The thermosensor and control box are located, in order, beneath the dash, next to the fuse box, and behind the grille.

EMISSION CONTROLS AND FUEL SYSTEM

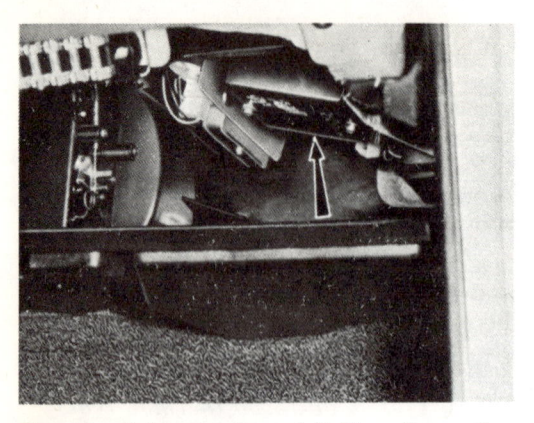

Control unit location (arrow) (© Toyo Kogyo Co., Ltd.)

Thermodetector location (arrow) (© Toyo Kogyo Co., Ltd.)

Component Testing

No. 1 Thermosensor—All Models

NOTE: *Begin this test procedure with the engine cold.*

1. Remove the air cleaner.
2. Examine the No. 1 thermosensor, which is located next to the thermostat housing, for leakage around the boot and for signs of wax leakage.
3. Disconnect the multiconnector from the thermosensor and place the prods of an ohmmeter on the thermosensor terminals. The ohmmeter should read over 7 k-ohms with the engine cold and less than 2.3 k-ohms after the engine has been warmed up.
4. Replace the thermosensor with a new one, if the reading on the ohmmeter is not within specifications.
5. If the No. 1 thermosensor is functioning properly, proceed with the appropriate test for the thermodetector below.

Themodetector

Use the following chart to determine the correct ohmmeter reading for the ambient temperature at the time of the test:

Thermadetector Resistance Specifications Chart

Ambient Temperature (° F)	Resistance (k-ohms ± 5%)
−4	10.0
+32	3.0
+68	1.2
+105	0.5

No. 1 Control Box—All Models

NOTE: *If all of the other components of the airflow control system are functioning properly and the system wiring and vacuum lines are in good condition, then the fault probably lies in the No. 1 control box. Perform the following tests to verify this.*

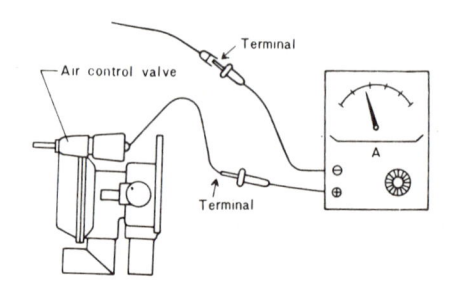

Testing the No. 1 control box (© Toyo Kogyo Co., Ltd.)

1. Disconnect the No. 1 thermosensor. Disconnect the idle switch multiconnector.
2. Start the engine and run it to the speeds specified below. The timing light should come on in these speed ranges:
   Manual Transmission: 3,600–4,400 rpm
   Automatic Transmission: 4,300–5,300 rpm
   NOTE: *These speeds should be held for an instant only.*
3. Connect an ammeter to the air control valve solenoid leads and to ground.
   a. Current should flow when the engine speed is between 900–

EMISSION CONTROLS AND FUEL SYSTEM

4,000 ±200 rpm (manual) or 750–5,200 (automatic);

b. Current flow should cease above 3,600–4,400 rpm (manual transmission) or 4,300–5,300 rpm (automatic transmission).

4. Short together the pins of the No. 1 thermosensor multiconnector with a jumper wire. Connect the timing light to the trailing side of the distributor, if it is not already in place.

a. The timing light should go on when the engine is below 3,600–4,400 rpm (automatic); rpm (manual) or below 4,300–5,200

b. On automatic transmission equipped models, connect an ammeter to the air control valve solenoid. Current should flow to the solenoid when the engine speed is below 3,400 ±200 rpm and should cease flowing above this speed.

5. Remove the jumper wire from the multiconnector and reconnect the No. 1 thermosensor. Reconnect the vacuum switch if it was disconnected.

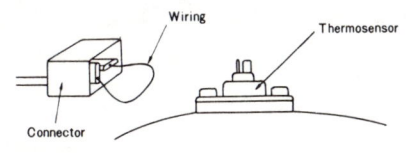

Short the pins of the No. 1 thermosensor together with a jumper wire (© Toyo Kogyo Co., Ltd.)

6. Connect the prods of the ammeter to the coasting valve solenoid terminals.

NOTE: *For a further description of coasting valve operation, see "Deceleration Control Systems", below.*

7. No current should flow to the solenoid with the engine at idle. Increase the engine speed; current should begin flowing between 1,250 and 1,550 rpm. Decrease engine speed; current should cease flowing between 1,300 and 1,100 rpm (1,400 rpm—automatic transmission).

If the No. 1 control box proves to be defective, replace it. Remember to disconnect all of the test equipment and reconnect the system components when the tests are completed.

Component Removal and Installation

NO. 1 THERMOSENSOR

1. Remove the air cleaner assembly.
2. If necessary, remove the starter

Arrow shows location of No. 1 thermosensor (© Toyo Kogyo Co., Ltd.)

motor as detailed under "Engine Electrical".

3. Unplug the thermosensor multiconnector.
4. Withdraw the boot from the thermosensor.
5. Unfasten its securing nuts and remove the switch.
6. Installation is the reverse of removal.

CONTROL BOX—1974–75

CAUTION: *Be sure that the ignition switch is turned off to prevent damage to the control box.*

1. Working from underneath the instrument panel, locate and disconnect the control box multiconnector.
2. Remove the screws which secure the control box.
3. Remove the control box.

Installation is performed in the reverse order of removal.

OTHER COMPONENTS

Any of the other components used in the airflow control system are removed by unfastening their multiconnectors and removing the screws which secure them.

DECELERATION CONTROL SYSTEM

The deceleration control system uses an anti-afterburn valve, a coasting valve, and an air supply valve. In addition, an idle sensing switch is fitted to the carburetor. The No. 1 control box is shared with the airflow control system.

The anti-afterburn valve, which is located on the intake manifold, is used to supply fresh air to the manifold during deceleration or when the engine is shut off, in order to prevent afterburning.

A coasting valve, which functions in a similar manner, is used to prevent an overly rich mixture during deceleration.

The coasting valve also vents the vacuum chamber of the air control valve during deceleration. The valve is operated by a solenoid which is controlled by the No. 1 control box and the idle sensing switch.

1974–75 models do not have a throttle positioner; they have an idle sensing switch attached to the carburetor in its place. When the throttle closes, its linkage contacts a plunger on the switch which completes the circuit from the No. 1 control box to the coasting valve thus causing the coasting valve to operate. On automatic transmission equipped models, it also determines trailing distributor operation.

A solenoid-operated air supply valve opens when the ignition is shut off to prevent the engine from dieseling (running on).

In addition to the above components, 1974–75 Rotary Pick-Ups have an altitude compensator which provides air to lean out the overly rich mixture which occurs at high altitudes.

On 1974 models with automatic transmission, a kick-down control system is used. Regardless of the gear selected, the transmission will not go above Second gear when the choke knob is pulled out.

Combination Anti-Afterburn and Coasting Valve—1974

1. Disconnect the hose which runs from the air cleaner to the combination valve at the air cleaner end.
2. Start the engine and run it at curb idle.
3. There should be no vacuum present at the end of the hose which you disconnected in Step 1.
4. Turn the engine off.
5. Disconnect the hose which runs from the coasting valve portion of the combination valve to the intake manifold from the coasting valve end and plug up the port.
6. Operate the engine at idle.
7. Disconnect the anti-afterburn valve solenoid connector.
8. Check for vacuum at the end of the hose which you disconnected in Step 1; there should be vacuum present. If not, the anti-afterburn valve is defective.
9. Turn the engine off. Reconnect the anti-afterburn valve electrical leads and the hose to the coasting valve.
10. Disconnect the intake manifold-to-anti-afterburn valve vacuum line at the valve end, and plug the vacuum fitting on the valve.
11. Start the engine and allow it to idle.
12. Disconnect the coasting valve solenoid at the multiconnector.
13. Hold your hand over the end of the vacuum line which you disconnected in Step 10. Vacuum should be felt; if not, replace the defective coasting valve.
14. Turn the engine off and reconnect the leads and hoses which were disconnected above.

Altitude Compensator—1975

1. Detach the air intake hose from the altitude compensator.
2. Start the engine and run it at idle.
3. Hold your finger over the altitude compensator air intake; the engine speed should decrease. If it doesn't, replace the compensator.
4. Reconnect the air intake hose, if the compensator is in good working order.

Idle Switch

1. Unfasten the idle switch leads.
2. Connect the test meter to the switch terminals.

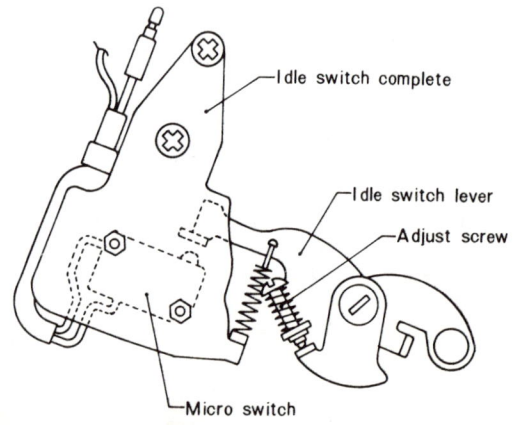

Idle switch—Rotary Pick-Up uses a multiconnector (© Toyo Kogyo Co., Ltd.)

3. With the engine at idle, the meter should indicate a completed circuit.
4. Depress the plunger on the idle switch; the circuit should be broken (no meter reading).

If the idle switch is not functioning properly, replace it with a new one.

EMISSION CONTROLS AND FUEL SYSTEM

Coolant Temperature Switch—1974–75

Start this test with the coolant temperature below 68°F.

1. Disconnect the electrical lead from the temperature switch.
2. Connect a test light between one terminal of the switch and a 12-volt battery. Ground the other terminal.
3. The test light should light.
4. Start the engine and allow it to warm up. Once the engine reaches normal operating temperaure, the test light should go out.
5. Replace the switch if it doesn't work as outlined.

Choke Switch (Semi-Automatic Choke)

1. Working underneath the instrument panel, disconnect the lead at the back of the choke switch.
2. Connect an ohmmeter to the terminals on the choke switch side of the connector.
3. With the choke knob *in* (off), the meter should show continuity (resistance reading).
4. Pull the choke knob out, about ½ in. for manual transmission cars or 1 in. for automatics. The meter should show no continuity (read zero).
5. Replace the switch if defective.

Component Removal and Installation

ANTI-AFTERBURN VALVE

1. Remove the air cleaner assembly.
2. Disconnect the air hoses and vacuum lines from the valve.
3. Unfasten the solenoid wiring.
4. Remove the securing nuts and withdraw the valve.

Arrow shows anti-afterburn valve (© Toyo Kogyo Co., Ltd.)

Installation is performed in the reverse order of removal.

COASTING VALVE

The coasting valve is removed and installed in the same manner as the anti-afterburn valve.

Arrow shows coasting valve (© Toyo Kogyo Co., Ltd.)

IDLE SWITCH

1. Remove the coasting valve. See the section above.
2. Remove the carburetor as detailed elsewhere, in this chapter.
3. Disconnect the wiring from the switch.
4. Unfasten the securing screws and remove the switch.

Arrow shows idle switch (© Toyo Kogyo Co., Ltd.)

Installation is performed in the reverse order of removal. After installing the switch, adjust it as outlined under "Adjustments", below.

AIR SUPPLY VALVE

1. Remove the air cleaner and the hot air duct.
2. Disconnect the air hose, the vacuum

EMISSION CONTROLS AND FUEL SYSTEM

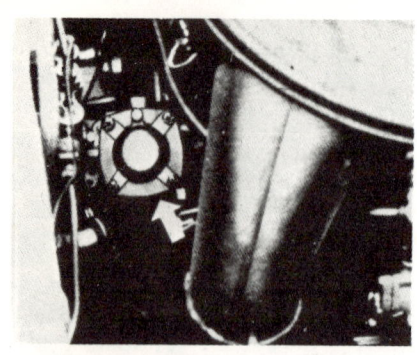

Arrow shows air valve (© Toyo Kogyo Co., Ltd.)

lines, and the solenoid wiring from the valve.

3. Unfasten the screws which secure the valve and remove it.

Air supply valve installation is performed in the reverse order of removal.

ALTITUDE COMPENSATOR

1. Disconnect both hoses from the altitude compensator. Be sure to note their positions for correct hook-up.

2. Unfasten the altitude compensator securing bolts.

Altitude compensator (© Toyo Kogyo Co., Ltd.)

3. Remove the compensator from its bracket.

Installation is the reverse of removal.

COOLANT TEMPERATURE SWITCH

1. Drain the coolant from the radiator enough to bring the coolant level below the temperature switch.
2. Remove the alternator and drive belt if they are in the way.
3. Disconnect the switch multiconnector.
4. Use an open-end wrench to remove the switch.
5. Installation is the reverse of removal.

Adjustments

IDLE SWITCH

1. Warm up the engine until the water temperature is at least 159°F.
2. Make sure that the mixture and idle speed are properly adjusted.
3. Adjust the idle speed to 1,075–1,100 rpm 1,200–1,300 rpm—automatic transmission) by rotating the throttle adjusting screw.
4. Rotate the idle switch adjusting screw until the switch changes from OFF to ON position.
5. Slowly turn the idle switch adjusting screw back to the point where the switch just changes from ON to OFF.
6. Turn the throttle screw back so that the engine returns to idle.

NOTE: *Be sure that the idle switch goes on when the idle speed is still above 1,000 rpm.*

EVAPORATIVE EMISSION CONTROL SYSTEM

The vapors rising from the gasoline in the fuel tank are vented into a separate condensing tank. There they condense and return to the fuel tank in liquid form when the engine is not running.

When the engine is running, the fuel vapors are sucked directly into the engine through the PCV valve and are burned along with the air/fuel mixture.

Any additional fuel vapors which are not handled by the condensing tank are stored in a charcoal cannister or filter which is incorporated into the air cleaner. When the engine is running, the charcoal is purged of its stored fuel vapor.

A check valve vents the fuel vapor into the atmosphere if pressure in the fuel tank becomes excessive.

System Testing

There are several things to check for if a malfunction of the evaporative emission control system is suspected.

1. Leaks may be traced by using an infrared hydrocarbon tester. Run the test probe along the lines and connections. The meter will indicate the presence of a leak by a high hydrocarbon (HC) reading. This method is much more accurate than a visual inspection which would indicate only the presence of a leak large enough to pass liquid.

EMISSION CONTROLS AND FUEL SYSTEM 117

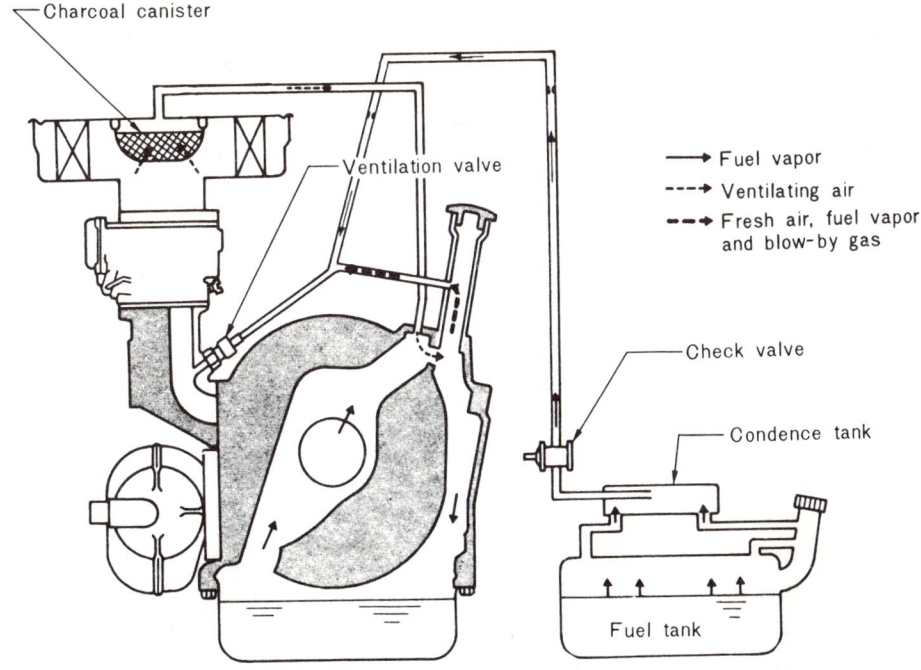

Evaporative emission control system (© Toyo Kogyo Co., Ltd.)

Charcoal canister (© Toyo Kogyo Co., Ltd.)

2. Leaks may be caused by any of the following, so always check these areas when looking for them:
 a. Defective or worn lines;
 b. Disconnected or pinched lines;
 c. Improperly routed lines;
 d. A defective check valve.

NOTE: *If it becomes necessary to replace any of the lines used in the evaporative emission control system, use only those hoses which are fuel-resistant or are marked "EVAP."*

3. If the fuel tank has collapsed, it may be the fault of clogged or pinched vent lines, a defective vapor separator, or a plugged or incorrect fuel filler cap.

Fuel System

ELECTRIC FUEL PUMP

An external electric fuel pump is mounted on the left frame rail adjacent to the fuel tank. Current is supplied to the pump through the ignition circuit and the pump will operate with the key in the RUN position.

Testing the Fuel Pump

To determine that the fuel pump is in good operating condition, tests for both volume and pressure should be performed. The tests are performed with the fuel pump installed, and the engine at normal operating temperature and idle speed.

Be sure that the fuel filter has been changed within the specified interval. If in doubt, install a new filter.

PRESSURE TEST

1. Remove the air cleaner.
2. Disconnect the fuel inlet line at the carburetor.
3. Connect a pressure gauge, a restrictor and a flexible hose between the fuel

EMISSION CONTROLS AND FUEL SYSTEM

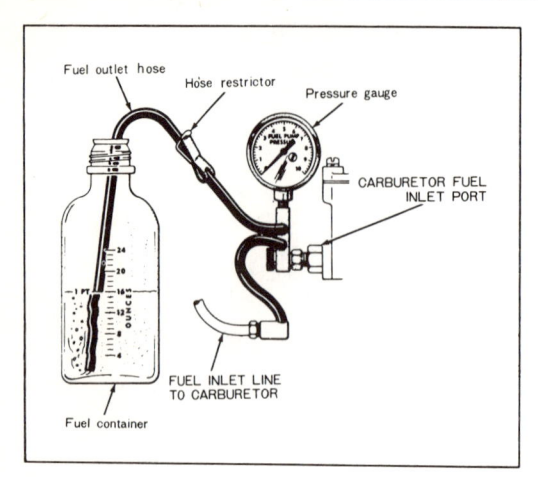

Testing the fuel pump for pressure and volume—B-1600 (© Toyo Kogyo Co., Ltd.)

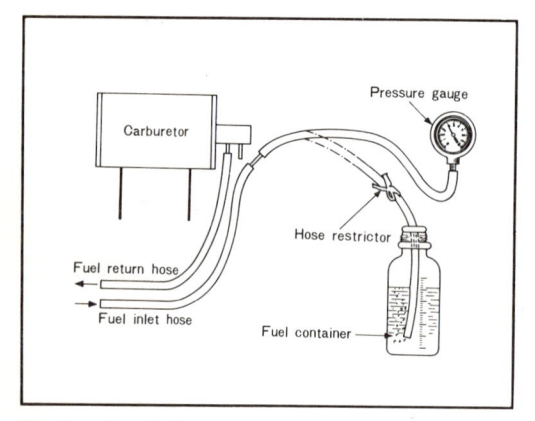

Testing the fuel pump—Rotary Pick-Up (© Toyo Kogyo Co., Ltd.)

filter and the carburetor. Position the flexible hose and restrictor so that the fuel can be discharged into a suitable graduated container.

4. Before taking a pressure reading, operate the engine at idle speed and vent the system into the container by momentarily opening the hose restrictor.

5. Close the hose restrictor and allow the pressure to stabilize and note the reading. It should be 2.8–3.6 psi or 3.6–5.0 psi on the Rotary Pick-Up.

6. If the pump pressure is not within specifications, and the fuel filter and fuel lines are not blocked, the pump is malfunctioning and should be replaced.

7. If the pressure is within specifications, perform the volume test.

Volume Test

8. Open the hose restrictor and expel the fuel into the container, while observing the time required to discharge 1 pint. Close the restrictor. Fuel pump volume should be approximately 2 pints/minute or 1.2 quarts/minutes on the Rotary Pick-Up.

9. If the pump volume is below specifications, repeat the test using an auxiliary fuel supply and a new filter. If the pump volume meets specifications while using the auxiliary fuel supply, check for a restriction in the fuel lines.

Removal and Installation

1. Remove the fuel pump shield from the frame. Disconnect the electrical leads from the pump.

2. Disconnect the inlet and outlet lines from the pump. Plug the lines.

3. Unbolt and remove the pump from its mounting bracket.

To install the fuel pump:

4. Position the fuel pump on the mounting bracket and install the bolts. Be sure that both mounting surfaces are clean.

5. Connect the inlet and outlet hoses.

6. Connect the electrical leads to the pump.

7. Install the fuel pump shield.

CARBURETOR

The Mazda Rotary Pick-Up uses a 4-barrel downdraft carburetor, while the B-1600 uses a 2-barrel downdraft unit.

Removal and Installation

B-1600

1. Remove the air cleaner and duct.

2. Disconnect the accelerator shaft from the throttle lever.

3. Disconnect and plug the fuel supply and fuel return lines and plug these.

4. Disconnect the leads from the throttle solenoid and deceleration valve at the quick-disconnects.

5. Disconnect the carburetor-to-distributor vacuum line.

6. Disconnect the throttle return spring.

7. Disconnect the choke cable.

8. Remove the carburetor attaching nuts from the intake manifold studs and remove the carburetor.

To install the carburetor:

EMISSION CONTROLS AND FUEL SYSTEM 119

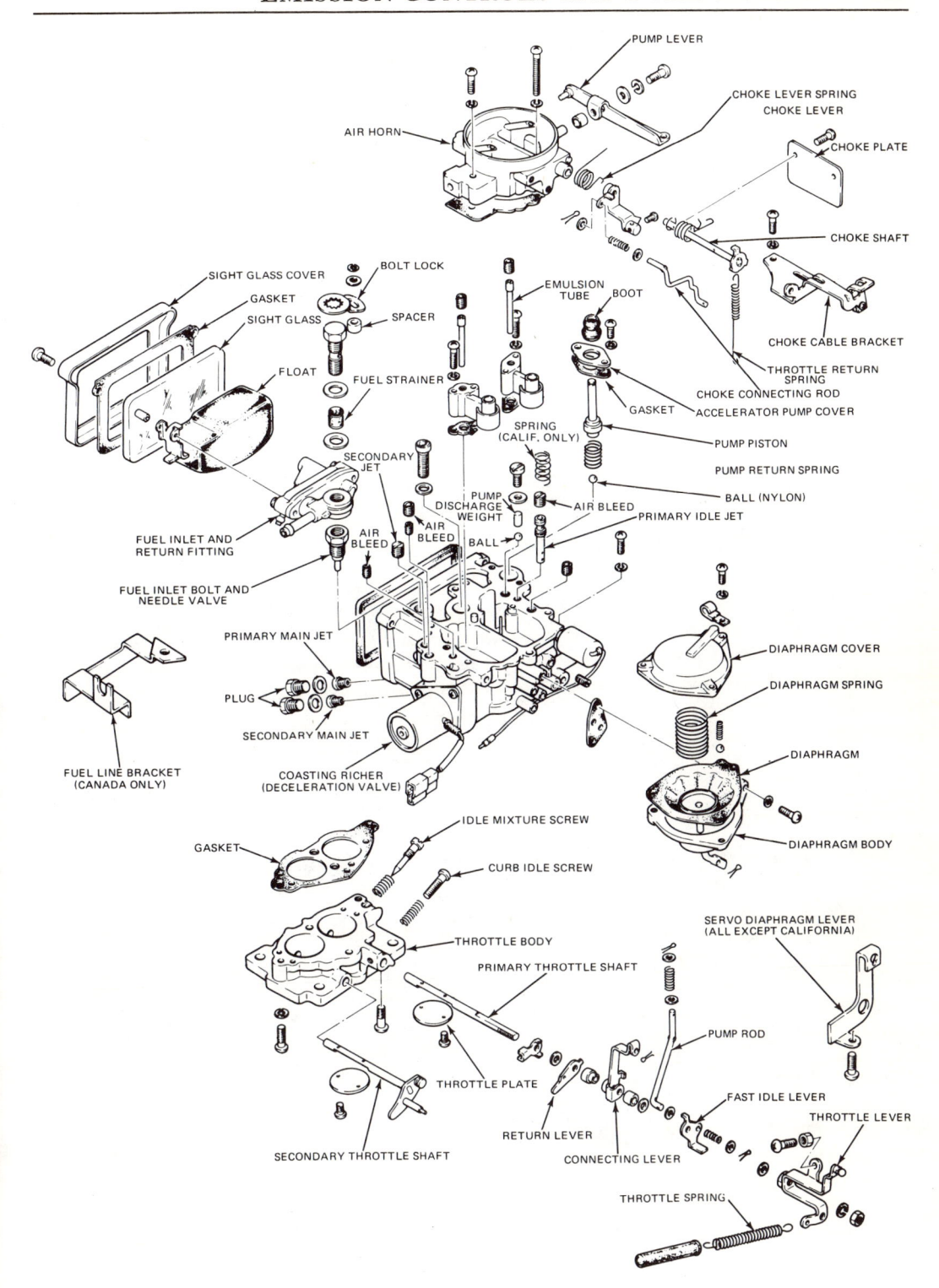

Exploded view of B-1600 carburetor (© Toyo Kogyo Co., Ltd.)

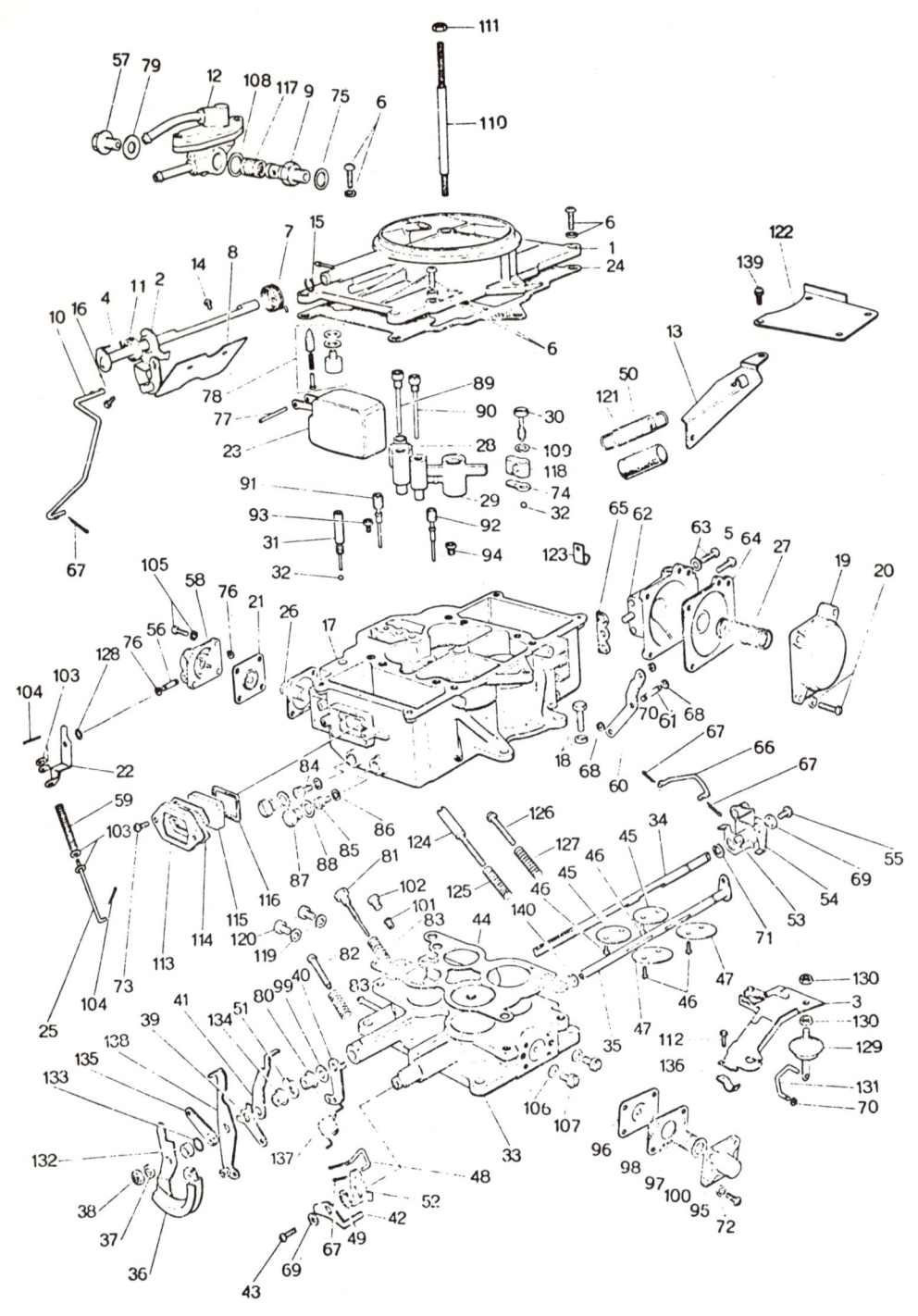

120 EMISSION CONTROLS AND FUEL SYSTEM

Exploded view of Rotary Pick-Up carburetor (© Toyo Kogyo Co., Ltd.)

1. Air horn
2. Choke valve lever
3. Clip
4. Choke lever shaft
5. Screw
6. Setscrew
7. Spring
8. Choke valve
9. Connector
10. Connecting rod
11. Spring
12. Fuel return valve
13. Hanger
14. Screw
15. Ring
16. Bolt
17. Carburetor body
18. Bolt
19. Diaphragm cover
20. Screw
21. Diaphragm
22. Accelerator pump arm
23. Float
24. Gasket
25. Connecting rod
26. Spring
27. Spring

EMISSION CONTROLS AND FUEL SYSTEM

9. Install a new carburetor gasket on the manifold.
10. Install the carburetor and tighten the carburetor attaching nuts.
11. Connect the throttle return spring.
12. Connect the accelerator shaft to the throttle shaft.
13. Connect the electrical leads to the throttle solenoid and deceleration valve.
14. Connect the distributor vacuum line.
15. Connect the fuel supply and fuel return lines.
16. Connect and adjust the choke cable.
17. Install the air cleaner and duct.
18. Start the engine and check for fuel leaks.

Rotary Pick-Up

1. Remove the air cleaner assembly, complete with its hoses and mounting bracket.
2. Detach the choke and accelerator cables from the carburetor.
3. Disconnect the fuel and vacuum lines from the carburetor.
4. Remove the oil line which runs to the metering oil pump, at the carburetor.
5. Unfasten the idle sensor switch wiring, if so equipped.
6. Remove the carburetor attaching nuts and/or bolts, gasket or heat insulator, and remove the carburetor.

Installation is performed in the reverse order of removal. Use a new gasket. Fill the float bowl with gasoline to aid in engine starting.

Overhaul

The following instructions are general overhaul procedures. Most good carburetor rebuilding kits come replete with exploded views and specific instructions.

Efficient carburetion depends greatly

28. Small venturi
29. Small venturi
30. Bolt
31. Check ball plug
32. Steel ball
33. Flange
34. Throttle shaft
35. Throttle shaft
36. Throttle lever
37. Spring washer
38. Nut
39. Lock
40. Adjusting arm
41. Starting lever
42. Arm
43. Screw
44. Gasket
45. Valve
46. Screw
47. Throttle valve
48. Throttle lever link
49. Ring
50. Throttle return spring
51. Arm
52. Retainer
53. Metering pump lever
54. Metering pump arm
55. Screw
56. Pin
57. Union bolt
58. Cover
59. Diaphragm spring
60. Diaphragm lever
61. Diaphragm pin
62. Diaphragm chamber
63. Screw
64. Diaphragm
65. Gasket
66. Connecting rod
67. Pin
68. Ring
69. Washer
70. Diaphragm stop ring
71. Diaphragm stop ring
72. Screw
73. Level gauge screw
74. Gasket
75. Gasket
76. Stop ring
77. Float pin
78. Needle valve seat
79. Gasket
80. Collar
81. Throttle adjusting screw
82. Idle adjusting screw
83. Spring
84. Main jet
85. Main jet
86. Gasket
87. Plug
88. Gasket
89. Air bleed
90. Air bleed
91. Slow jet
92. Step jet
93. Air bleed screw
94. Air bleed step
95. Cover
96. Diaphragm
97. Spring
98. Gasket
99. Washer
100. Shim
101. Jet
102. Bleed plug
103. Retainer
104. Pin
105. Screw
106. Gasket
107. Plug
108. Gasket
109. Gasket
110. Bolt
111. Nut
113. Cover
114. Gasket
115. Sight glass
116. Gasket
117. Filter
118. Accelerator nozzle
119. Gasket
120. Plug
121. Cover
122. Coasting valve bracket
123. Clip
124. Screw
125. Spring
126. Screw
127. Spring
128. Shim
129. Throttle positioner
130. Nut
131. Rod
132. Collar
133. Shim
134. Collar
135. Arm
136. Plate
137. Retaining spring
138. Lever
139. Setscrew
140. Ring

on careful cleaning and inspection during overhaul, since dirt, gum, water, or varnish in or on the carburetor parts are often responsible for poor performance.

Overhaul your carburetor in a clean, dust-free area. Carefully disassemble the carburetor, referring often to the exploded views. Keep all similar and lookalike parts segregated during disassembly and cleaning to avoid accidental interchange during assembly. Make a note of all jet sizes.

When the carburetor is disassembled, wash all parts (except diaphragms, electric choke units, pump plunger, and any other plastic, leather, fiber, or rubber parts) in clean carburetor solvent. Do not leave parts in the solvent any longer than is necessary to sufficiently loosen the deposits. Excessive cleaning may remove the special finish from the float bowl and choke valve bodies, leaving these parts unfit for service. Rinse all parts in clean solvent and blow them dry with compressed air or allow them to air dry. Wipe clean all cork, plastic, leather, and fiber parts with a clean, lint-free cloth.

Blow out all passages and jets with compressed air and be sure that there are no restrictions or blockages. Never use wire or similar tools to clean jets, fuel passages, or air bleeds. Clean all jets and valves separately to avoid accidental interchange.

Check all parts for wear or damage. If wear or damage is found, replace the defective parts. Especially check the following:

1. Check the float needle and seat for wear. If wear is found, replace the complete assembly.
2. Check the float hinge pin for wear and the float(s) for dents or distortion. Replace the float if fuel has leaked into it.
3. Check the throttle and choke shaft bores for wear or an out-of-round condition. Damage or wear to the throttle arm, shaft, or shaft bore will often require replacement of the throttle body. These parts require a close tolerance of fit; wear may allow air leakage, which could affect starting and idling.

   NOTE: *Throttle shafts and bushings are not included in overhaul kits. They can be purchased separately.*

4. Inspect the idle mixture adjusting needles for burrs or grooves. Any such condition requires replacement of the needle, since you will not be able to obtain a satisfactory idle.
5. Test the accelerator pump check valves. They should pass air one way but not the other. Test for proper seating by blowing and sucking on the valve. Replace the valve if necessary. If the valve is satisfactory, wash the valve again to remove breath moisture.
6. Check the bowl cover for warped surfaces with a straightedge.
7. Closely inspect the valves and seats for wear and damage, replacing as necessary.
8. After the carburetor is assembled, check the choke valve for freedom of operation.

Carburetor overhaul kits are recommended for each overhaul. These kits contain all gaskets and new parts to replace those that deteriorate most rapidly. Failure to replace all parts supplied with the kit (especially gaskets) can result in poor performance later.

Some carburetor manufacturers supply overhaul kits of three basic types: minor repair; major repair; and gasket kits. Basically, they contain the following:

Minor Repair Kits:
    All gaskets
    Float needle valve
    Volume control screw
    All diaphragms
    Spring for the pump diaphragm

Major Repair Kits:
    All jets and gaskets
    All diaphragms
    Float needle valve
    Volume control screw
    Pump ball valve
    Main jet carrier
    Float
    Complete intermediate rod
    Intermediate pump lever
    Complete injector tube
    Some cover hold-down screws and washers

Gasket Kits:
    All gaskets

After cleaning and checking all components, reassemble the carburetor, using new parts and referring to the exploded view. When reassembling, make sure that all screws and jets are tight in

EMISSION CONTROLS AND FUEL SYSTEM

their seats, but do not overtighten as the tips will be distorted. Tighten all screws gradually, in rotation. Do not tighten needle valves into their seats; uneven jetting will result. Always use new gaskets. Be sure to adjust the float level when reassembling.

CARBURETOR ADJUSTMENTS

B-1600

FLOAT AND FUEL LEVEL

1. With the engine running, check the fuel level in the sight glass (in the fuel bowl).
2. If the fuel level is not at the specified mark on the sight glass,remove the carburetor from the truck.

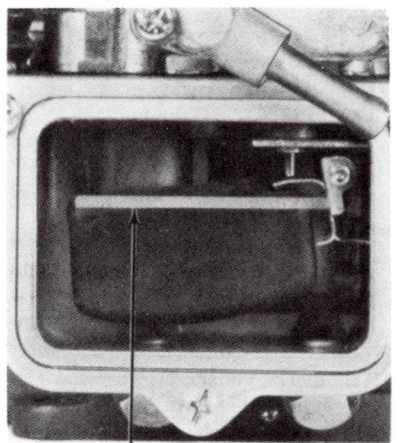

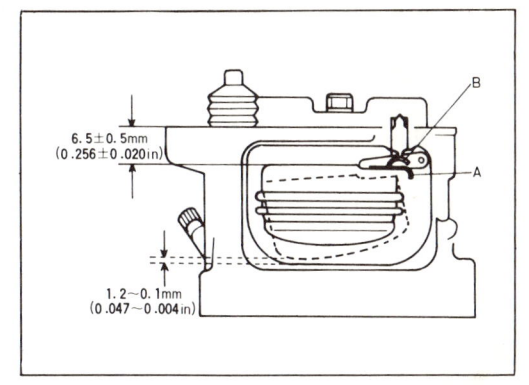

Fuel and float level—B-1600. Bend the float tab "A" to adjust float drop and tab "B" to adjust float level. (© Toyo Kogyo Co., Ltd.)

Fuel level mark on the sight glass—B-1600 (© Toyo Kogyo Co., Ltd.)

3. Remove the fuel bowl cover.
4. Invert the carburetor and lower the float until the tang on the float just contacts the needle valve.
5. Measure the clearance between the float and the edge of the bowl.
6. If the clearance is not as specified, bend the float tang until the proper clearance is obtained.
7. Install the fuel bowl cover.
8. Reinstall the carburetor on the truck.
9. Recheck the fuel level at the sight glass.

FAST IDLE

The fast idle can be adjusted by turning the fast idle adjusting screw. Check the choke plate for free operation.

Fast idle adjusting screw (arrow)—B-1600 (© Toyo Kogyo Co., Ltd.)

ACCELERATOR LINKAGE

Inspect the throttle linkage for free operation. Remove the air cleaner. With the accelerator fully depressed, the position of the throttle plates should be vertical.

SECONDARY THROTTLE VALVE

When the primary throttle valve opening angle is 55° from the fully closed po-

Throttle linkage adjustment screw—B-1600 (© Toyo Kogyo Co., Ltd.)

EMISSION CONTROLS AND FUEL SYSTEM

sition, the throttle lever link should contact the throttle arm. Adjust by bending the throttle lever link.

Rotary Pick-Up

Fast Idle

1. Pull the choke knob all the way out.
2. Measure the clearance between the primary throttle plate and the wall of the primary throttle bore. The clearance can be measured with a suitable drill bit.

Check the fuel level in the sight glass—Rotary Pick-Up (© Toyo Kogyo Co., Ltd.)

Fast idle adjustment (by opening angle)—Rotary Pick-Up (© Toyo Kogyo Co., Ltd.)

1. Pulled by choke wire
2. Link
3. Choke shaft lever
4. Choke lever
5. Fast idle rod
   (Bend this rod for adjustment)
6. Fast idle lever
7. Throttle lever

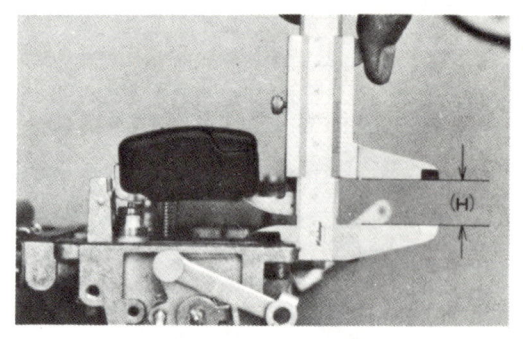

Checking the float level (H) with the air horn removed—Rotary Pick-Up (© Toyo Kogyo Co., Ltd.)

2. If the fuel levels are not within the specified marks on the sight glass, remove the air horn with the floats.
3. Invert the air horn and let the float hang so that it just contacts the needle valve.
4. Measure the clearance between the float and the air horn gasket, which should be 0.043 in.

Bend the float seat lip to adjust the clearance if necessary.

5. Install the air horn and recheck the fuel levels in the sight glass.

3. The clearance should be 0.0398–0.0524 in. (#61-#55 drill) for trucks with manual transmission, or 0.0480–0.0618 in. (#55-#53 drill) for trucks with automatic transmission.
4. If the clearance is not as specified, adjust the fast idle by bending the connecting rod to obtain the proper clearance.

Float Level

1. With the engine running, check the fuel level in the sight glass, using a mirror.

Checking the float drop (arrows)—Rotary Pick-Up (© Toyo Kogyo Co., Ltd.)

Float Drop

1. Remove the air horn with the floats and allow the floats to hang free.
2. Measure the clearance between the bottom of the float and the air horn gasket. The clearance should be 2.03–2.07 in.
3. If not, adjust the distance by bending the float stopper.
4. Install the air horn and recheck the fuel level in the sight glass.

On the Rotary Pick-Up, adjust the float drop at the float stopper B and the float level seat lip (A) (© Toyo Kogyo Co., Ltd.)

Carburetor Specifications

Part	B-1600	Rotary Pick-Up
Throttle Bore Diameter (in.)		
Primary	1.10	1.10
Secondary	1.26	1.34
Venturi Diameter (in.)		
Primary	0.91	0.87
Secondary	1.10	1.10
Main Jet		
Primary	#110	#106
Secondary	#160	#140
Main Air Bleed		
Primary	50	80
Secondary	80	160
Idle Jet		
Primary	#48	#50
Secondary	#80	#90
Idle Air Bleed		
Primary	150 (1972, #160)	190
Secondary	160 (1972, #130)	150
Power Valve	#55 (1972, #70)	——
Fast Idle (in.)	Throttle valve open 22°	0.040–0.052 (MT); 0.048–0.062 (AT)
Float Level (in.)	0.0236–0.0276	0.043

(MT) Manual transmission
(AT) Automatic transmission
—— Not applicable
CO concentration at idle (Rotary Pick-Up): 0.1–2.0%
HC concentration at idle (Rotary Pick-Up): less than 200 ppm (parts per million)
CO concentration at idle (B-1600): 1.5–2.5%—1972: (1.5–3.5%)

Chapter Six
Clutch and Transmission

Manual Transmission

The B-1600 and the Rotary Pick-Up both use a four-speed manual transmission, synchronized in all forward gears. Both transmissions are of the type known as "top loaders." There is no external shift linkage, and therefore, no provision for linkage or shifter adjustment.

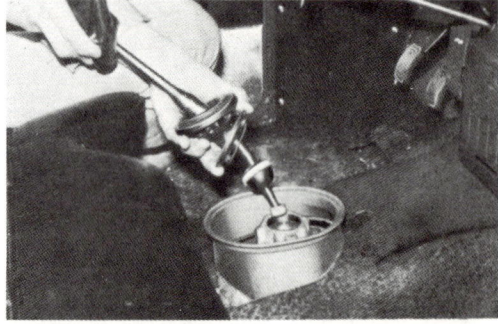

Removing or installing the gearshift lever (© Toyo Kogyo Co., Ltd.)

Removal and Installation

B-1600

1. Raise and support the truck. Drain the lubricant from the transmission.
2. Disconnect the ground wire from the battery.
3. Remove the gearshift lever boot.
4. Unbolt the cover plate from the gearshift lever retainer.
5. Pull the gearshift lever, shim and bushing straight up and away from the gearshift lever retainer.
6. Disconnect the wires from the starter motor and back-up light switch.
7. Disconnect the speedometer cable from the extension housing.
8. Remove the driveshaft.
9. Unbolt the exhaust pipe from the bracket on the transmission case.
10. Disconnect the exhaust pipe at the exhaust manifold.
11 Unhook the clutch release fork return spring and remove the clutch release cylinder from the clutch housing.
12. Remove the starter.
13. Support the transmission with a jack.
14. Unbolt the transmission from the rear of the engine.
15. Place a jack under the engine, protecting the oil pan with a block of wood.
16. Unbolt the transmission from the crossmember.
17. Unbolt and remove the crossmember.

CLUTCH AND TRANSMISSION

18. Lower the jack and slide the transmission rearward until the mainshaft clears the clutch disc.
19. Remove the transmission from under the truck.
20. Installation is the reverse of removal.

Rotary Pick-Up

1. Remove the knob from the gearshift lever.
2. Remove the gearshift lever boot.
3. Unbolt the retainer cover from the gearshift lever retainer.
4. Pull the gearshift lever, shim and bushing straight up and away from the gearshift lever retainer.
5. Disconnect the battery ground wire.
6. Remove the bolt attaching the power brake vacuum pipe to the clutch housing.
7. Disconnect the ground strap from the transmission case.
8. Remove the clutch release cylinder.
9. Remove the one upper bolt holding the starter and the three upper bolts and nuts securing the transmission to the engine.
10. Raise and support the truck.
11. Disconnect the wires from the starter motor and the back-up light switch wires.
12. Unbolt and remove the heat insulator from the front exhaust pipe.
13. Disconnect the exhaust pipe from the brackets.
14. Disconnect the exhaust pipe front flange from the exhaust manifold. Remove the front exhaust pipe.
15. Remove the driveshaft.
16. Insert a transmission oil plug into the extension housing.
17. Remove the starter.
18. Install a jack under the engine and support the engine.
19. Unbolt the transmission support from the body.
20. Remove the two lower bolts holding the transmission to the engine.
21. Slide the transmission rearward until the mainshaft clears the clutch disc and remove the transmission from under the truck.
22. Installation is the reverse of removal.

Clutch

The clutch is a dry single disc type, consisting of a clutch disc, clutch cover and pressure plate and a clutch release mechanism. It is hydraulically-operated by a firewall-mounted master cylinder and a clutch release slave cylinder mounted on the clutch housing.

Clutch Pedal Free-Play Adjustment

All Models

The free-play of the clutch pedal before the pushrod contacts the piston in the master cylinder should be 0.02–0.12 in.

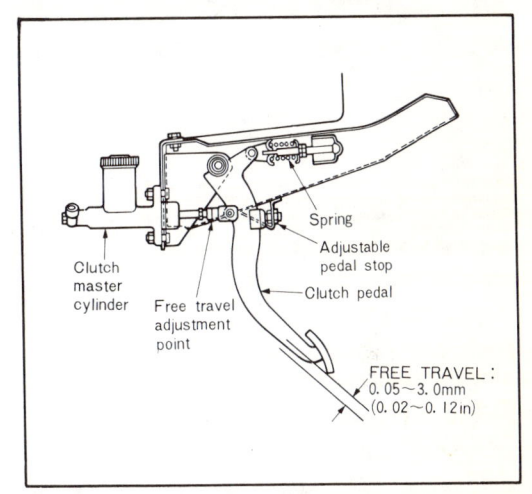

Clutch pedal free-play adjustment—B-1600 (© Toyo Kogyo Co., Ltd.)

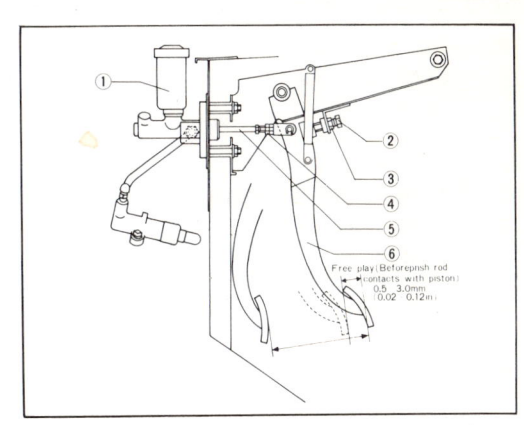

Clutch pedal free-play adjustment—Rotary Pick-Up (© Toyo Kogyo Co., Ltd.)
1. Master cylinder   4. Locknut
2. Height adjusting bolt   5. Rod
3. Locknut   6. Pedal

CLUTCH AND TRANSMISSION

To adjust the free-play, loosen the locknut and turn the pushrod until the proper adjustment is obtained. Tighten the locknut after the adjustment is complete.

Clutch Release Lever Adjustment

ALL MODELS

NOTE: *This adjustment must be maintained to prevent release bearing and clutch damage.*

1. Raise and support the truck.
2. Disconnect the release lever return spring at the lever.

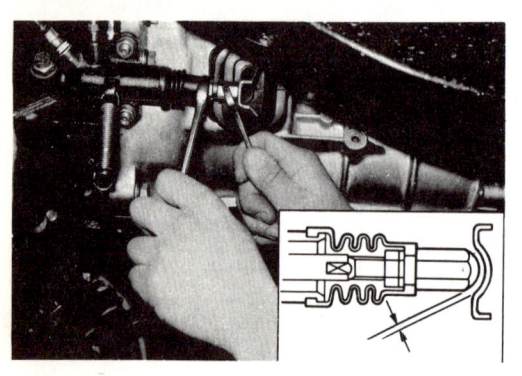

Adjusting clutch release fork—free-play (© Toyo Kogyo Co., Ltd.)

3. Loosen the locknut and rotate the adjusting nut until a clearance of 0.14–0.18 in. is obtained between the bullet nosed end of the adjusting nut and the release lever.
4. Tighten the locknut and hook the return spring.
5. Lower the truck.

Removal and Installation

ALL MODELS

1. Remove the transmission.
2. Remove the four attaching and two pilot bolts holding the clutch cover to the flywheel. Loosen the bolts evenly and a turn or two at a time. If the clutch cover is to be reinstalled, mark the flywheel and clutch cover to show the location of the two pilot holes.
3. Remove the clutch disc.

To install the clutch:

4. Install the clutch disc on the flywheel. Do not touch the facing or allow the facing to come in contact with grease or oil. The clutch disc can be aligned

Installing the clutch disc (typical) using a dummy shaft (49 0813 310). Hold the flywheel with a commercial tool similar to 49 0118 271A. (© Toyo Kogyo Co., Ltd.)

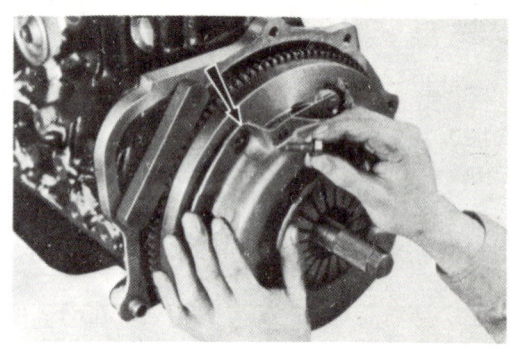

Installing the pressure plate. Be sure to align the 0 marks (arrow) or matchmarks. (© Toyo Kogyo Co., Ltd.)

using a tool made for that purpose, or with an old mainshaft.

5. Install the clutch cover on the flywheel and install the four standard bolts and the two pilot bolts.
6. To avoid distorting the pressure plate, tighten the bolts evenly a few turns at a time until they are all tight.
7. Torque the bolts to 13–20 ft lbs using a crossing pattern.
8. Remove the aligning tool.
9. Apply a light film of lubricant to the release bearing, release lever contact area on the release bearing hub and to the input shaft bearing retainer.
10. Install the transmission.
11. Check the operation of the clutch and if necessary, adjust the pedal free-play and the release lever.

CLUTCH MASTER CYLINDER

Bleeding the Hydraulic System

The clutch hydraulic system must be bled whenever the line has been disconnected or air has entered the system.

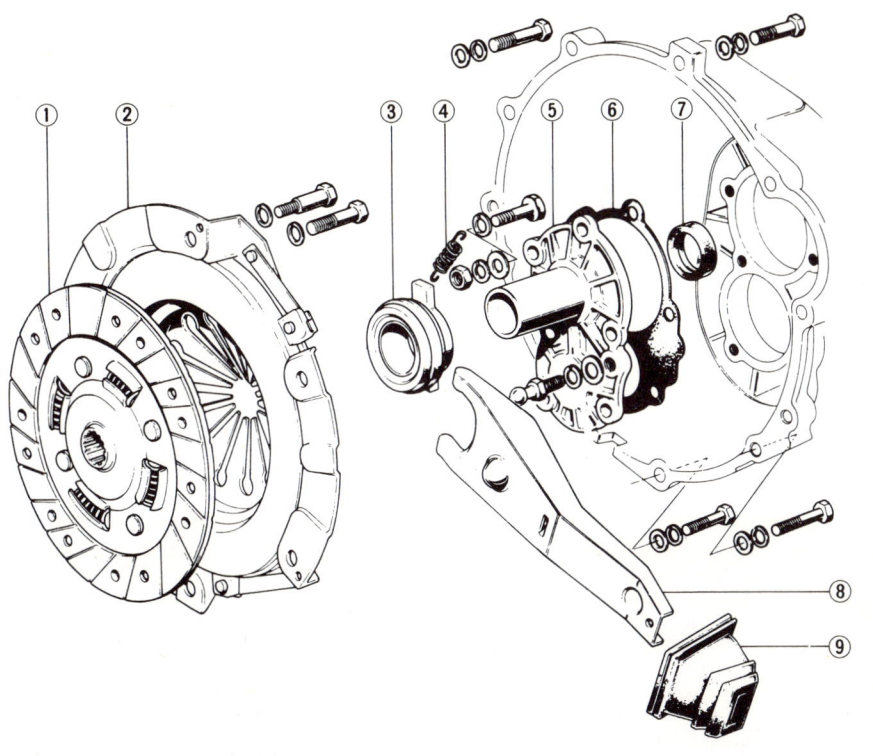

CLUTCH AND TRANSMISSION

1. Clutch disc
2. Clutch cover and pressure plate assembly
3. Release bearing
4. Spring
5. Front cover
6. Gasket
7. Oil seal
8. Release fork
9. Dust cover

Exploded view of clutch—B-1600 (© Toyo Kogyo Co., Ltd.)

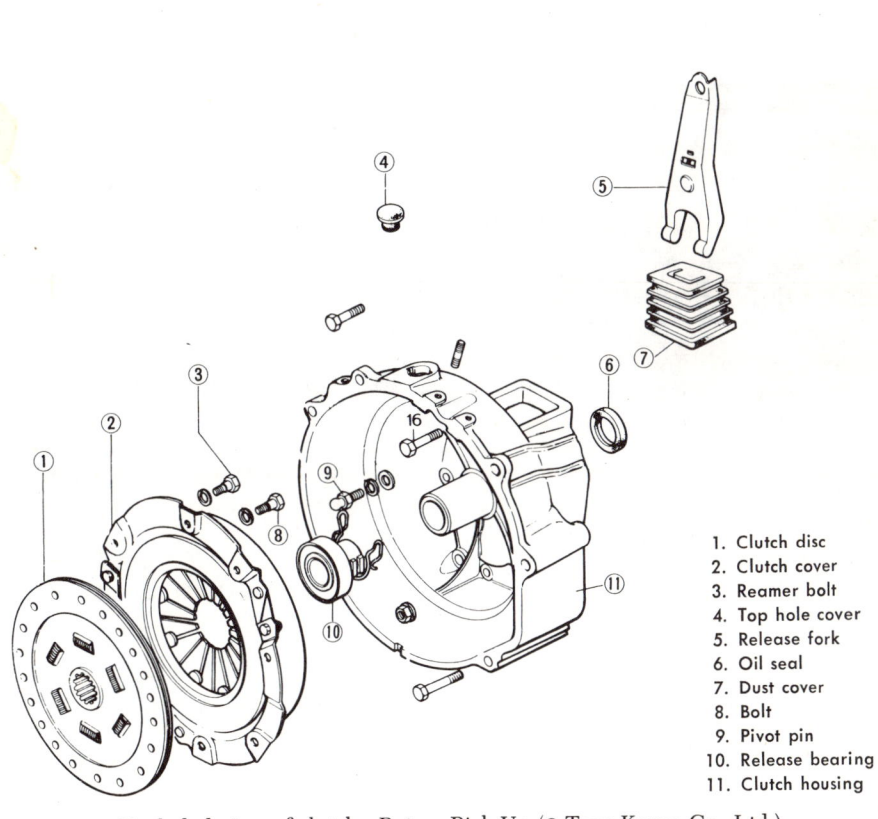

1. Clutch disc
2. Clutch cover
3. Reamer bolt
4. Top hole cover
5. Release fork
6. Oil seal
7. Dust cover
8. Bolt
9. Pivot pin
10. Release bearing
11. Clutch housing

Exploded view of clutch—Rotary Pick-Up (© Toyo Kogyo Co., Ltd.)

CLUTCH AND TRANSMISSION

To bleed the system, remove the rubber cap from the bleeder valve and attach a rubber hose to the valve. Submerge the other end of the hose in a large jar of clean brake fluid. Open the bleeder valve. Depress the clutch pedal and allow it to return slowly. Continue this pumping action and watch the jar of brake fluid. When air bubbles stop appearing, close the bleeder valve and remove the tube.

During the bleeding process, the master cylinder must be kept at least 3/4 full. After the bleeding operation is finished, install the cap on the bleeder valve and fill the master cylinder to the proper level. Always use fresh brake fluid, and above all, do not use the fluid that was in the jar for bleeding, since it contains air. Install the master cylinder reservoir cap.

Removal and Installation

ALL MODELS

1. Disconnect and plug the fluid outlet line at the outlet fitting on the master cylinder one-way valve.
2. Remove the nuts and bolts attaching the master cylinder to the firewall.

Typical master cylinder. Disconnect and plug the fluid connection and remove the nuts. (© Toyo Kogyo Co., Ltd.)

3. Remove the cylinder straight out away from the firewall.

To install the master cylinder:

4. Start the pedal pushrod into the master cylinder and position the master cylinder on the firewall.
5. Install the attaching nuts and bolts. Torque the nuts to 12–17 ft lbs.
6. Connect the fluid outlet line to the master cylinder fitting.
7. Bleed the hydraulic system.
8. Check the clutch pedal free-travel and adjust as necessary.

Overhaul

ALL MODELS

1. Remove the master cylinder.
2. Clean the outside of the cylinder thoroughly and drain the fluid.
3. Remove the dust cover.
4. Use a screwdriver to remove the piston stop-ring. Remove the stop washer.
5. Remove the piston, piston cup and piston return spring from the cylinder.
6. Carefully remove and disassemble the one-way valve.
7. Wash all parts (except rubber parts) in clean alcohol or brake fluid. Never use mineral spirits of any kind to clean a master cylinder.
8. Check the rubber cups. If they have become worn, softened or swelled, replace them.
9. Check the clearance between the cylinder bore and piston. If it exceeds 0.006 in., replace the cylinder or piston.
10. Be sure that the one-way valve is free to operate.

To assemble the master cylinder:

11. Dip the piston and cups in clean brake fluid.
12. Install the return spring in the cylinder bore.
13. Install the primary cup so that the flat side of the cup is toward the piston.
14. Install the secondary cup on the piston and insert the cup and piston into the cylinder.
15. Install the stop washer and stop-ring.
16. Assemble and install the one-way valve.
17. Fill the reservoir with clean brake fluid and operate the piston with a screwdriver until fluid is ejected through the outlet fitting.
18. Install the master cylinder.
19. Bleed the hydraulic system.

CLUTCH SLAVE CYLINDER

Removal and Installation

ALL MODELS

1. Disconnect and plug the slave cylinder inlet line at the slave cylinder.

CLUTCH AND TRANSMISSION 131

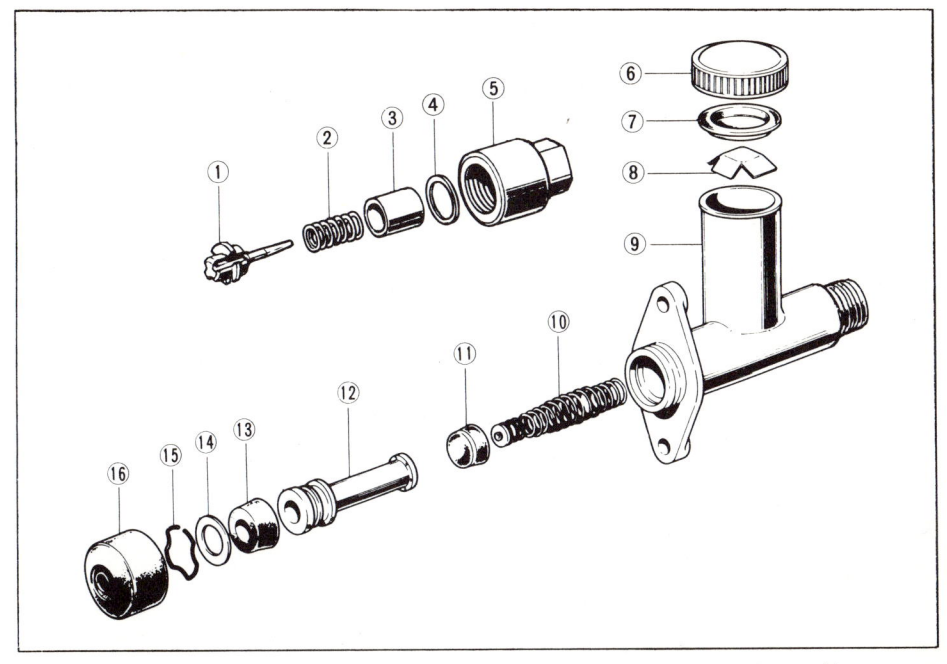

Exploded view of clutch master cylinder—B-1600 (© Toyo Kogyo Co., Ltd.)

1. Pin
2. Spring
3. Piston
4. Gasket
5. Nut
6. Filler cap
7. Baffle
8. Baffle plate
9. Cylinder and reservoir
10. Return spring
11. Primary cup
12. Piston
13. Secondary cup
14. Washer
15. Stop ring
16. Dust boot

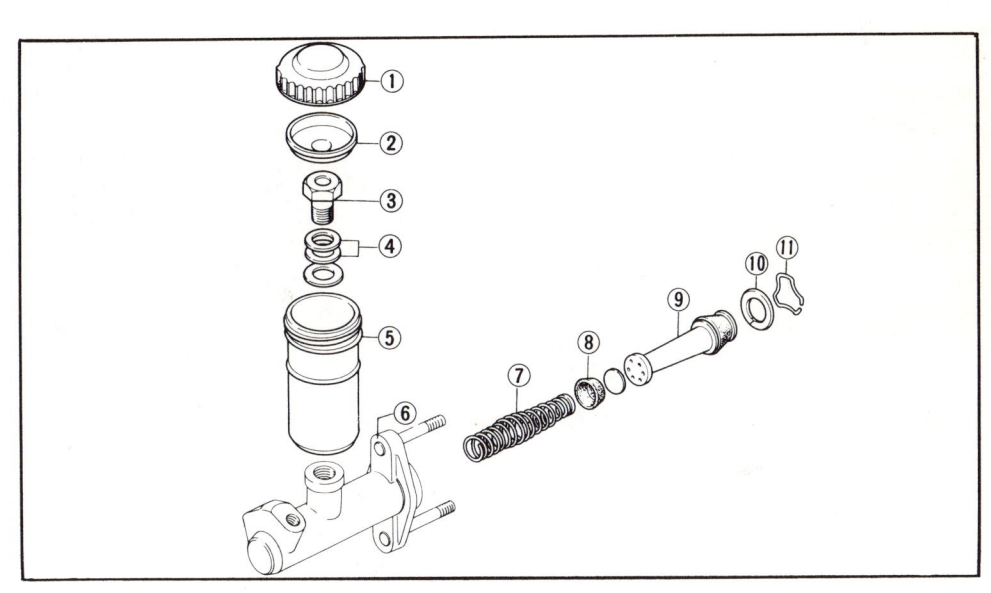

Exploded view of clutch master cylinder—Rotary Pick-Up (© Toyo Kogyo Co., Ltd.)

1. Cap
2. Fluid baffle
3. Bolt
4. Washer
5. Reservoir
6. Cylinder
7. Spring
8. Primary piston cup
9. Piston and secondary cup assembly
10. Piston stop washer
11. Piston stop wire

CLUTCH AND TRANSMISSION

2. Unhook the release lever return spring.

3. Remove the nuts and washers attaching the slave cylinder to the clutch housing.

To install the slave cylinder:

4. Install the slave cylinder on the clutch housing, torquing the nuts to 12–17 ft lbs.

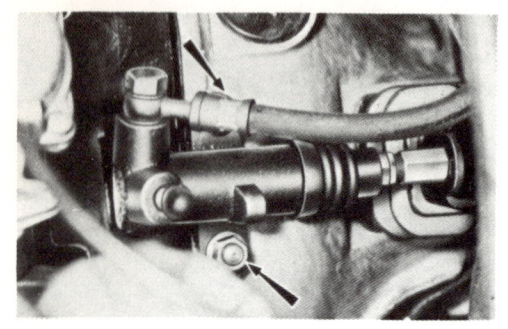

Remove the clutch slave cylinder. Disconnect and plug the fluid connection (upper arrow). (© Toyo Kogyo Co., Ltd.)

5. Connect the slave cylinder inlet line to the slave cylinder.
6. Fill the master cylinder and bleed the hydraulic system.
7. Check and adjust the release lever.
8. Connect the return spring.

Overhaul

ALL MODELS

1. Remove the slave cylinder.
2. Clean the outside thoroughly.

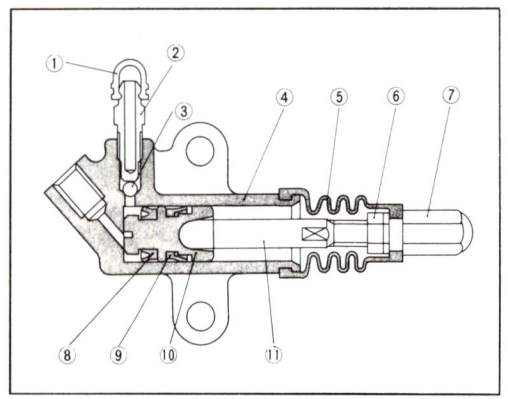

Cross-section of clutch slave cylinder—B-1600 shown (© Toyo Kogyo Co., Ltd.)

1. Cap
2. Bleeder screw
3. Valve
4. Cylinder
5. Dust nut
6. Locknut
7. Adjusting nut
8. Primary cup
9. Secondary cup
10. Piston
11. Release rod

3. Remove the dust cover and release rod.
4. Remove the piston from the cylinder.
5. Disassemble the bleeder valve.
6. Inspect the cylinder, using Steps 7–9 of the "Master Cylinder Overhaul" procedure.

To assemble the slave cylinder:

7. Dip the pistons and cups in clean brake fluid.
8. Assemble the cups to the piston as shown and install the piston.
9. Install the release rod and release rod boot.
10. Install the steel ball and bleeder into the bleeder orifice. Install the bleeder cap.
11. Install the slave cylinder

Automatic Transmission

Mazda Rotary Pick-Ups use a JATCO R3A automatic transmission as optional equipment in 1974–75. It is a 3-speed unit with manual selection of 1st and 2nd gears possible.

Kick-Down Switch and Downshift Solenoid Adjustment

1. Make sure that the accelerator pedal goes through the entire stroke properly.
2. Turn the ignition switch ON.
3. Depress the accelerator pedal as far as possible. As the throttle nears the wide-open position, the contact point of the kick-down switch should be closed with a light click from the solenoid. The

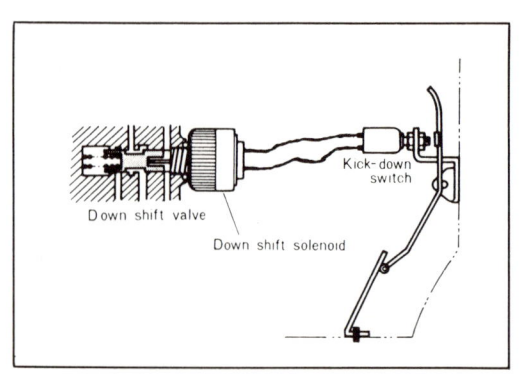

Automatic transmission kick-down switch and downshift solenoid (© Toyo Kogyo Co., Ltd.)

CLUTCH AND TRANSMISSION

kick-down switch should begin to operate at about 7/8 of full pedal travel.

4. If not, loosen the kick-down switch attaching nut and adjust the switch.

5. Tighten the attaching nut after the adjustment.

6. If the switch still produces no audible click, indicating engagement, the solenoid is probably defective and should be replaced.

Manual Linkage Adjustment

1. Put the gearshift lever in Neutral (the slot of the manual shaft is positioned vertically).

2. Raise and support the truck.

3. Adjust the position of the manual lever by turning the T-joint so that the manual lever is in Neutral.

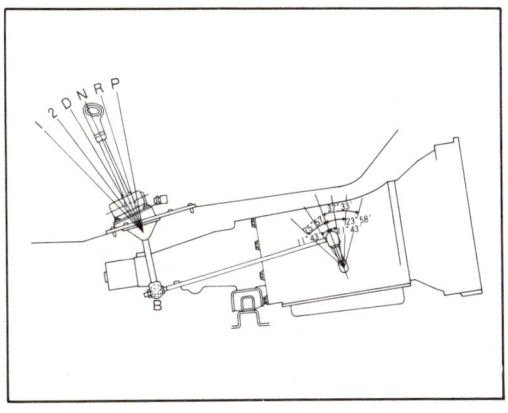

Auto transmission manual linkage (© Toyo Kogyo Co., Ltd.)

4. Make sure that the manual lever engages Park and be sure that the linkage is not loose.

5. Lower the truck and check the operation of the linkage.

Inhibitor Switch Adjustment

The inhibitor (neutral safety switch) allows the engine to be started only in Park or Neutral.

1. Remove the housing from the shift lever.

2. Adjust the shift lever so that there is 0–0.012 in. clearance between the pin and the guide plate, when the lever is in Neutral.

Auto transmission inhibitor switch adjustment (© Toyo Kogyo Co., Ltd.)

3. Adjust the inhibitor switch so that the pin hole in the switch body is aligned with the pin hole of the sliding plate when the shift lever is in Neutral.

4. Check the adjustment by trying to start the engine in all gears. It should only start in Park or Neutral.

5. Reinstall the housing on the shift lever.

Pan Removal and Installation

1. Raise and support the truck.

2. Place a drain pan under the transmission pan.

3. Remove the pan attaching bolts (except the two at the front). Loosen the two at the front slightly. Allow the fluid to drain.

4. Remove the pan.

5. Remove and discard the gasket.

6. Install a new pan gasket and install the pan on the transmission.

7. Lower the truck and fill the transmission with fluid. Check the transmission operation.

Chapter Seven
Drive Train

Driveshaft and U-Joints

ALL MODELS

The driveshaft assembly consists of the front shaft, the rear shaft, a center support bearing and U-joints and yokes. The rear end of the driveshaft is attached to the companion flange at the rear axle through a U-joint and at the front, to the mainshaft by means of a sliding yoke. This arrangement provides for fore-and-aft movement of the driveshaft as the truck moves up and down. The center of the driveshaft is supported by the bearing attached to the underbody of the truck.

Removal and Installation

1. Remove the bolts attaching the driveshaft to the companion flange of the rear axle. Mark the driveshaft and companion flange for correct alignment when it is installed.
2. Remove the center support bearing bracket from the underbody.
3. Pull the driveshaft rearward and remove it from the transmission. Plug the extension housing.

To install the transmission:
4. Position the driveshaft and slide the front yoke into the extension housing of the transmission.
5. Attach the center support bearing bracket.
6. Install the rear shaft to the companion flange and torque the bolts to 39–47 ft lbs. Be sure that the alignment marks made during removal are aligned.

U-Joint Overhaul

1. Remove the driveshaft from the vehicle and place it in a vise, being careful not to damage it.
2. Remove the snap-rings which retain the bearings in the flange and in the driveshaft.
3. Remove the driveshaft tube from the vise and position the U-joint in the vise with a socket smaller than the bearing cap on one side and a socket larger than the bearing cap on the other side.
4. Slowly tighten the jaws of the vise so that the smaller socket forces the U-joint spider and the opposite bearing into the larger socket.

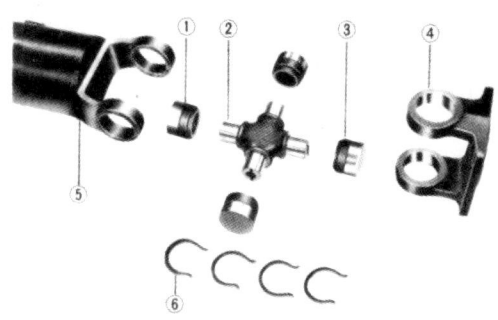

Exploded view of U-joint (© Toyo Kogyo Co., Ltd.)

1. Bearing
2. Spider
3. Grease seal
4. Yoke
5. Driveshaft
6. Snap-ring

DRIVE TRAIN 135

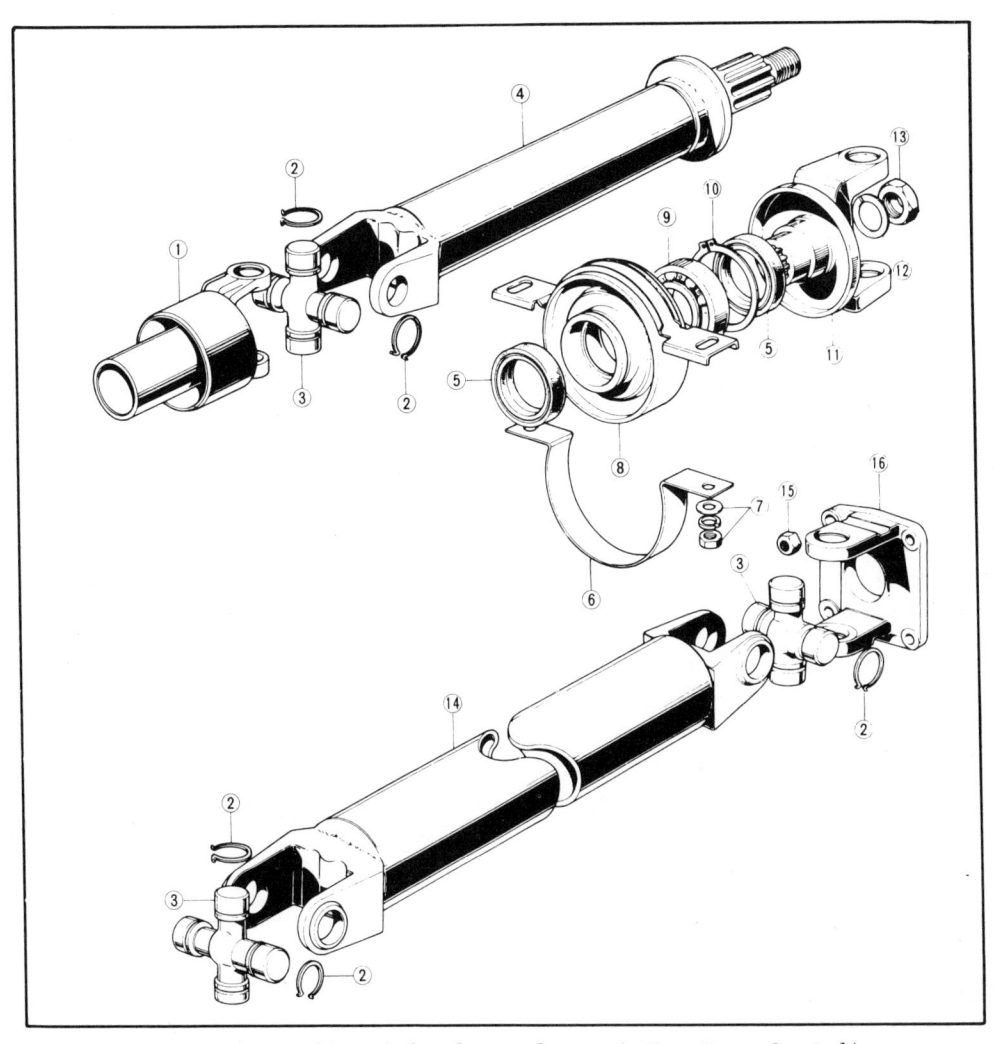

Exploded view of driveshaft and center bearing (© Toyo Kogyo Co., Ltd.)

1. Sliding yoke
2. Snap-ring
3. Universal joint
4. Front shaft
5. Grease seal
6. Protector
7. Nut and washer
8. Center bearing support
9. Bearing
10. Snap-ring
11. Yoke (center)
12. Washer
13. Nut
14. Rear shaft
15. Nut
16. Yoke (rear)

5. Remove the other side of the spider in the same manner (if applicable) and remove the spider assembly from the driveshaft. Discard the spider assemblies.

6. Clean all foreign matter from the yoke areas at the end of the driveshaft(s).

7. Start the new spider and one of the bearing cap assemblies into a yoke by positioning the yoke in a vise with the spider positioned in place with one of the bearing cap assemblies positioned over one of the holes in the yoke. Slowly close the vise, pressing the bearing cap assembly in the yoke. Press the cap in far enough so that the retaining snap-ring can be installed. Use the smaller socket to recess the bearing cap.

8. Open the vise and position the opposite bearing cap assembly over the proper hole in the yoke with the socket that is smaller than the diameter of the bearing cap located on the cap. Slowly close the vise, pressing the bearing cap into the hole in the yoke with the socket. Make sure that the spider assembly is in line with the bearing cap as it is pressed in. Press the bearing cap in far enough

so that the retaining snap-ring can be installed. Snap-rings are available in 0.057–0.064 in. thicknesses to assure good centering of the yokes and spiders, preventing out-of-balance. When selecting snap-rings, to give a suitable slight drag fit (not binding), use similar snap-rings in any given yoke. For example, do not use a 0.059 in. snap-ring opposite a 0.063 in. snap-ring, as this would create an out-of-balance condition.

9. Install all remaining U-joints in the same manner. The nut attaching the yoke and bearing to the front coupling shaft should be torqued to 115–130 ft lbs.

10. Install the driveshaft and grease the new U-joints.

Rear Axle

The Mazda uses a removable carrier axle with a hypoid ring and pinion and a semi-floating axle.

AXLE SHAFT

Removal and Installation

1. Raise and support the truck.
2. Remove the rear wheel and brake drum.
3. Remove the brake shoes.
4. Remove the parking brake cable retainer.
5. Disconnect and plug the hydraulic brake lines at the wheel cylinders.
6. Unbolt the backing plate and bearing housing.
7. Slide the complete axle shaft from the housing. If necessary, remove the oil seal from the housing.

To install the axle shaft:

8. Install a new axle oil seal in the housing if the old one was removed.
9. Install the axle shaft assembly.
10. Using two bolts and nuts, temporarily install the bearing housing and backing plate to the housing flange.
11. Check the axle shaft end-play with a dial indicator mounted on the backing plate.
12. If only one axle shaft has been removed, the end-play should be 0.002–

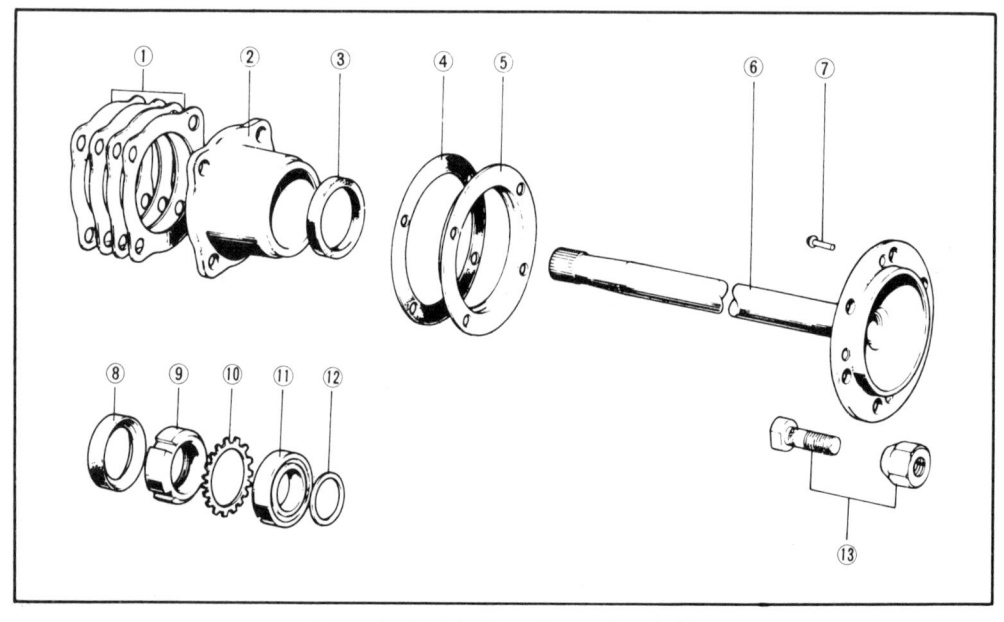

Rear axle shaft (© Toyo Kogyo Co., Ltd.)

1. Shims
2. Bearing housing
3. Oil seal (outer)
4. Gasket
5. Baffle
6. Axle shaft
7. Rivet
8. Oil seal (inner)
9. Locknut
10. Lockwasher
11. Bearing
12. Spacer
13. Hub bolt and nut

DRIVE TRAIN 137

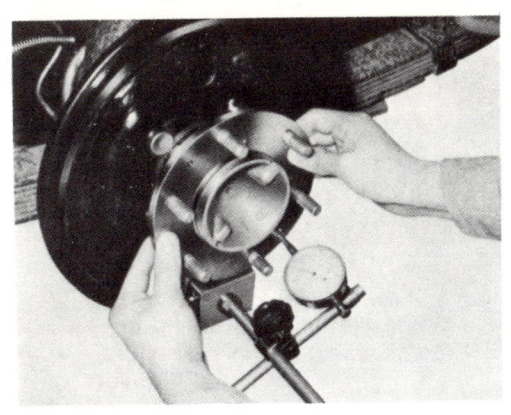

Checking rear axle shaft end-play (© Toyo Kogyo Co., Ltd.)

0.006 in. If both axle shafts have been removed, check the end-play after the first shaft is installed. It should be 0.026–0.033 in. The end-play of the second shaft should then be 0.002–0.006 in. Shims are available to adjust the end-play.

13. After adjusting the end-play, install all bolts and torque them to 12–16 ft lbs.
14. Install the brake shoes.
15. Install the brake drum and wheel.
16. Connect the brake lines.
17. Bleed the brakes.
18. Lower the truck and road-test it.

DIFFERENTIAL

Differential service is best left to those extremely familiar with their vagaries and idiosyncrasies. A great many specialized tools are required as well as a good deal of experience.

Introduction

The rear axle must transmit power through 90°. To accomplish this, straight

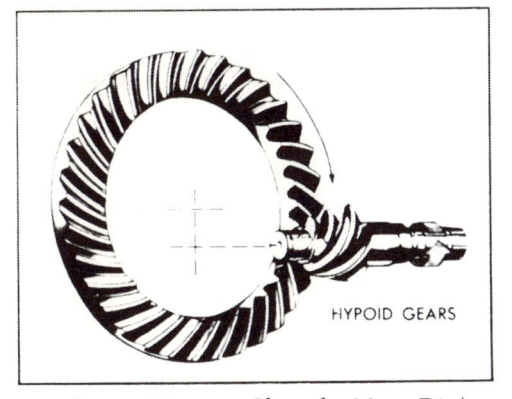

Hypoid gears (Courtesy Chevrolet Motor Div.)

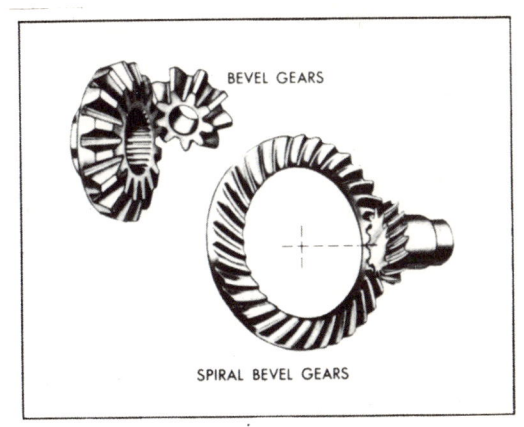

Bevel and Spiral bevel gears (Courtesy Chevrolet Motor Div.)

cut bevel gears or spiral bevel gears were used. This type of gear is satisfactory for differential side gears, but since the centerline of the gears must intersect, they rapidly became unsuited for ring and pinion gears. The lowering of the driveshaft brought about a variation of the bevel gear, which is called the hypoid gear. This type of gear does not require a meeting of the gear centerlines and can therefore be underslung, relative to the centerline of the ring gear.

Operation

The differential is an arrangement of gears which permits the rear wheels to turn at different speeds when cornering and divides the torque between the axle shafts. The differential gears are mounted on a pinion shaft and the gears are free to rotate on this shaft. The pinion shaft is fitted in a bore in the differential case and is at right angles to the axle shafts.

Power flow through the differential is as follows. The drive pinion, which is turned by the driveshaft, turns the ring gear. The ring gear, which is bolted to the differential case, rotates the case. The differential pinion forces the pinion gears against the side gears. In cases where both wheels have equal traction, the pinion gears do not rotate on the pinion shaft, because the input force of the pinion gear is divided equally between the two side gears. Consequently the pinion gears revolve with the pinion shaft, although they do not revolve on the pinion shaft itself. The side gears, which are splined to the axle shafts, and meshed with the pinion gears, rotate the axle shafts.

When it becomes necessary to turn a corner, the differential becomes effective and allows the axle shafts to rotate at different speeds. As the inner wheel slows down, the side gear splined to the inner wheel axle shaft also slows down. The pinion gears act as balancing levers by maintaining equal tooth loads to both gears while allowing unequal speeds of rotation at the axle shafts. If the vehicle speed remains constant, and the inner wheel slows down to 90 percent of vehicle speed, the outer wheel will speed up to 110 percent.

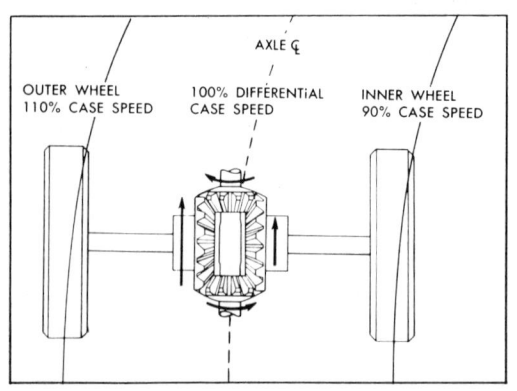

Differential operation during cornering (Courtesy Chevrolet Motor Div.)

Limited-Slip Differential Operation

Limited-slip differentials provide driving force to the wheel with the best traction before the other wheel begins to spin. This is accomplished through clutch plates or cones. The clutch plates or cones are located between the side gears and inner wall of the differential case. When they are squeezed together through the spring tension and outward force from the side gears, three reactions occur. Resistance on the side gears causes more torque to be exerted on the clutch packs or clutch cones. Rapid one-wheel spin cannot occur, because the side gear is forced to turn at the same speed as the case. Most important, with the side gear and the differential case turning at the same speed, the other wheel is forced to rotate in the same direction and at the same speed as the differential case. Thus driving force is applied to the wheel with the better traction.

NOTE: *Whenever the rear of a vehicle with a limited-slip rear axle is jacked or supported, both wheels must be raised off the ground. Movement of either wheel in contact with the ground can cause the vehicle to move.*

Determining Gear Ratio

Normally, the gear ratio of an axle installed in a vehicle is listed somewhere; in service manuals, on an option list, or on a tag somewhere on the axle.

Determining the axle ratio of any given axle is an esoteric subject, relatively useless until you have to know. But, as a "junkyard art," it is invaluable.

The rear axle ratio is said to have a certain ratio, say, 4.11. It is called a 4.11 rear although the 4.11 actually means 4.11:1. This means that the driveshaft will turn 4.11 times for every turn of the rear wheel. The number 4.11 is determined by dividing the number of teeth on the pinion gear into the number of teeth on the ring gear. In the case of a 4.11, there could be 9 teeth on the pinion and 37 teeth on the ring gear ($37 \div 9 = 4.11$). This provides a sure way (although troublesome—except to those who are really interested) of determining your rear axle ratio. You must drain the rear axle and remove the rear cover, if it has one, and count the teeth on the ring and pinion.

An easier method is to jack and support the vehicle so that BOTH rear wheels are off the ground. Make a chalk mark on the rear wheel and the driveshaft. Block the front wheels, set the parking brake and put the transmission in Neutral. Turn the rear wheel one complete revolution and count the number of turns that the driveshaft makes. The number of turns that the driveshaft makes in one complete revolution of the rear wheel is an *approximation* of the rear axle ratio.

Differential Diagnosis

The most essential part of rear axle service is proper diagnosis of the problem. Bent or broken axle shafts or broken gears pose little problem, but isolating an axle noise and correctly interpreting the problem can be extremely difficult, even for an experienced mechanic.

DRIVE TRAIN

Any gear driven unit will produce a certain amount of noise, therefore, a specific diagnosis for each individual unit is the best practice. Acceptable or normal noise can be classified as a slight noise heard only at certain speeds or under unusual conditions. This noise tends to reach a peak at 40–60 mph, depending on the road condition, load, gear ratio and tire size. Frequently, other noises are mistakenly diagnosed as coming from the rear axle. Vehicle noises from tires, transmission, driveshaft, U-joints and front and rear wheel bearings will often be mistaken as emanating from the rear axle. Raising the tire pressure to eliminate tire noise (although this will not silence mud or snow treads), listening for noise at varying speeds and road conditions and listening for noise at drive and coast conditions will aid in diagnosing alleged rear axle noises.

EXTERNAL NOISE ELIMINATION

It is advisable to make a thorough road test to determine whether the noise originates in the rear axle or whether it originates from the tires, engine, transmission, wheel bearings or road surface. Noise originating from other places cannot be corrected by overhauling the rear axle.

ROAD NOISE

Brick roads or rough surfaced concrete, may cause a noise which can be mistaken as coming from the rear axle. Driving on a different type of road, (smooth asphalt or dirt) will determine whether the road is the cause of the noise. Road noise is usually the same on drive or coast conditions.

TIRE NOISE

Tire noise can be mistaken as rear axle noises, even though the tires on the front are at fault. Snow tread and mud tread tires or tires worn unevenly will frequently cause vibrations which seem to originate elsewhere; *temporarily, and for test purposes only,* inflate the tires to 40–50 lbs. This will significantly alter the noise produced by the tires, but will not alter noise from the rear axle. Noises from the rear axle will normally cease at speeds below 30 mph on coast, while tire noise will continue at lower tone as car speed is decreased. The rear axle noise will usually change from drive conditions to coast conditions, while tire noise will not. Do not forget to lower the tire pressure to normal after the test is complete.

ENGINE AND TRANSMISSION NOISE

Engine and transmission noises also seem to originate in the rear axle. Road test the vehicle and determine at which speeds the noise is most pronounced. Stop the car in a quiet place to avoid interfering noises. With the transmission in Neutral, run the engine slowly through the engine speeds corresponding to the car speed at which the noise was most noticeable. If a similar noise was produced with the car standing still, the noise is not in the rear axle, but somewhere in the engine or transmission.

FRONT WHEEL BEARING NOISE

Front wheel bearing noises, sometimes confused with rear axle noises, will not change when comparing drive and coast conditions. While holding the car speed steady, lightly apply the footbrake. This will often cause wheel bearing noise to lessen, as some of the weight is taken off the bearing. Front wheel bearings are easily checked by jacking up the wheels and spinning the wheels. Shaking the wheels will also determine if the wheel bearings are excessively loose.

REAR AXLE NOISES

If a logical test of the vehicle shows that the noise is not caused by external items, it can be assumed that the noise originates from the rear axle. The rear axle should be tested on a smooth level road to avoid road noise. It is not advisable to test the axle by jacking up the rear wheels and running the car.

True rear axle noises generally fall into two classes; gear noise and bearing noises, and can be caused by faulty driveshaft, faulty wheel bearings, worn differential or pinion shaft bearings, U-joint misalignment, worn differential

DRIVE TRAIN

side gears and pinions, or mismatched, improperly adjusted, or scored ring and pinion gears.

Rear Wheel Bearing Noise

A rough rear wheel bearing causes a vibration or growl which will continue with the car coasting or in Neutral. A brinelled rear wheel bearing will also cause a knock or click approximately every two revolutions of the rear wheel, due to the fact that the bearing rollers do not travel at the same speed as the rear wheel and axle. Jack up the rear wheels and spin the wheel slowly, listening for signs of a rough or brinelled wheel bearing.

Differential Side Gear and Pinion Noise

Differential side gears and pinions seldom cause noise, since their movement is relatively slight on straight ahead driving. Noise produced by these gears will be more noticeable on turns.

Pinion Bearing Noise

Pinion bearing failures can be distinguished by their speed of rotation, which is higher than side bearings or axle bearings. Rough or brinelled pinion bearings cause a continuous low pitch whirring or scraping noise beginning at low speeds.

Side Bearing Noise

Side bearings produce a constant rough noise, which is slower than the pinion bearing noise. Side bearing noise may also fluctuate in the above rear wheel bearing test.

Gear Noise

Two basic types of gear noise exist. First, is the type produced by bent or broken gear teeth which have been forcibly damaged. The noise from this type of damage is audible over the entire speed range. Scoring or damage to the hypoid gear teeth generally results from insufficient lubricant, improper lubricant, improper break-in, insufficient gear backlash, improper ring and pinion gear alignment or loss of torque on the drive pinion nut. If not corrected, the scoring will lead to eventual erosion or fracture of the gear teeth. Hypoid gear tooth fracture can also be caused by extended overloading of the gear set (fatigue fracture) or by shock overloading (sudden failure). Differential and side gears

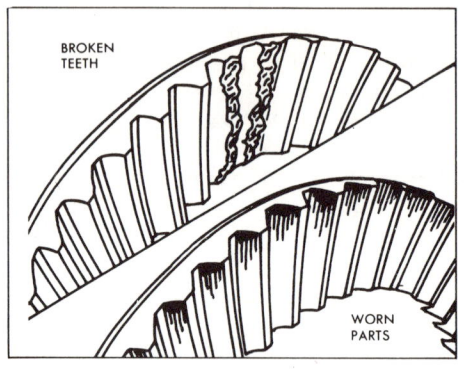

Broken teeth and worn parts can produce gear noise (Courtesy Chevrolet Motor Div.)

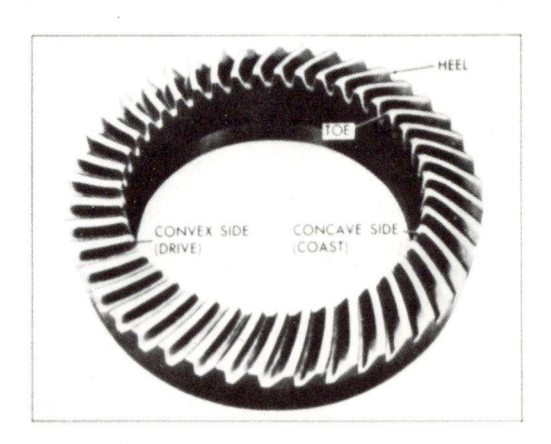

Gear tooth nomenclature (Courtesy Chevrolet Motor Div.)

rarely give trouble, but common causes of differential failure are shock loading, extended overloading and differential pinion seizure at the cross-shaft, resulting from excessive wheel spin and consequent lubricant breakdown.

The second type of gear noise pertains to the mesh pattern between the ring and pinion gears. This type of abnormal gear noise can be recognized as a cycling pitch or whine audible in either drive, float or coast conditions. Gear noises can be recognized as they tend to peak out in a narrow speed range and remain constant in pitch, whereas bearing noises tend to vary in pitch with ve-

DRIVE TRAIN 141

hicle speeds. Noises produced by the ring and pinion gear will generally follow the pattern below.

  a. Drive Noise: Produced under vehicle acceleration.

  b. Coast Noise: Produced while the car coasts with a closed throttle.

  c. Float Noise: Occurs while maintaining constant car speed (just enough to keep speed constant) on a level road.

  d. Drive, Coast and Float Noise: These noises will vary in tone with speed and be very rough or irregular if the differential or pinion shaft bearings are worn.

Bearing Failure Chart

General Wear

Cause	Serviceability
Wear on races and rollers caused by fine abrasives	Clean all parts and check seals. Install new bearing if old one is rough or noisy.

Normal wear pattern (© Chevrolet Div. G.M. Corp.)

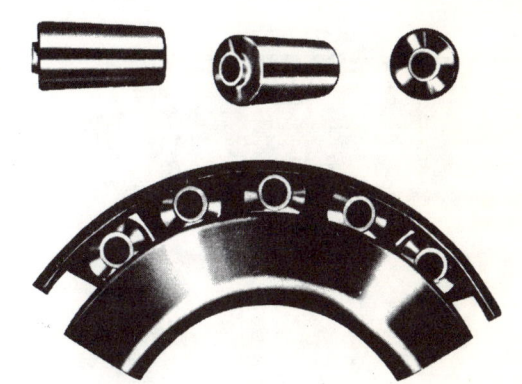

Step wear (© Chevrolet Div. G.M. Corp.)

Step Wear

Cause	Serviceability
Wear pattern on roller ends caused by fine abrasives	Clean all parts and check seals. Install new bearings if old one is rough or noisy.

Indentations

Cause	Serviceability
Surface depressions on races and rollers caused by hard foreign particles	Clean all parts and check seals. Install new bearing if old one is rough or noisy.

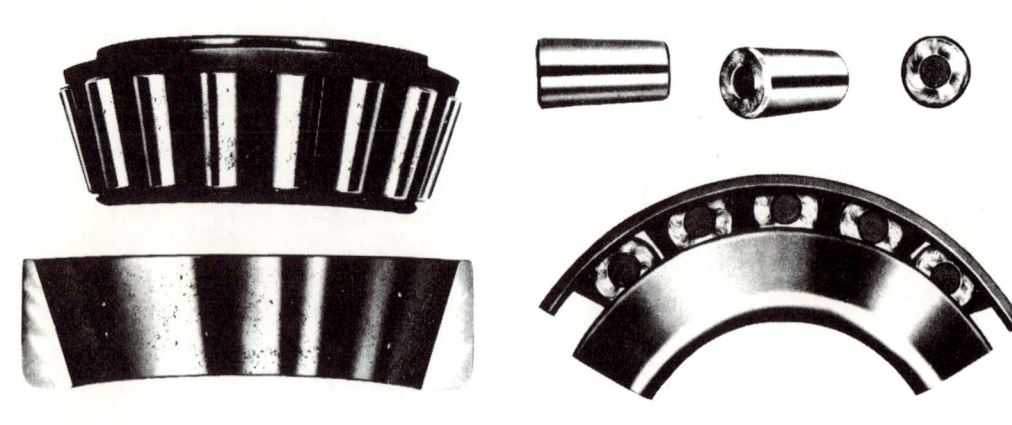

142 DRIVE TRAIN

Indentations (Chevrolet Div. G.M. Corp.)

Galling (© Chevrolet Div. G.M. Corp.)

Galling

Cause	Serviceability
Metal smears on roller ends due to overheating from improper lubricant or overloading	Install a new bearing. Check seals and use proper lubricant.

Etching (© Chevrolet Div. G.M. Corp.)

Cage wear (© Chevrolet Div. G.M. Corp.)

Etching

Cause	Serviceability
Bearing surfaces appear gray or gray-black with related etching	Install new bearing and check seals. Use proper lubricant.

Cage Wear

Cause	Serviceability
Wear around outside diameter of cage and rollers caused by foreign material and poor lubrication	Clean all parts, check seals, and install new bearing.

DRIVE TRAIN

Fatigue Spalling

Cause	Serviceability
Flaking of surface metal due to fatigue	Clean all parts and install new bearing.

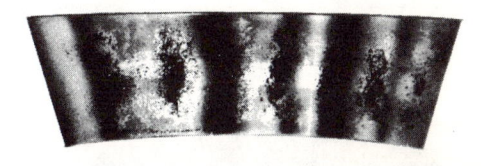

Fatigue spalling (© Chevrolet Div. G.M. Corp.) 　　Heat discoloration (© Chevrolet Div. G.M. Corp.)

Heat Discoloration

Cause	Serviceability
Discoloration from faint yellow to dark blue due to overload or lubricant breakdown. Softening of races or rollers also	Check for softening of parts by drawing a file over suspected area. The file will glide easily over hard metal, but will cut soft metal. If overheating is evident, install new bearings. Check seals and other parts.

Stain Discoloration

Cause	Serviceability
Stain discoloration ranging from light brown to black, caused by lubricant breakdown or moisture	Reuse bearings if stains can be removed by light polishing and no overheating exists. Check seals.

Stain discoloration (© Chevrolet Div. G.M. Corp.) 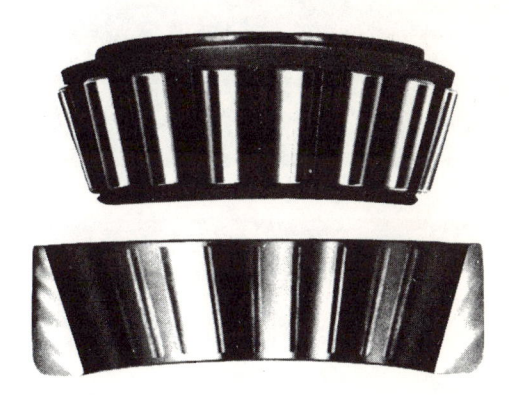　　Brinelling (© Chevrolet Div. G.M. Corp.)

144 DRIVE TRAIN

Brinelling

Cause	Serviceability
Surface indentations in race caused by rollers under impact load or vibration while the bearing is not rotating	If the old bearing is rough or noisy, install a new bearing.

Bent Cage

Cause	Serviceability
Improper handling	Install a new bearing.

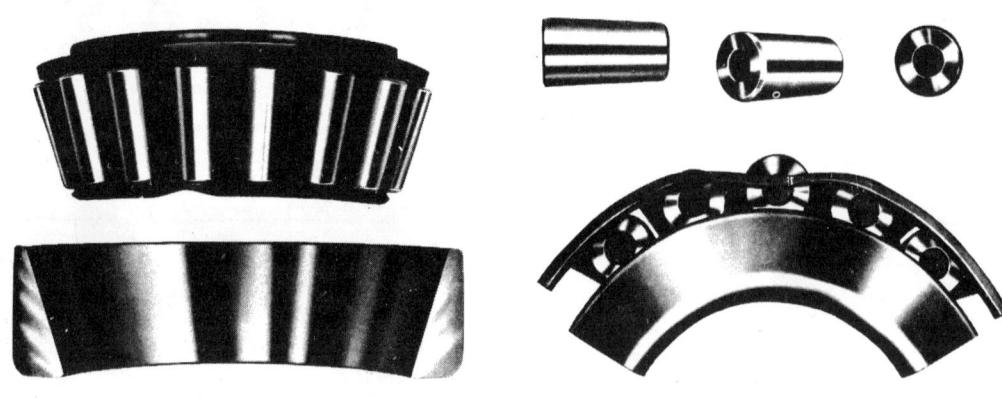

Bent cage (© Chevrolet Div. G.M. Corp.)

Misalignment

Cause	Serviceability
Outer race misaligned as shown	Install a new bearing and be sure races and bearing are properly seated.

Misalignment (© Chevrolet Div. G.M. Corp.)

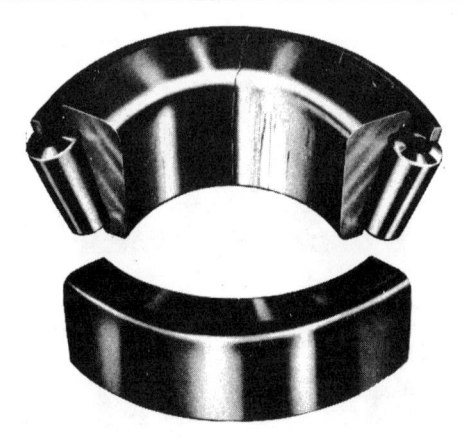

Cracked inner race (© Chevrolet Div. G.M. Corp.)

DRIVE TRAIN 145

Cracked Inner Race

Cause	Serviceability
Crack due to improper fit, cocked bearing, or poor bearing seats	Install a new bearing and be sure it is seated properly.

Frettage

Cause	Serviceability
Corrosion due to small movement of parts with no lubrication	Clean parts and check seals. Install a new bearing and be sure of proper lubrication.

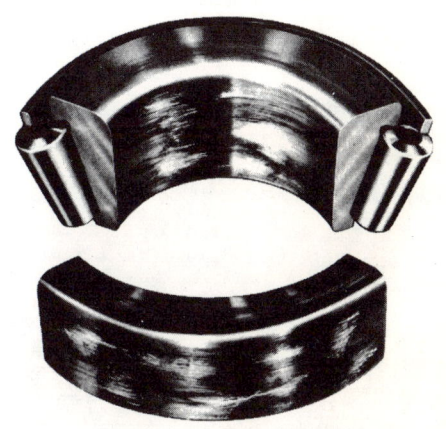

Frettage (© Chevrolet Div. G.M. Corp.)

Smears (© Chevrolet Div. G.M. Corp.)

Smears

Cause	Serviceability
Metal smears due to slippage caused by poor fit, improper lubrication, overloading, or handling damage	Clean parts, install new bearing, and check for proper fit and lubrication.

DRIVE TRAIN

GENERAL DRIVE AXLE DIAGNOSTIC GUIDE
(Also see following text for further differential diagnosis.)

CONDITION	POSSIBLE CAUSE	CORRECTION
REAR WHEEL NOISE	(a) Loose Wheel.	(a) Tighten loose wheel nuts.
	(b) Spalled wheel bearing cup or cone.	(b) Check rear wheel bearings. If spalled or worn, replace.
	(c) Defective or brinelled wheel bearing.	(c) Defective or brinelled bearings must be replaced. Check rear axle shaft end-play.
	(d) Excessive axle shaft end-play.	(d) Readjust axle shaft end play.
	(e) Bent or sprung axle shaft flange.	(e) Replace bent or sprung axle shaft.
SCORING OF DIFFERENTIAL GEARS AND PINIONS	(a) Insufficient lubrication.	(a) Replace scored gears. Scoring marks on the pressure face of gear teeth or in the bore are caused by instantaneous fusing of the mating surfaces. Scored gears should be replaced. Fill rear axle to required capacity with proper lubricant.
	(b) Improper grade of lubricant.	(b) Replace scored gears. Inspect all gears and bearings for possible damage. Clean and refill axle to required capacity with proper lubricant.
	(c) Excessive spinning of one wheel.	(c) Replace scored gears. Inspect all gears, pinion bores and shaft for scoring, or bearings for possible damage.
TOOTH BREAKAGE (RING GEAR AND PINION)	(a) Overloading.	(a) Replace gears. Examine other gears and bearings for possible damage. Avoid future overloading.
	(b) Erratic clutch operation.	(b) Replace gears, and examine remaining parts for possible damage. Avoid erratic clutch operation.
	(c) Ice-spotted pavements.	(c) Replace gears. Examine remaining parts for possible damage. Replace parts as required.
	(d) Improper adjustment.	(d) Replace gears. Examine other parts for possible damage. Be sure ring gear and pinion backlash is correct.
REAR AXLE NOISE	(a) Insufficient lubricant.	(a) Refill rear axle with correct amount of the proper lubricant. Also check for leaks and correct as necessary.
	(b) Improper ring gear and pinion adjustment.	(b) Check ring gear and pinion tooth contact.
	(c) Unmatched ring gear and pinion.	(c) Remove unmatched ring gear and pinion. Replace with a new matched gear and pinion set.
	(d) Worn teeth on ring gear or pinion.	(d) Check teeth on ring gear and pinion for contact. If necessary, replace with new matched set.
	(e) End-play in drive pinion bearings.	(e) Adjust drive pinion bearing preload.
	(f) Side play in differential bearings.	(f) Adjust differential bearing preload.
	(g) Incorrect drive gearlash.	(g) Correct drive gear lash.
	(h) Limited-Slip differential — moan and chatter.	(h) Drain and flush lubricant. Refill with proper lubricant.

DRIVE TRAIN

CONDITION	POSSIBLE CAUSE	CORRECTION
Loss of Lubricant	(a) Lubricant level too high.	(a) Drain excess lubricant.
	(b) Worn axle shaft oil seals.	(b) Replace worn oil seals with new ones. Prepare new seals before replacement.
	(c) Cracked rear axle housing.	(c) Repair or replace housing as required.
	(d) Worn drive pinion oil seal.	(d) Replace worn drive pinion oil seal with a new one.
	(e) Scored and worn companion flange.	(e) Replace worn or scored companion flange and oil seal.
	(f) Clogged vent.	(f) Remove obstructions.
	(g) Loose carrier housing bolts or housing cover screws.	(g) Tighten bolts or cover screws to specifications and fill to correct level with proper lubricant.
Overheating of Unit	(a) Lubricant level too low.	(a) Refill rear axle.
	(b) Incorrect grade of lubricant.	(b) Drain, flush and refill rear axle with correct amount of the proper lubricant.
	(c) Bearings adjusted too tightly.	(c) Readjust bearings.
	(d) Excessive wear in gears.	(d) Check gears for excessive wear or scoring. Replace as necessary.
	(e) Insufficient ring gear-to-pinion clearance.	(e) Readjust ring gear and pinion backlash and check gears for possible scoring.

NOISE DIAGNOSIS CHART

PROBLEM	CAUSE
1. Identical noise in Drive or Coast conditions	1. Road noise Tire noise Front wheel bearing noise
2. Noise changes on a different type of road	2. Road noise Tire noise
3. Noise tone lowers as car speed is lowered	3. Tire noise
4. Similar noise is produced with car standing and driving	4. Engine noise Transmission noise
5. Vibration	5. Rough rear wheel bearing Unbalanced or damaged driveshaft Unbalanced tire Worn universal joint in driveshaft Misaligned drive shaft at companion flange Excessive companion flange runout
6. A knock or click approximately every two revolutions of rear wheel	6. Brinelled rear wheel bearing
7. Noise most pronounced on turns	7. Differential side gear and pinion wear or damage
8. A continuous low pitch whirring or scraping noise starting at relatively low speed	8. Damaged or worn pinion bearing
9. Drive noise, coast noise or float noise	9. Damaged or worn ring and pinion gear
10. Clunk on acceleration or deceleration	10. Worn differential cross-shaft in case
11. Clunk on stops	11. Insufficient grease in driveshaft slip yoke
12. Groan in Forward or Reverse	12. Improper differential lubricant
13. Chatter on turns	13. Improper differential lubricant Worn clutch plates
14. Clunk or knock during operation on rough roads.	14. Excessive end-play of axle shafts to differential cross-shaft

Chapter Eight
Suspension and Steering

Front Suspension

ALL MODELS

The Mazda front suspension uses a wishbone-type suspension arm with a coil spring. Shock absorbers are hydraulic double-action.

FRONT SHOCK ABSORBER

Testing

The simplest test for any shock absorber is to bounce the suspect corner of the vehicle until it is bouncing quickly. Let go of the vehicle and count the number of bounces before it comes to rest. A good shock absorber should come to rest in 2–3 bounces at the most.

As an alternative:
1. Remove the shock absorber.
2. Hold the shock in an upright position and work it up and down 4–5 times through its full travel.
3. If strong resistance is felt, the shock is functioning properly. If no resistance is felt, or, if there is a sudden free movement in the stroke, replace the shock absorber with a new one. It is also a good idea to replace a shock absorber if an excessive amount of oil is visible on its exterior.

Removal and Installation

1. Raise and support the truck.
2. Remove the nuts attaching the upper end of the shock absorber to the crossmember.
3. Remove the rubber bushings and washers.
4. Remove the bolts attaching the lower end of the shock absorber to the lower control arm.
5. Remove the shock from under the lower control arm.

To install the shock absorber:
6. Replace any worn or damaged bushings.
7. From under the lower control arm, install the shock with bushings and attach the shock to the lower control arm.

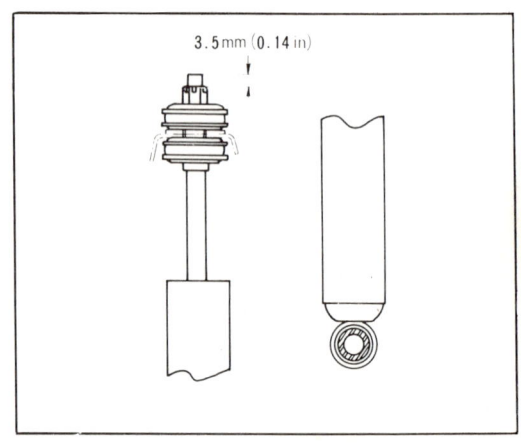

Tightening of front shock absorber nut—B-1600 (© Toyo Kogyo Co., Ltd.)

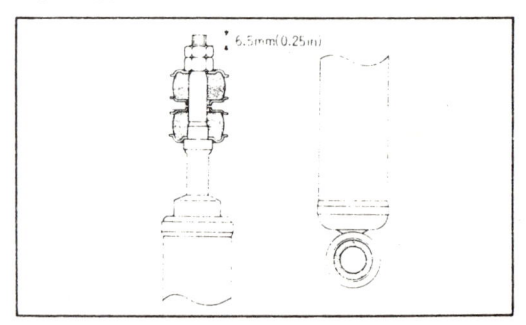

Tightening of front shock absorber nut—Rotary Pick-Up (© Toyo Kogyo Co., Ltd.)

SUSPENSION AND STEERING 149

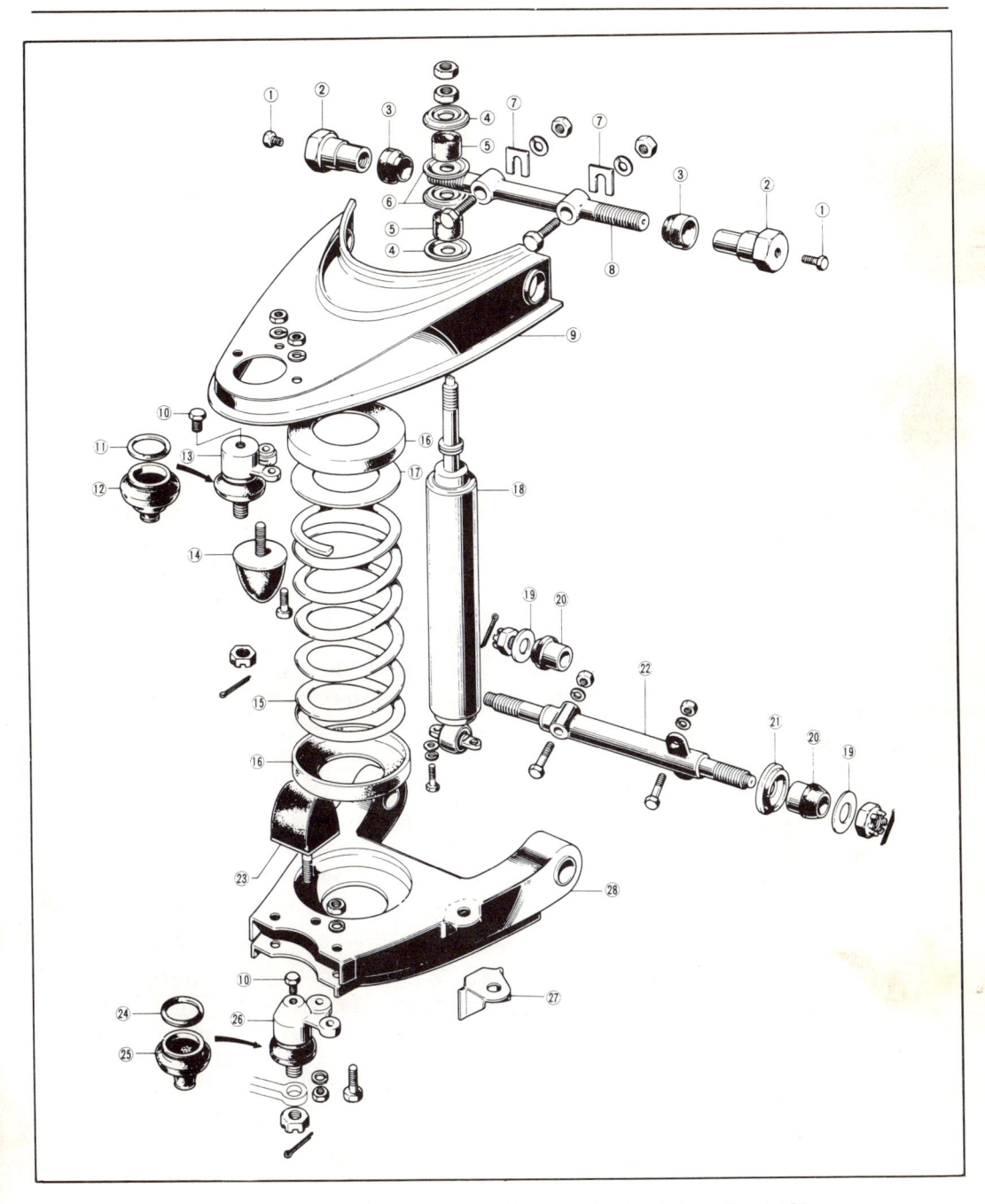

Exploded view of front suspension—all models (© Toyo Kogyo Co., Ltd.)

1. Plug
2. Threaded bushing
3. Dust seal
4. Retainer
5. Bush
6. Retainer
7. Adjusting shim
8. Upper arm shaft
9. Upper arm
10. Plug
11. Set ring
12. Dust seal
13. Ball joint assembly
14. Stopper
15. Coil spring
16. Seat
17. Adjusting plate
18. Shock absorber
19. Washer
20. Bush
21. Stopper
22. Lower arm shaft
23. Stopper
24. Set ring
25. Dust seal
26. Ball joint
27. Bracket
28. Lower arm

SUSPENSION AND STEERING

8. Attach the upper end of the shock to the crossmember. Tighten the shock absorber as shown.
9. Lower the truck.

UPPER CONTROL ARM

Removal and Installation.

1. Raise and support the truck.
2. Position jackstands under the lower control arm.
3. Lower the vehicle on the jackstands until the upper control arm is off the bumper stop.
4. Remove the wheel. Install a chain around the coil spring as a safety measure.
5. Remove the cotter pin and nut retaining the upper ball joint.
6. Break the tapered fit loose by striking it with a hammer and separate the ball joint from the spindle.
7. From under the hood, remove the two upper arm retaining bolts and remove the arm from the vehicle. Note the number and position of shims.
8. Remove the three ball joint retaining bolts and remove the ball joint from the upper arm.

To install the upper control arm:

9. Install the ball joint in the upper control arm.
10. Position the upper control arm in the truck and install the alignment shims from where they were removed. Install the retaining nuts and bolts on the shaft and torque them to 62–76 ft lbs.
11. Position the spindle on the ball joint and install the retaining nut and cotter pin.
12. Remove the safety chain.
13. Install the wheel.
14. Remove the jackstands and lower the truck. Have the front end alignment checked.

LOWER CONTROL ARM

Removal and Installation

1. Raise the front of the truck and position jackstands under both sides of the frame just behind the lower control arms.
2. Remove the wheel.
3. Remove the lower shock absorber retaining bolts and push the shock up into the spring.

Disconnect the stabilizer bar at the arrows (© Toyo Kogyo Co., Ltd.)

4. Remove the front stabilizer bar retaining bolt, nut and bushings and disconnect the stabilizer bar from the lower control arm.
5. Position a floor jack under the lower control arm and raise the arm to take the spring pressure off. Install a safety chain on the spring.
6. Unbolt the ball joint from the lower control arm.
7. Pull the spindle and ball joint away from the lower arm.
8. If necessary, the lower ball joint can be removed by removing the cotter pin and nut and loosening the ball joint with a hammer.
9. Carefully lower the control arm on the jack, being careful that the spring does not fly out.
10. Remove the three lower control arm retaining bolts and remove the lower control arm.

To install the lower control arm:

11. Position the lower control arm in place and install the three retaining bolts and nuts. Do not tighten. If removed, install the ball joint.
12. Position the spring on the lower control arm and in the upper frame retaining pocket.
13. Use a C-clamp to clamp the spring to the lower control arm.
14. Raise the lower control arm with a floor jack and position the ball joint and spindle in the lower arm.
15. Loosely install the three lower arm-to-ball joint bolts. Remove the safety chain from the spring, and remove the floor jack and C-clamp.
16. Torque the three ball joint retaining nuts to 60–70 ft lbs.
17. Pull the shock absorber down and install the bolts and nuts.

SUSPENSION AND STEERING 151

18. Install the stabilizer bar on the lower control arm.
19. Install the front wheel. Lower the truck and have the front wheel alignment checked.

BALL JOINTS

Checking

1. Check the ball joint dust seals and replace them if they are defective.
2. Check the end-play of the upper and lower ball joints. If the end-play exceeds 0.039 in., replace the ball joint.

Greasing the ball joint (© Toyo Kogyo Co., Ltd.)

Replacement

Use the applicable procedures under "Upper Control Arm Removal and Installation," or "Lower Control Arm Removal and Installation."

FRONT END ALIGNMENT

Caster

Caster is the forward or rearward tilt of the upper ball joint. Rearward tilt is referred to as positive caster, while forward tilt is referred to as negative caster.

Caster is adjusted by changing the shim(s) between the upper arm shaft and the frame, or, by turning the shaft until the correct angle is obtained.

Camber

Camber is the outward tilting of the front wheels, at the top, from the vertical.

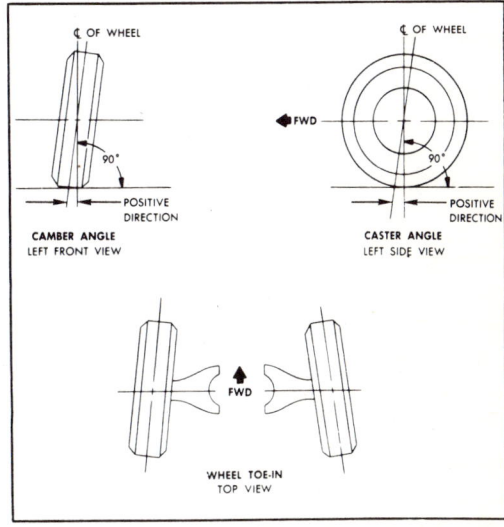

Caster, camber and toe-in (Courtesy Chevrolet Motor Div.)

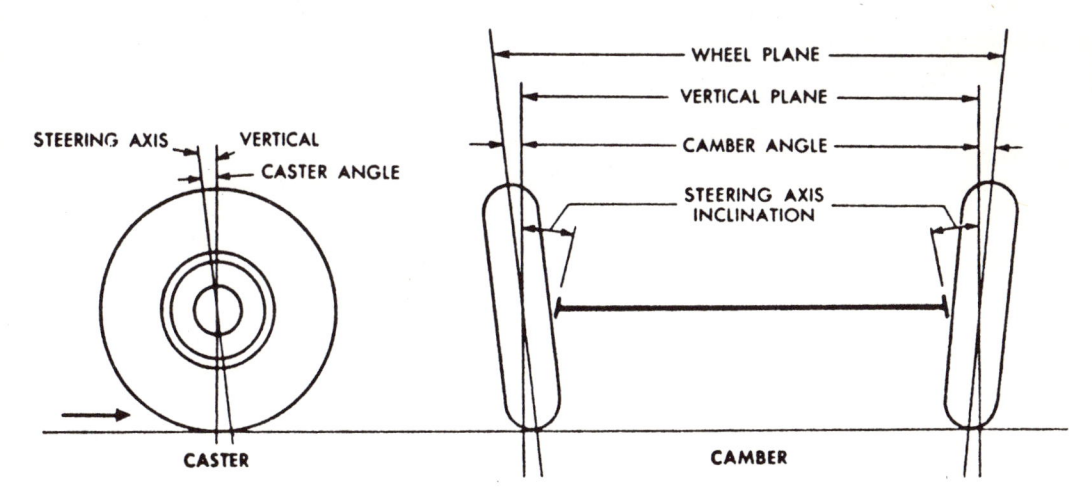

Steering geometry (Courtesy Chevrolet Motor Div.)

SUSPENSION AND STEERING

Camber is adjusted by adding or substracting the shim(s) between the upper arm shaft and the frame. Shims are available in thicknesses of 0.039 in., 0.063 in., 0.079 in., and 0.126 in.

Toe-In

Toe-in is the amount, measured in a fraction of an inch, that the wheels are closer together in the front than at the rear.

Toe-in can be increased or decreased by changing the length of the tie-rods. Threaded sleeves on the tie-rods are provided for this purpose. The clamps on the tie-rods must be positioned to prevent interference with the center link on the Rotary Pick-Up.

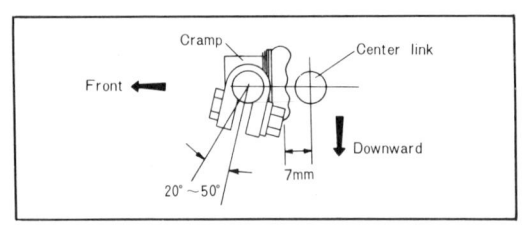

Tie-rod clamp position—Rotary Pick-Up (© Toyo Kogyo Co., Ltd.)

Front Wheel Turning Angle

The turning stop screws are located at the steering knuckle. If necessary, the screws can be adjusted to alter the turning angle.

NOTE: *This should not be attempted unless you are equipped with the necessary measuring equipment and a knowledge of front end alignment.*

Rear Suspension

ALL MODELS

The rear suspension consists of semi-elliptic leaf springs and hydraulic double-action shock absorbers.

SPRINGS

Removal and Installation

1. Raise and support the truck, allowing the spring to hang freely.
2. Support the rear axle with jackstands.
3. Disconnect the rear shock absorber at the lower mount.
4. Remove the spring clip nuts and the spring plate.
5. Remove the spring pin nut and remove the two bolts and nuts attaching the spring pin to the frame bracket.
6. Remove the spring pin and remove the front end of the spring from the truck.

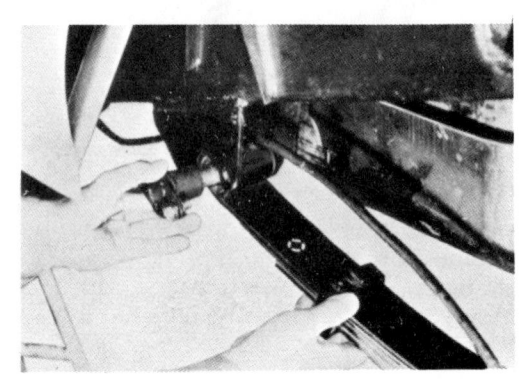

Removing or installing spring pin (© Toyo Kogyo Co., Ltd.)

Wheel Alignment Specifications

Year	Model	Caster Range (deg)	Caster Pref Setting (deg)	Camber Range (deg)	Camber Pref Setting (deg)	Toe-in (in.)	Front Wheel Turning Angle (deg) Inward	Front Wheel Turning Angle (deg) Outward
1972–75	B-1600	½P to 1–½P	1P	1P to 2P	1–½P	0–0.24	35–½	33
1974–75	Rotary Pick-Up	1–½P to 2–½P	2P	0 to ¾P	¼P	0–0.24	33–¼	32–½

P—Positive

SUSPENSION AND STEERING 153

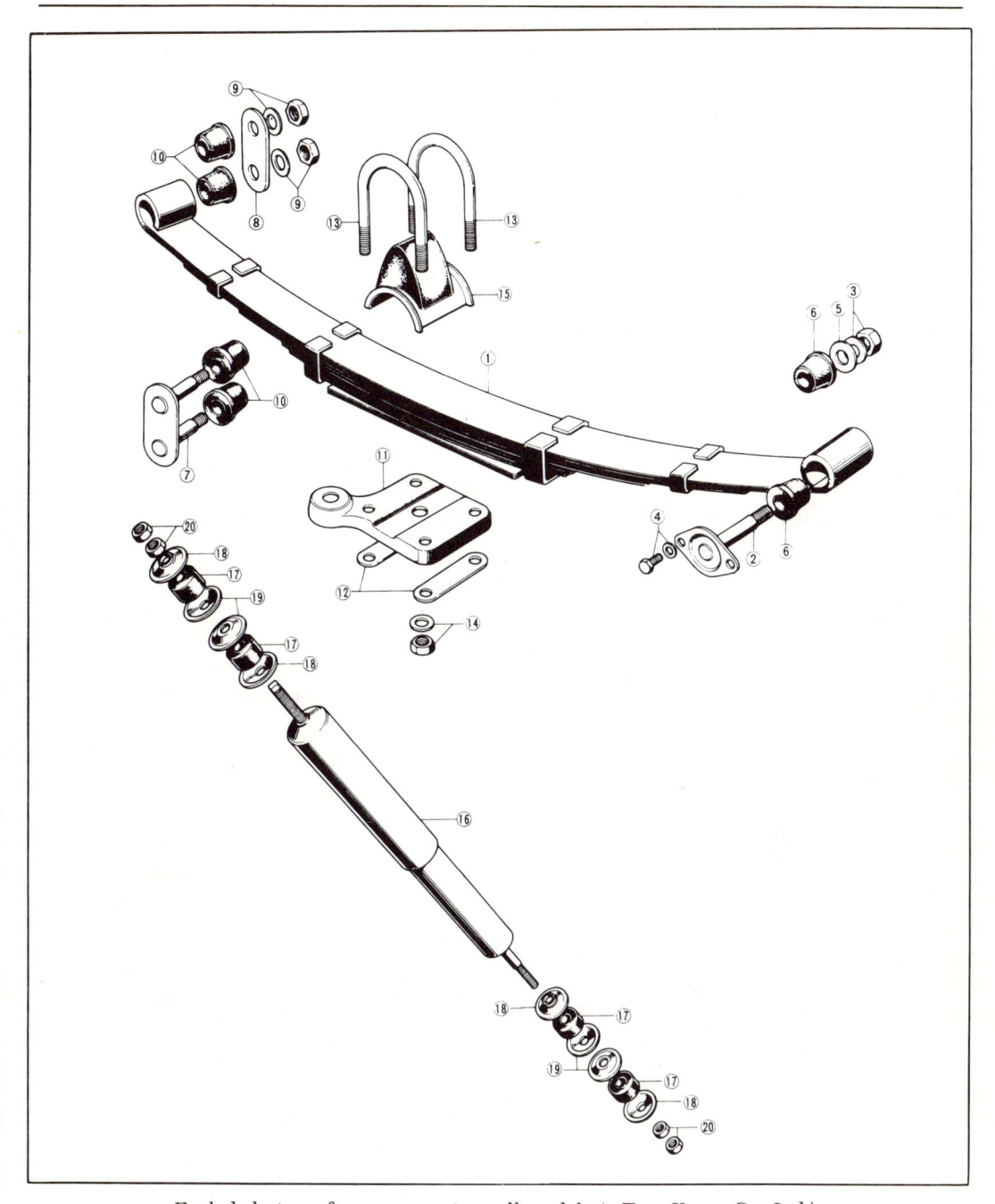

Exploded view of rear suspension—all models (© Toyo Kogyo Co., Ltd.)

1. Rear spring
2. Spring pin assembly
3. Nut
4. Bolt
5. Spacer
6. Bush
7. Shackle plate assembly
8. Shackle plate
9. Nut and washer
10. Bush
11. Spring clamp
12. Shim
13. U bolt
14. Nut and washer
15. Stopper rubber
16. Shock absorber
17. Bush
18. Retainer
19. Centering washer
20. Nut

SUSPENSION AND STEERING

7. Remove the shackle plate nuts and the shackle plate.
8. Remove the spring from the truck.

To install the spring:

9. Install the rubber bushings in the front eye of the spring and position it in the frame bracket. Align the holes of the bushings with the hole of the frame bracket.
10. Insert the spring pin from the outside through the rubber bushing.
11. Install the spring pin plate to the frame bracket and torque the nuts to 15–18 ft lbs.
12. Install the rubber bushings in the rear spring eye and shackle plate. Install the spring and shackle plate to the frame bracket. Do not tighten the nuts.
13. Lower the rear axle and place the center hole of the axle spring clip plate over the head of the spring center bolt.
14. Install the spring plate under the spring and install the spring clips. Torque the nuts to 46–58 ft lbs.
15. Connect the shock absorber at the lower mount and torque the mount to 18–26 ft lbs.
16. Lower the vehicle and bounce it several times to seat the springs.
17. Tighten the spring pin nuts to 62–76 ft lbs and shackle plate nuts to 44–58 ft lbs.

SHOCK ABSORBER

Testing

See "Front Shock Absorber Testing."

Removal and Installation

1. Raise and support the truck.
2. Remove the nuts, washers and

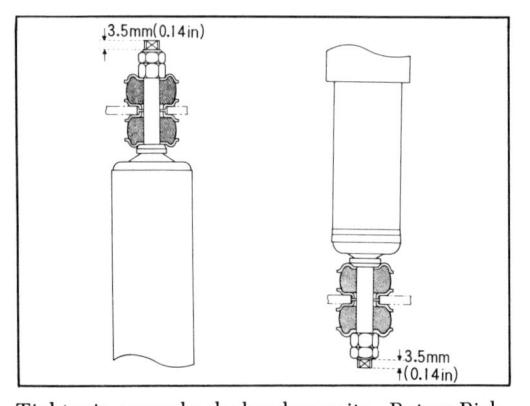

Tightening rear shock absorber units—Rotary Pick-Up (© Toyo Kogyo Co., Ltd.)

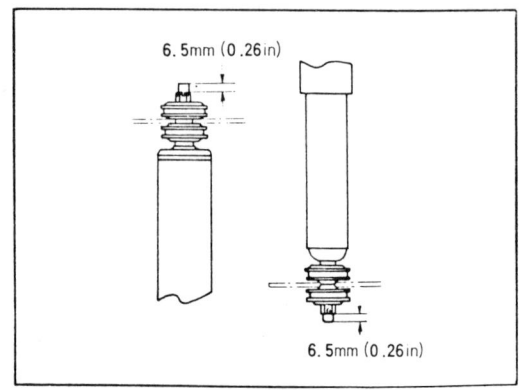

Tightening rear shock absorber units—B-1600 (© Toyo Kogyo Co., Ltd.)

bushings from the upper and lower shock mounts.
3. Compress the shock absorber and remove it.

To install the shock absorber:

4. If the rubber bushings are worn or damaged, use new ones.
5. Compress the shock absorber and install it in the truck.
6. Install the rubber bushings, washers and nuts on both the upper and lower mounts. Torque all mounts as shown.
7. Lower the truck.

Steering

The steering system consists of a recirculating ball nut gear, a steering column and linkage.

STEERING WHEEL

Removal and Installation

B-1600

1. Disconnect the negative battery cable.
2. Remove the horn button by turning it counterclockwise. Remove the horn contact spring.
3. Matchmark the steering wheel and shaft.
4. Remove the wheel attaching nut and remove the steering wheel with a puller.
5. Installation is the reverse of removal. Use the matchmarks to assemble properly. Torque the steering wheel nut to 22–29 ft lbs.

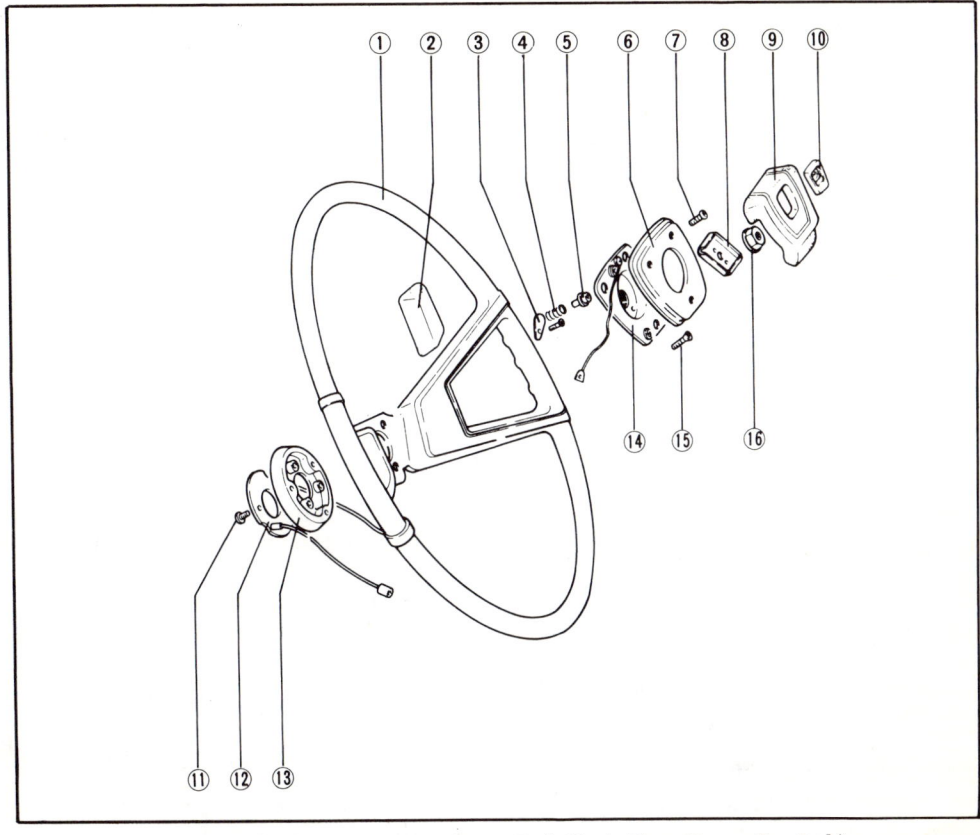

SUSPENSION AND STEERING

Steering wheel components—Rotary Pick-Up (© Toyo Kogyo Co., Ltd.)

1. Steering wheel
2. Horn button
3. Ground plate
4. Spring
5. Insulator
6. Cap set
7. Screw
8. Spring cap
9. Horn cap
10. Emblem
11. Tapping screw
12. Terminal
13. Wheel core cover
14. Set plate
15. Screw
16. Steering wheel nut

ROTARY PICK-UP

1. Pull the steering wheel pad toward the top of the wheel. Disconnect the negative battery cable.
2. Remove the horn button and contact assembly.
3. Matchmark the steering wheel and shaft.
4. Remove the steering wheel nut and remove the wheel with a puller.

NOTE: *Do not pound on the column shaft.*

5. Installation is the reverse of removal. Torque the steering wheel nut to 22–29 ft lbs.

Checking Steering Wheel Play

The free-play at the outer circumference of the steering wheel should be 0.6–1.0 in. Place the front wheels straight ahead and slowly turn the steering wheel. The free-play should be measured at the point when the front wheels begin to move. If excessive play is evident, check the following:
 a. Ball joints;
 b. Worn idler arm bushings;
 c. Loose wheel bearings, or;
 d. Improperly adjusted steering gear.

IGNITION SWITCH
Removal and Installation
B-1600 ONLY

1. Disconnect the negative battery cable.
2. Reach under the instrument panel and pull the wire connector from the rear of the switch.

SUSPENSION AND STEERING

3. Hold the switch body from behind the instrument panel and remove the black retaining nut.
4. Remove the switch from behind the instrument panel.

To install the ignition switch:

5. Install the switch from behind the instrument panel.
6. Hold the switch body behind the instrument panel and install the retaining nut.
7. Connect the multiple connector to the rear of the switch.
8. Connect the battery cable and check the operation of the switch.

STEERING LINKAGE

Idler Arm

REMOVAL AND INSTALLATION

1. Raise and support the front of the truck.
2. Remove the cotter pin and nut attaching the center link to the idler arm.
3. Disconnect the center link from the idler arm with a ball joint puller.
4. Remove the bolts attaching the idler arm and remove the idler arm.
5. Installation is the reverse of removal. Torque the idler arm attaching bolts to 32–40 ft lbs.

Pitman Arm

REMOVAL AND INSTALLATION

1. Raise and support the front of the truck.
2. Remove the cotter pin and nut attaching the center link to the pitman arm.
3. Disconnect the center link from the pitman arm with a ball joint puller.
4. Remove the pitman arm attaching nut.
5. Remove the pitman arm from the steering sector shaft.
6. Installation is the reverse of removal. Be sure to align the marks on the pitman arm and sector shaft. Tighten the pitman arm attaching nut to 108–130 ft lbs. The nut should always be tightened to the next slot if the cotter pin does not fit properly.

Center Link

REMOVAL AND INSTALLATION

1. Raise and support the front of the truck.
2. Remove the center link from both tie-rods, pitman arm and the idler arm by removing the cotter pins and nuts.
3. Installation is the reverse of removal.

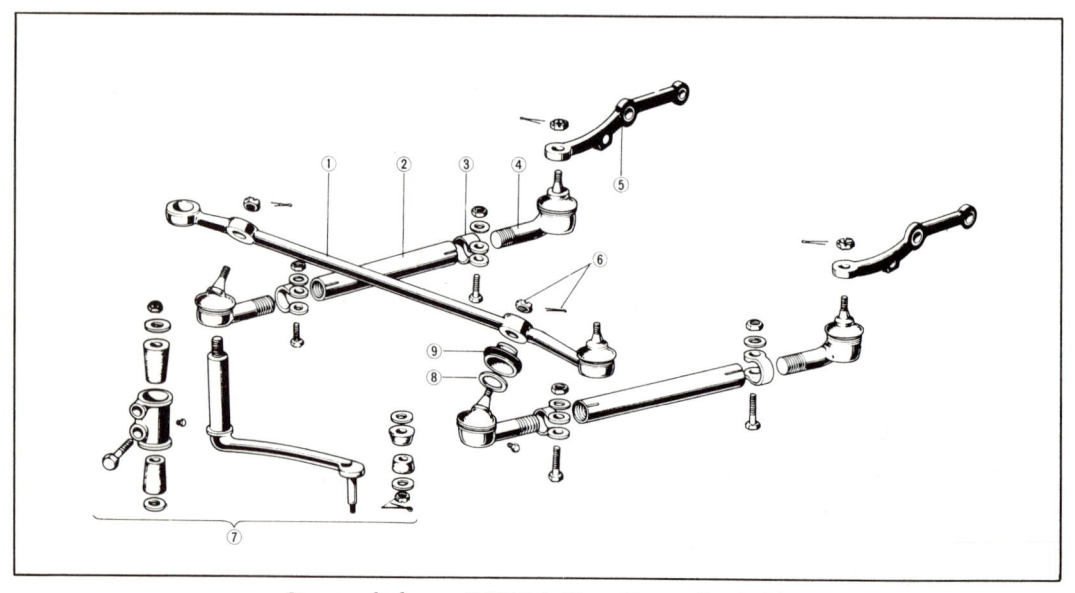

Steering linkage—B-1600 (© Toyo Kogyo Co., Ltd.)

1. Center link
2. Tie-rod
3. Clamp, bolt and nut
4. Ball joint
5. Knuckle arm
6. Nut and split pin
7. Idler arm assembly
8. Set ring
9. Boot

SUSPENSION AND STEERING 157

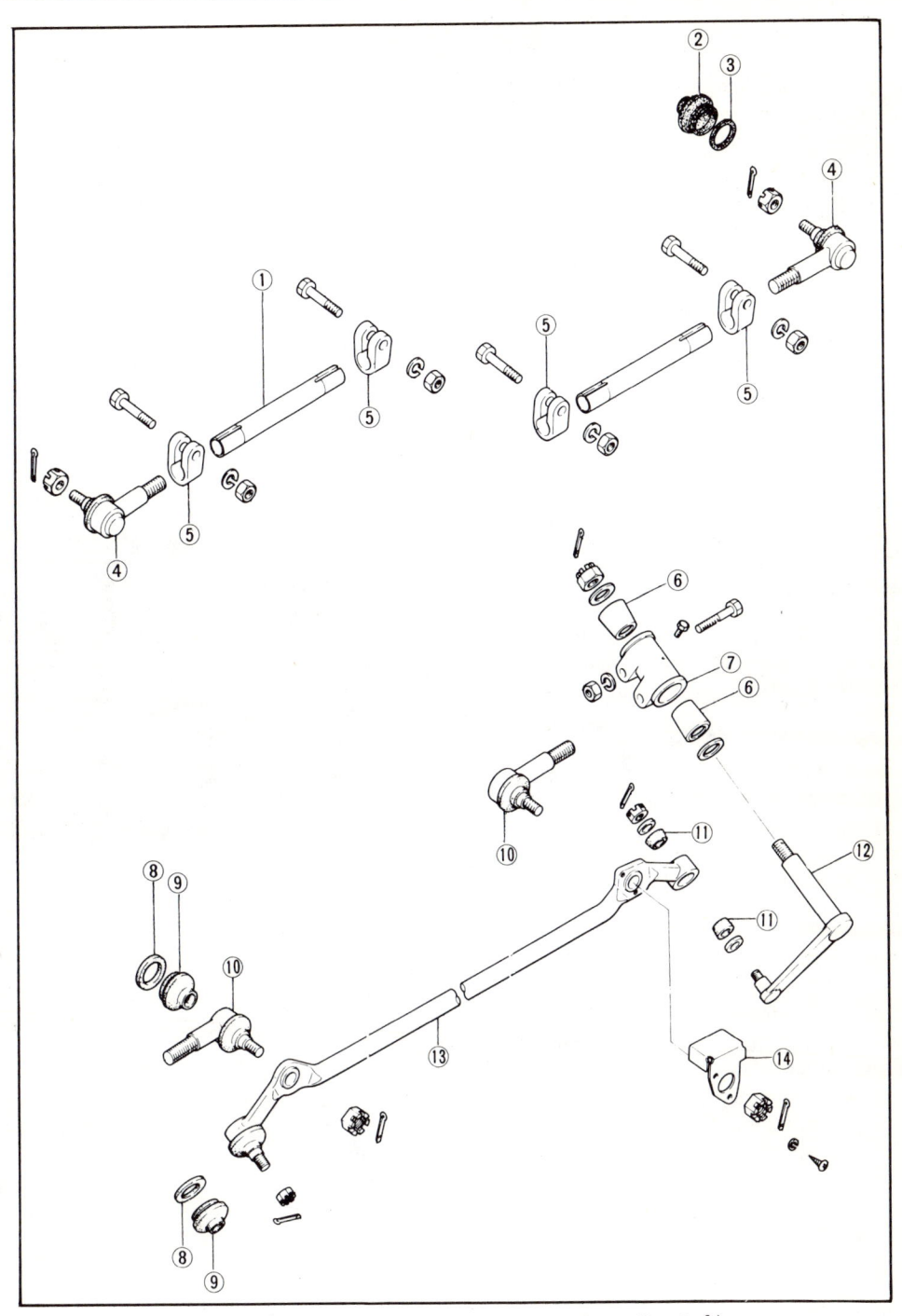

Steering linkage—Rotary Pick-Up (© Toyo Kogyo Co., Ltd.)

1. Tie-rod
2. Dust seal
3. Dust seal ring
4. Ball joint
5. Tie-rod clamp
6. Tapered bush
7. Idler bracket
8. Dust seal ring
9. Dust seal
10. Ball joint
11. Tapered bush
12. Idler arm
13. Center link
14. Insulator

Chapter Nine
Brakes

B1600 Sport Truck

Brake System

The B-1600 uses front and rear drum brakes with single piston front wheel cylinders and dual piston rear wheel cylinders.

The Rotary Pick-Up uses disc brakes in the front with drum brakes at the rear. The rear drum brakes also use a dual piston wheel cylinder.

Both trucks use a foot-operated parking brake acting on the rear brake shoes.

ADJUSTMENT

Front Drum Brakes

The brake shoes should be at normal room temperature. Adjust each front brake shoe as follows.

1. Raise and support the truck. The wheels must be free to turn freely.
2. Remove the adjusting slot covers from the brake backing plate.
3. Insert a brake adjusting spoon (a screwdriver will do in a pinch) to grab the starwheel of the wheel cylinder.
4. Rotate the starwheel of one wheel cylinder toward the inside of the brake drum until the wheel is locked. Then back off the starwheel 5 notches.
5. Repeat Step 4 for each wheel cylinder of each wheel.
6. Install the adjusting slot covers.
7. Check the brake adjustment by spinning the wheel by hand. There should be no drag.
8. Lower the truck.

Brake adjustment—drum brakes (© Toyo Kogyo Co., Ltd.)

Front Disc Brakes

Disc brakes are inherently self-adjusting and no adjustments are required or possible.

Rear Drum Brakes

The brake shoes should be at normal room temperature. Make the adjustment as follows.

1. Be sure that the parking brake is fully released. Disconnect the equalizer clevis pin.
2. Raise and support the truck so that the wheels are free to turn.
3. Remove the adjusting slot covers from the brake backing plate.
4. Insert a brake spoon (or screwdriver) into the lower adjusting slot to contact the starwheel of the lower wheel cylinder.
5. Turn the lower wheel cylinder starwheel to expand the brake shoe until it locks against the drum. Back the starwheel off 5 notches. Check the wheel,

Brake Specifications
(All Measurements are given in in.)

Year	Model	Master Cylinder Bore	Wheel Cylinder or Caliper Piston Bore - Front Disc	Front Drum	Rear Disc	Rear Drum	Brake Disc or Drum Diameter - Front Disc	Front Drum	Rear Disc	Rear Drum	New Pad or Lining Thickness
1972–75	B-1600	0.750	—	1.0	—	0.813	—	10.2364 ①	—	10.2364 ①	0.217 ②
1974–75	Rotary Pick-Up	0.875	2.1248	—	—	0.750	10.079 ③	—	—	10.2364 ①	0.551 (front) 0.217 (rear) ④

① Wear limit: 10.2758 in.
② Wear limit: 0.039 in.
③ Thickness of the brake disc is 0.4724 in. Minimum allowable thickness is 0.4331 in. Maximum allowable run-out is 0.0039 in.
④ Disc brake pad wear limit: 0.276 in.
  Brake shoe wear limit: 0.039 in.
— Not applicable

BRAKES

by rotating it, to be sure that there is no drag.

6. Repeat Step 5 for each wheel cylinder of each wheel.

7. Connect the parking brake equalizer clevis pin and check the parking brake adjustment.

8. Install the adjusting hole covers.

9. Lower the truck and road-test the brakes. Readjust if necessary.

BRAKE PEDAL FREE-TRAVEL ADJUSTMENT

B-1600

There should be 0.02–0.12 in. of brake pedal free-travel before the pushrod contacts the piston.

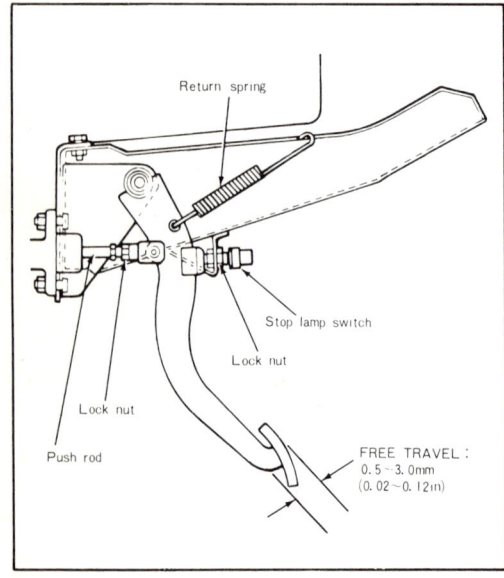

Brake pedal free-play adjustment—B-1600 (© Toyo Kogyo Co., Ltd.)

1. Loosen the locknut on the master cylinder pushrod at the clevis, which attaches the pushrod to the pedal.

2. Turn the master cylinder pushrod either in or out to obtain the specified clearance.

3. When the adjustment is complete, tighten the locknut to 8–13 ft lbs.

Rotary Pick-Up

1. Disconnect the stoplight switch at the terminals.

2. Loosen the locknut and adjust the brake pedal height to 7.5 in. between the pedal and floor mat by turning the stoplight switch and pushrod.

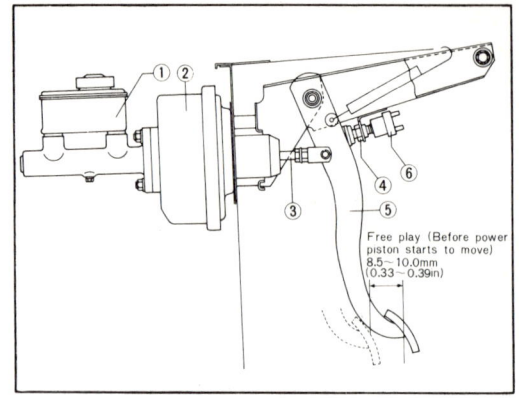

Brake pedal free-play adjustment—Rotary Pick-Up (© Toyo Kogyo Co., Ltd.)

1. Master cylinder
2. Power brake unit
3. Pushrod
4. Locknut
5. Brake pedal
6. Stoplight switch

3. Tighten the locknut.

4. Connect the stoplight switch wire.

Hydraulic System

MASTER CYLINDER

Removal and Installation

ALL MODELS

1. Disconnect and plug the brake lines.

2. Remove the two nuts and lockwashers which secure the master cylinder to the firewall.

3. Lift the master cylinder and boot outward and upward away from the firewall and brake pushrod.

To install the master cylinder:

4. Install the master cylinder and boot on the firewall, while carefully guiding

To remove the master cylinder, disconnect and plug the lines (arrows) and unbolt the unit (upper arrow) (© Toyo Kogyo Co., Ltd.)

BRAKES 161

the brake pushrod into contact with the master cylinder piston.

5. Install the two nuts and lockwashers and tighten the nuts to 11–17 ft lbs.

6. Connect the brake lines to the master cylinder outlet ports.

7. Bleed the brake system.

8. Check the brake pedal free-travel adjustment.

Overhaul

ALL MODELS

1. Remove the master cylinder.
2. Remove the master cylinder reservoir and drain the master cylinder.
3. Remove the two grommets from the master cylinder body.
4. Remove the dust boot.
5. Use a small screwdriver to remove the piston stop ring.
6. Remove the piston stop washer, primary piston and primary piston return spring.
7. Loosen but do not remove the secondary piston stop screw.
8. Push the secondary piston in and remove the stop screw. Insert a guide pin in its place. Remove the secondary piston and secondary return spring.
9. Remove the outlet port fittings, gaskets, check valves and check valve springs.
10. Clean all the parts (except rubber) in isopropyl alcohol. Do not use mineral base fluids. Allow all parts to air dry.

To assemble the master cylinder:

11. Dip all parts (except rubber) in clean brake fluid before assembly.
12. Install the check valve spring and check valves into the cylinder outlets and install the outlet port fittings and gaskets.
13. Position the secondary piston return spring on the secondary piston and install the assembly spring first. It may be necessary to use a guide pin in the secondary piston stop bolt hole.
14. Position the primary piston spring on the primary piston and install the assembly, spring first into the cylinder.
15. Install the piston stop washer and piston stop ring.

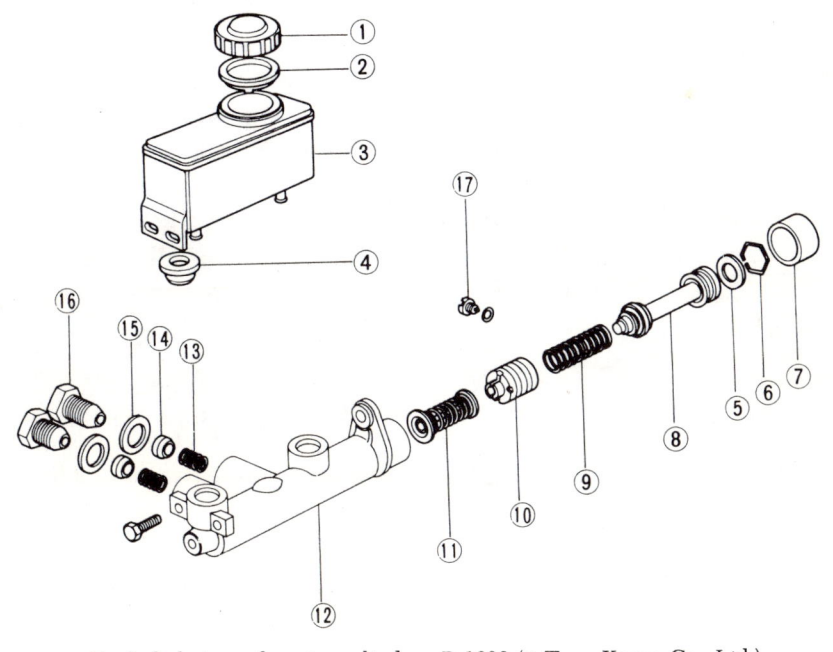

Exploded view of master cylinder—B-1600 (© Toyo Kogyo Co., Ltd.)

1. Filler cap
2. Baffle
3. Reservoir
4. Grommet
5. Washer
6. Stop ring
7. Dust boot
8. Primary piston
9. Spring
10. Secondary piston
11. Valve and spring
12. Cylinder
13. Spring
14. Check valve
15. Gasket
16. Outlet fitting
17. Stop bolt

BRAKES

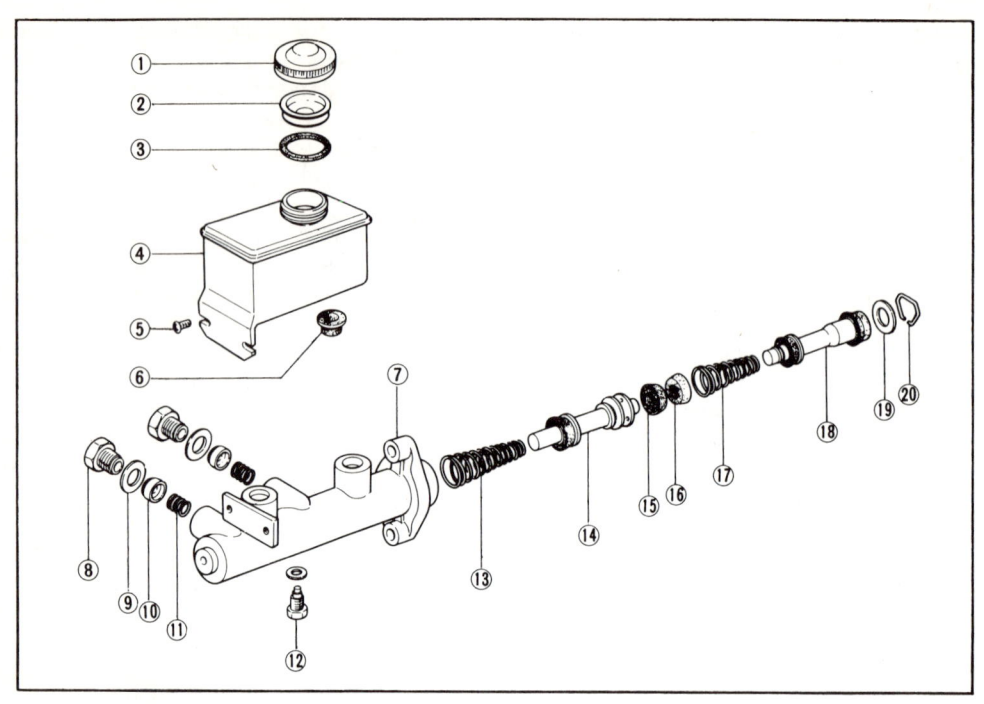

Exploded view of master cylinder—Rotary Pick-Up (© Toyo Kogyo Co., Ltd.)

1. Reservoir cap
2. Fluid baffle
3. Packing
4. Reservoir
5. Bolt
6. Bushing
7. Cylinder
8. Joint bolt
9. Gasket
10. Check valve
11. Spring
12. Secondary piston stop bolt and O-ring
13. Spring
14. Secondary piston
15. Secondary piston cup
16. Secondary piston cup
17. Spring
18. Primary piston
19. Stop washer
20. Snap-ring

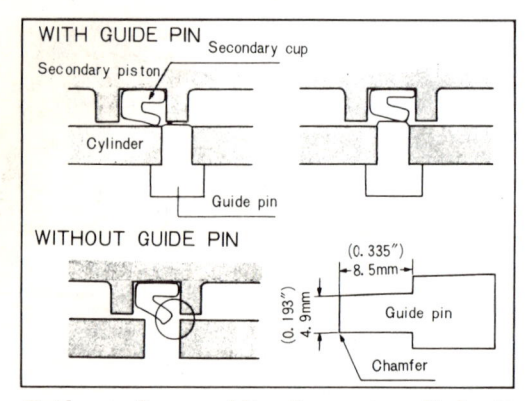

Guide pin for assembling the master cylinder (© Toyo Kogyo Co., Ltd.)

16. Install the secondary piston stop bolt.
17. Install the two grommets in the cylinder body.
18. Install the reservoir so that the outlet tubes are seated in the grommets.
19. Fill the master cylinder and pump the piston with a screwdriver until fluid flows from the outlet ports.
20. Install the master cylinder and bleed the brakes.

PRESSURE DIFFERENTIAL VALVE

Removal and Installation

1. Disconnect the warning light switch connector from the warning light switch.
2. Disconnect the brake inlet and outlet lines. Plug the lines.
3. Remove the valve assembly-to-cowl attaching bolt and remove the valve and switch assembly.

To install the valve and switch:

4. Position the valve and switch on the cowl. Install the retaining bolt.
5. Connect the brake lines to the valve.
6. Connect the warning light to the switch wiring connector.
7. Depress the brake pedal several times, then bleed the brake system.
8. Fill the master cylinder and check for proper operation.

Centralizing the Pressure Differential Valve

Normally, the brake warning light will remain ON after any repairs to the brake system, or after bleeding the brakes. This is caused by the pressure differential valve remaining in the off center position.

To centralize the pressure differential valve and turn the warning light OFF:
1. Turn the ignition switch to ON.
2. Check the fluid levels in the master cylinder reservoirs and fill them to within ¼ in. of the top, if necessary.
3. Depress the brake pedal and the piston will center itself, causing the warning light to go out.
4. Turn the ignition switch OFF.
5. Before driving the truck, check the operation of the brakes to be sure that a firm pedal has been obtained.

BLEEDING

All Models

The primary and secondary (front and rear) systems are independent systems and are bled separately. Bleed the longest line first on an individual system. In the case of the rear brakes, bleed at the lower right rear wheel cylinder then at the upper right rear wheel cylinder.

During the bleeding operation, do not allow the master cylinder to run dry. Keep the master cylinder reservoirs full of extra heavy-duty brake fluid. Immediately after bleeding, throw out the fluid that was bled from the system. It is useless since it contains air bubbles.

Bleeding the brakes—(rear brakes shown) (© Toyo Kogyo Co., Ltd.)

Do not use the secondary piston stop screw located on the side of the master cylinder to bleed with, as damage to the secondary piston could result.

1. Bleed the rear (secondary) brake system first. Remove the bleeder fitting cap and attach a rubber hose snugly over the fitting at the right rear lower wheel cylinder.
2. Submerge the end of the hose in a jar of clean brake fluid. Open the bleeder valve ¾ turn.
3. Push the brake pedal down slowly through its full travel. Close the bleeder fitting and let the pedal return. Repeat this operation until air bubbles cease to appear at the submerged end of the bleeder tube.
4. When the fluid is completely free of bubbles, close the bleeder fitting, remove the tube and install the bleeder fitting cap.
5. Repeat this procedure at the upper right wheel cylinder.
6. Repeat the procedure at the left rear wheel cylinders. Refill the master cylinder reservoir after each wheel cylinder is bled.
7. Bleed the primary (front) brake system in the same manner, ending by bleeding each left front wheel.
8. When the bleeding operation is complete, the master cylinder should be filled to within ¼ in. of the top. Install the master cylinder cover.
9. Centralize the pressure differential valve.

Front Drum Brakes

BRAKE DRUM

Removal and Installation

1. Raise and support the truck.
2. Remove the wheel.
3. Remove the brake drum attaching screws and install them in the tapped holes in the brake drum.
4. Turn these screws in evenly to force the brake drum away from the wheel hub.
5. Remove and inspect the brake drum. See "Inspection."

To install the brake drum:

BRAKES

Brake drum removal (© Toyo Kogyo Co., Ltd.)

6. Install the brake drum with the attaching screw holes aligned with the holes in the hub.
7. Transfer the attaching screws from the tapped holes in the brake drum to the attaching holes in the hub.
8. Tighten the screws evenly to secure the hub.
9. Install the wheel.
10. Lower the truck and check the brake adjustment.

Inspection

1. Brush all dust from the inside of the brake drum.
2. Check the brake drum diameter with a brake drum gauge. Replace any drums which have a diameter greater than 10.2758 in.
3. Inspect the brake drums for cracks. Replace any cracked drums.
4. Look carefully for any scoring of the drums. If the drums are scored, have them reground by a shop.

BRAKE SHOES

Inspection

1. If compressed air is available, blow out the accumulated dust and grit.
2. Inspect for excessive lining wear or shoe damage. Replace any cracked shoes.
3. If the lining is worn to within 0.039 in. of the shoe or if the shoes are damaged, they must be replaced.
4. Replace any linings that are contaminated with grease or brake fluid from leaking wheel cylinders. Replace linings in axle sets only.
5. Check the condition of the shoes, retracting springs and hold-down springs for signs of overheating. If the shoes have a slight blue color, this indicates overheating and replacement of the springs as well as the linings is recommended.
6. If signs of overheating are present, the wheel cylinders should be rebuilt as a precaution against future problems.

Removal and Installation

1. Raise and support the truck.
2. Remove the wheel.
3. Remove the brake drum.
4. Remove the brake shoe retracting springs.
5. Remove the shoe retaining spring guide pin and the retaining spring, by holding the guide pin to the backing plate and compressing and turning the spring 90°. A brake spring tool to do this easily is available, inexpensively, from most auto parts stores.
6. Remove the brake shoes, noting their positions.

Front brake shoes installed—B-1600. The slots in the shoes (arrows) should face the adjuster. (© Toyo Kogyo Co., Ltd.)

To install new brake shoes:

7. Lubricate the threads of the adjusting screw with brake paste and one or two spots on the adjuster wheel inside threads. Lubricate the backing plate shoe pads.
8. Position each brake shoe on the brake backing plate so that the slot in the shoe web is toward the starwheel in the wheel cylinder.
9. Install the shoe retaining spring guide pin. Install the retaining spring over the guide pin, hold the guide pin in

BRAKES

place and depress the retaining spring. Turn it 90° to lock the spring in place.

10. Install the brake shoe retracting spring. Be careful not to bend the springs or stretch the hooks.
11. Install the brake drum.
12. Install the wheel.
13. Adjust the brakes.
14. Bleed the brakes.
15. Lower the truck and check for proper operation.

WHEEL CYLINDER

Removal and Installation

1. Raise and support the truck.
2. Remove the wheel.
3. Remove the brake drum and brake shoes.
4. Disconnect and plug the brake line at the wheel cylinder.
5. Remove the stud nuts and bolt attaching the wheel cylinder to the backing plate and remove the wheel cylinder.

To install the wheel cylinder:

6. Install the wheel cylinder on the backing plate.
7. Clean the end of the brake line and attach it to the wheel cylinder. Tighten the tube fitting nut.
8. Install the links in the end of the wheel cylinder.
9. Install the shoes and adjuster assemblies.
10. Install the brake drum and wheel.
11. Adjust the brakes.
12. Bleed the brakes and centralize the pressure differential valve.
13. Lower the truck.

Overhaul

1. Remove the wheel cylinder.
2. Remove the piston and adjusting screw with the boot attached to the cylinder. Separate the adjuster and boot from the adjuster.
3. Using compressed air (if possible), blow the piston cup, cup expander and spring. Lay the cylinder face down and apply air pressure to the brake line port.
4. Wash all parts in ispropyl alcohol, except the rubber boot.
5. Examine the cylinder bore, piston and adjuster for wear, roughness or damage. Check the clearance between the piston and cylinder bore. If the clearance is greater than 0.006 in., replace with new parts. Discard the piston cups.

To assemble the wheel cylinder:

6. Lubricate the cylinder bore, adjuster and new piston cup with clean brake fluid.
7. Position the piston return spring in the piston cup expander. Install the return spring, piston cup expander and

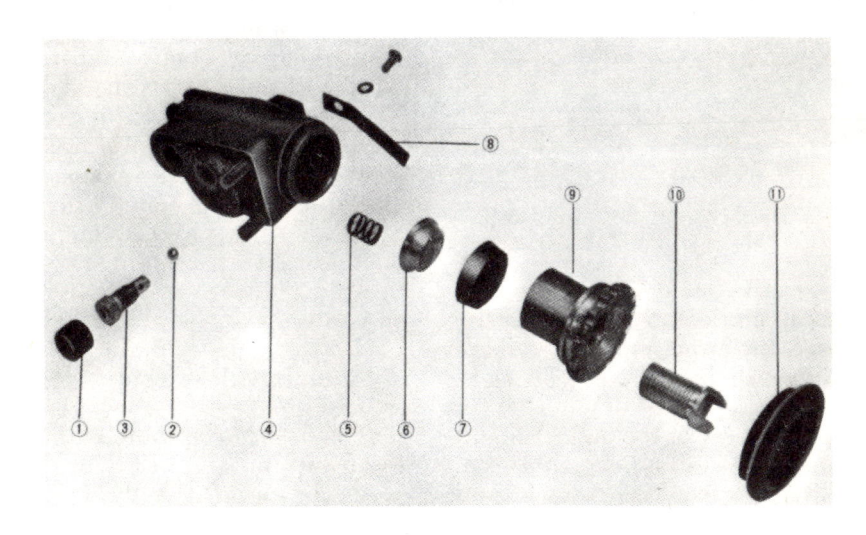

Front wheel cylinder—B-1600 (© Toyo Kogyo Co., Ltd.)

1. Cap
2. Bleeder screw
3. Steel ball
4. Cylinder
5. Spring
6. Filling block
7. Piston cup
8. Set spring
9. Piston and star wheel
10. Screw
11. Dust boot

BRAKES

piston cup in the cylinder. The flat side of the piston cup goes toward the piston.

8. Install the piston boot to the piston adjuster (smaller lip of the boot in the groove of the piston adjuster).

9. Insert the piston adjuster into the cylinder and install the larger lip of the boot in the groove on the cylinder body.

10. Install the adjusting screw in the piston adjuster.

11. Install the wheel cylinder.

FRONT WHEEL BEARINGS

Adjustment

The front wheel bearings should be adjusted if the wheel is loose on the spindle or if the wheel does not rotate freely. In addition, they should be checked and repacked at the suggested interval. See "Maintenance," Chapter 1.

1. Raise and support the truck.
2. Remove the wheel and tire.
3. Attach a spring scale onto a hub bolt.
4. Pull the spring scale squarely and read the pull as the hub begins to turn. It should be 1.3–2.4 lbs.

Checking front wheel bearing preload—B-1600 (© Toyo Kogyo Co., Ltd.)

5. If the reading is not correct, remove the grease cap and cotter pin. Adjust the bearings with the large nut on the end of the spindle until the proper reading is obtained.
6. Align the holes of the adjusting nut and spindle and install a new cotter pin.
7. Install the grease cap, wheel and tire.
8. Lower the truck.

Alternate Procedure

If a spring scale is not available, the following procedure can be used.

1. Raise and support the truck.
2. Remove the wheel and tire and the grease cap.
3. Remove the cotter pin.
4. Rotate the hub and tighten the adjusting nut until the hub binds.
5. Back the adjusting nut off $1/6$ turn. Be sure that the hub rotates freely with no side play.
6. Align the holes of the nut and spindle and install a new cotter pin.
7. Install the grease cap, wheel and tire.
8. Lower the truck.

Removal, Installation and Packing

1. Raise and support the truck.
2. Remove the wheel cover.
3. Remove the wheel and tire.
4. Remove the grease cap from the hub. Remove the cotter pin, nut lock, adjusting nut and flat washer from the spindle.
5. Remove the hub and drum from the wheel spindle.
6. Remove and discard the old grease retainer. Remove the inner bearing cone and roller from the hub.
7. Clean the grease from the inner and outer bearing cups with solvent and inspect the cups for scratches, pits, or wear.
8. If the cups are worn or damaged, remove them with a drift.
9. Thoroughly clean the inner and outer bearing cones and rollers. DO NOT SPIN THE BEARINGS TO DRY THEM. Allow them to air dry.
10. Inspect the cones and rollers for wear and replace as necessary. See the "Bearing Failure Chart" in Chapter 7. The cone and roller assemblies should be replaced as a set. Do not use new bearings or cups with old bearings or cups.
11. Clean the spindle and the inside of the hub with solvent to remove all of the old grease.
12. Cover the spindle with a cloth and clean the dirt from the dust shield. Remove the cloth carefully. Do not get dirt on the spindle.
13. If the inner or outer bearing cups were removed, install the new replacement cups in the hub. Be sure that they are seated squarely and properly.
14. Pack the inside of the hub with

BRAKES 167

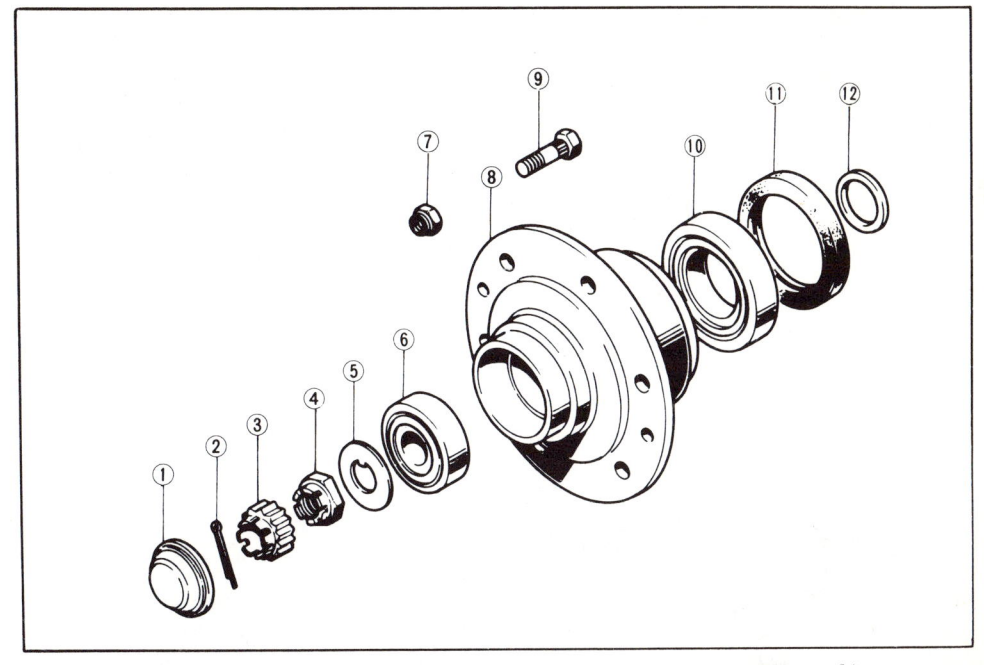

Exploded view of front wheel bearing—B-1600 (© Toyo Kogyo Co., Ltd.)

1. Grease cap
2. Split pin
3. Nut lock
4. Adjusting nut
5. Thrust washer
6. Outer bearing
7. Wheel nut
8. Front wheel hub
9. Hub bolt
10. Inner bearing
11. Grease seal
12. Spacer

wheel bearing grease. Add grease to the hub until grease is flush with the inside diameter of both bearing cups.

NOTE: *It is important that all the old grease is removed because the more popular lithium base grease is not compatible with the sodium base grease which was originally installed.*

15. Pack the bearing cone and roller with wheel bearing grease. Work as much grease as possible between the cone and rollers. Lubricate the outside cone surfaces with grease.
16. Install the inner bearing cone and roller in the inner cup. Apply a light film of grease to the grease seal and install the seal. Be sure that the seal is properly seated.
17. Install the hub and drum on the spindle. Keep the hub centered on the spindle to prevent damaging the grease seal.
18. Install the outer bearing cone and roller and the flat washer on the spindle. Install the adjusting nut.
19. Install the wheel and tire.
20. Adjust the wheel bearings.
21. Install the hub cap.
22. Before driving the truck, pump the brake pedal several times to restore normal brake lining-to-drum clearance and normal brake pedal pressure.

Front Disc Brakes

DISC BRAKE PAD

Removal and Installation

The disc brake pads should be inspected whenever the wheels are removed for any reason. The pad should be replaced when the thickness of the pad and backing plate is 0.315 in. or less.

1. Raise and support the truck.
2. Remove the wheel and tire.
3. Remove the retaining pins and hold-down plates.
4. Remove the caliper and anti-rattle spring and remove the pads.

To install the pads, proceed as follows:

5. Remove the rubber cap from the bleeder screw and connect a hose to the bleeder screw. Submerge the other end of the hose in a suitable container.

BRAKES

Remove the retaining pins (© Toyo Kogyo Co., Ltd.)

Remove the hold-down plates (© Toyo Kogyo Co., Ltd.)

Remove the caliper (© Toyo Kogyo Co., Ltd.)

Remove the brake pads (© Toyo Kogyo Co., Ltd.)

6. Open the bleeder screw.
7. Press the piston back into the caliper using an instrument which will not scratch the piston (piece of wood, etc.).
8. Tighten the bleeder screw and remove the hose.
9. Install the new brake pads and shims in the caliper. Brake pads should be replaced on both wheels at the same time. Do not mix different types of pads.
10. Install the anti-rattle spring.
11. Install the caliper.
12. Install the hold-down plates and retainers.
13. Install the wheel and tire.
14. Lower the truck.

DISC BRAKE CALIPER

Removal and Installation

1. Raise and support the truck.
2. Remove the wheel and tire.
3. Disconnect and plug the brake line.
4. Remove the caliper and the pads from the caliper.
5. If necessary, the caliper bracket can be removed by unbolting the two bolts.
6. Installation is the reverse of removal.

Caliper bracket attaching bolts (arrows) (© Toyo Kogyo Co., Ltd.)

Overhaul

1. Clean the outside of the caliper.
2. Place a piece of hardwood in front of the piston to prevent damaging the piston.
3. The piston can be removed by applying air pressure to the fluid port behind the piston. If the piston is seized, tap lightly around the piston while applying air pressure.

NOTE: *Use caution while applying air pressure. Do not use excessive air*

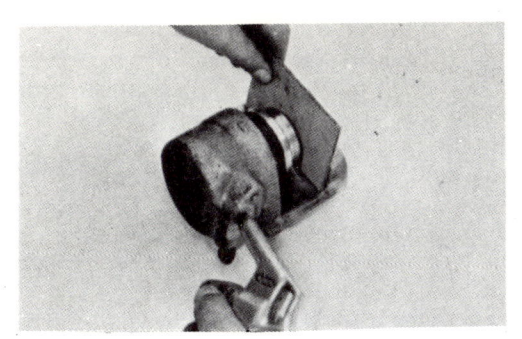

BRAKES 169

Removing the piston from the caliper (© Toyo Kogyo Co., Ltd.)

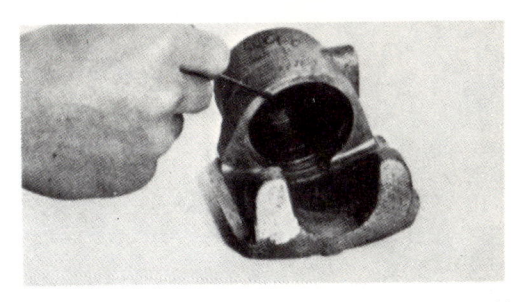

Removing the piston seal (© Toyo Kogyo Co., Ltd.)

pressure as physical harm could result.

4. Remove the dust boot from the piston.

5. Remove the retainer and dust boot from the caliper.
6. Remove the piston seal from the caliper bore.
7. If necessary, remove the bleeder screw.

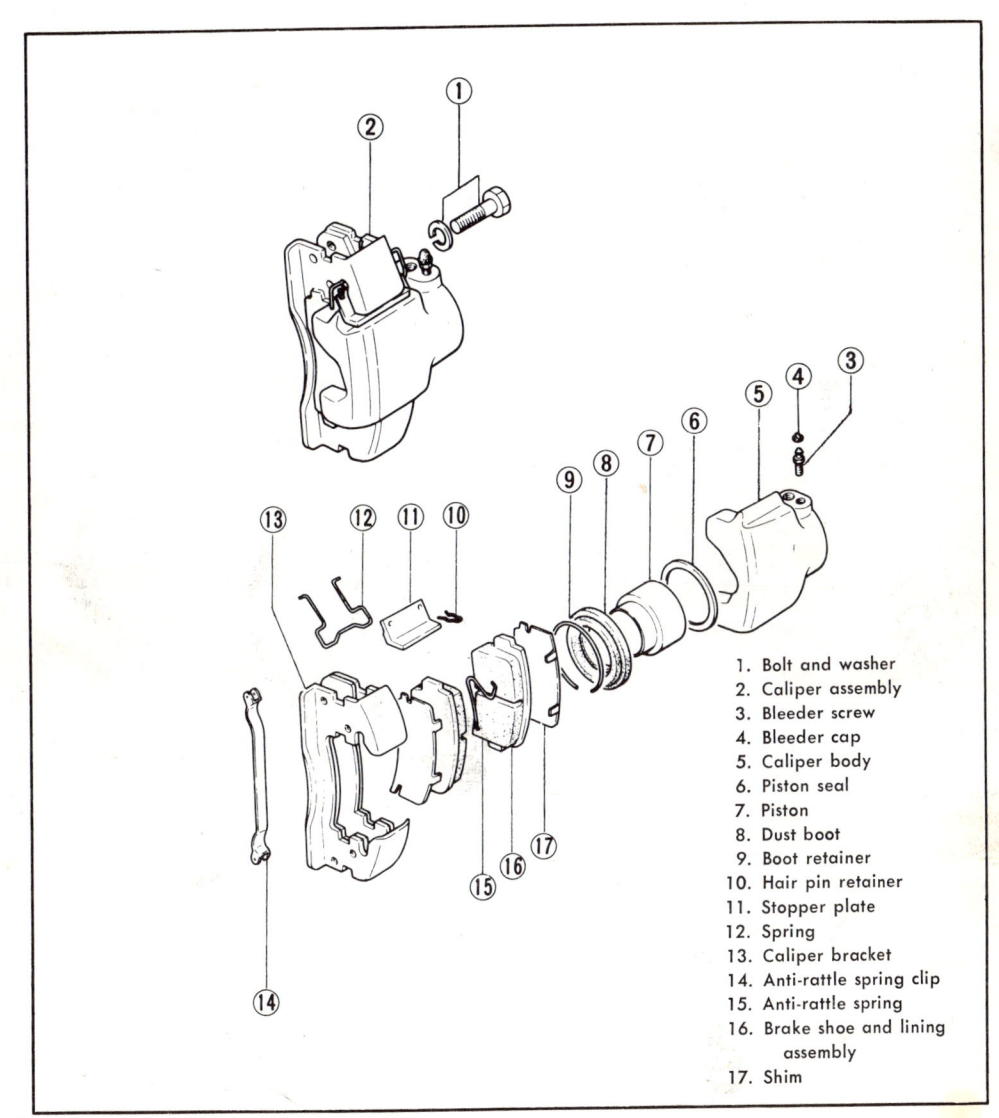

1. Bolt and washer
2. Caliper assembly
3. Bleeder screw
4. Bleeder cap
5. Caliper body
6. Piston seal
7. Piston
8. Dust boot
9. Boot retainer
10. Hair pin retainer
11. Stopper plate
12. Spring
13. Caliper bracket
14. Anti-rattle spring clip
15. Anti-rattle spring
16. Brake shoe and lining assembly
17. Shim

Exploded view of front disc brake assembly (© Toyo Kogyo Co., Ltd.)

BRAKES

8. Clean all the disassembled parts in clean brake fluid and air dry.
9. Inspect the caliper bore for scoring or damage. Minor damage can be corrected by LIGHT polishing with crocus cloth.
10. Discard the old piston seal and dust boot. Use new ones during reassembly.

To assemble the caliper:

11. Lubricate the piston seal with brake fluid and install it in the caliper groove.
12. Be sure that the seal is not twisted.
13. Lubricate the piston and caliper bore with brake fluid and insert the piston.

Installing the retainer (© Toyo Kogyo Co., Ltd.)

Installing the piston (© Toyo Kogyo Co., Ltd.)

14. Install the dust boot and retainer. The flange on the dust boot should fit the caliper groove squarely.
15. If the bleeder screw was removed, install it.

BRAKE DISC

Removal and Installation

1. Raise and support the truck.
2. Remove the wheel and tire.
3. Remove the grease cap.
4. Remove the caliper from the disc. It is not necessary to disconnect the brake line from the caliper. The caliper can be wired from the frame and suspended.
5. Remove the caliper bracket.
6. Remove the grease cap. Remove the cotter pin, nut lock, adjusting nut and flat washer from the spindle.
7. Pull the hub and rotor assembly from the spindle.
8. Remove the outer bearing from the hub.

Remove the outer bearing from the hub (© Toyo Kogyo Co., Ltd.)

9. Clean the spindle and inside of the hub with solvent to remove the old grease.
10. Matchmark the hub and rotor.
11. Remove the bolts attaching the hub to the rotor and remove the rotor from the hub.

To install the rotor:

12. Check the rotor for thickness. If the thickness is less than 0.433 in., it should be replaced with a new rotor.
13. Pack the inside of the hub with lithium grease. Pack the inner rollers and outer rollers with lithium grease, making sure that the spaces between the rollers are filled.
14. Install the inner bearing in the inner bearing cup.
15. Install the spacer and grease seal in the hub.
16. Install the hub on the rotor. Install the attaching bolts and tighten them to 32–41 ft lbs.
17. Install the hub and rotor on the spindle.
18. Install the outer bearing, flat washer, and adjusting nut.
19. Adjust the wheel bearings.

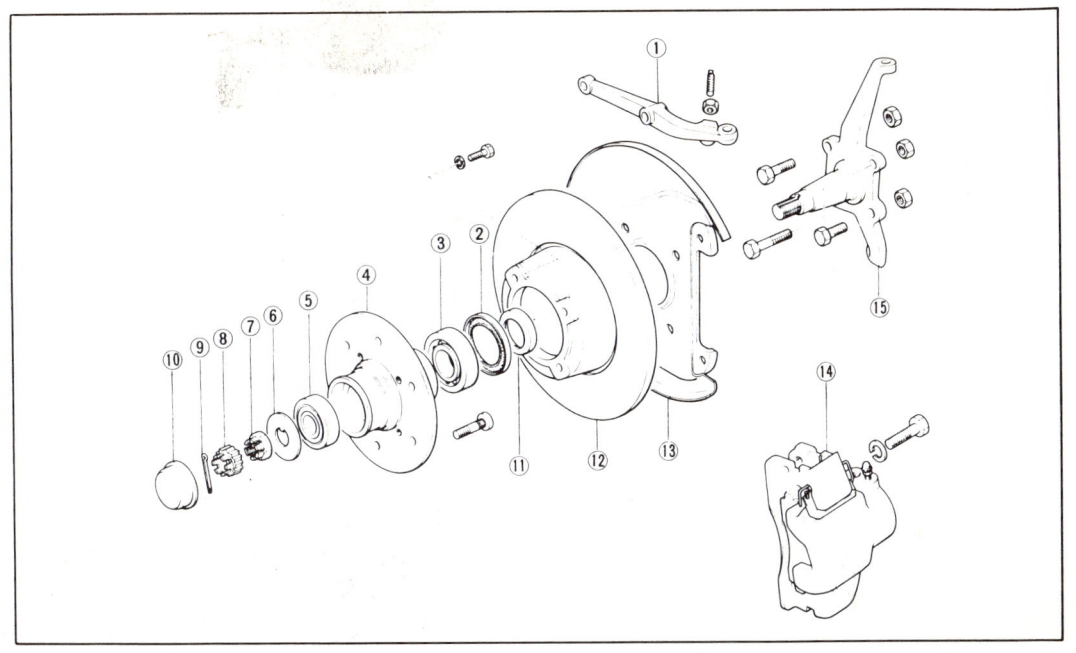

Exploded view of front disc brake caliper, rotor, and bearings (© Toyo Kogyo Co., Ltd.)

1. Knuckle
2. Grease seal
3. Inner bearing
4. Hub
5. Outer bearing
6. Washer
7. Adjusting nut
8. Nut lock
9. Cotter pin
10. Grease cap
11. Spacer
12. Rotor
13. Caliper mounting adaptor
14. Caliper assembly
15. Steering knuckle

20. Install the nut lock and a new cotter pin. Pack the grease cap with lithium grease and install the grease cap.
21. Install the caliper.
22. Install the wheel and tire.
23. Lower the truck.
24. Pump the brake pedal several times to restore normal pad-to-disc clearance and normal pedal travel.

FRONT WHEEL BEARINGS

Adjustment

The front wheel bearings should be adjusted if the wheel is loose on the spindle or if the wheel does not rotate freely.

1. Raise and support the truck.
2. Remove the wheel and tire.
3. Remove the grease cap.
4. Remove the cotter pin and nut lock. Discard the cotter pin.
5. Loosen the adjusting nut three turns.
6. Rock the hub and rotor assembly to push the brake pads away from the rotor.
7. Rotate the hub and rotor and tighten the adjusting nut to seat the bearings. This occurs when the hub begins to bind.
8. Back the adjusting nut off $1/6$ turn. Install the nut lock and a new cotter pin. The bearing preload should be 3.5–7.0 in. lbs when checked with a spring scale.
9. Check the wheel rotation. If the wheel rotates properly (with no play or binding) install the grease cap.
10. Install the wheel and tire.
11. Lower the truck.
12. Pump the brake pedal several times to restore normal pad-to-disc clearance and to restore normal pedal height.

Rear Drum Brakes

BRAKE DRUMS

Inspection

Inspect the rear brake drums in the same manner as the front brake drums. See "Front Brake Drum Inspection."

Removal and Installation

Rear brake drum removal is identical to front brake drum removal. See the

BRAKES

procedures under "Front Brake Drum Removal." Be sure that the parking brake is fully released.

REAR BRAKE SHOES

Inspection

Inspect the rear brake shoes in the same manner as for the front brake shoes. See the procedures under "Front Brake Shoe Inspection."

Removal and Installation

1. Raise and support the truck. Release the parking brake.
2. Remove the wheel.
3. Remove the brake drum.
4. Remove the shoe retracting springs.
5. Remove the shoe retaining spring guide pins and retaining spring by holding the guide pin to the backing plate, and compressing and turning the retaining spring 90°. A tool to do this easily is available inexpensively at most auto supply stores.
6. Remove the parking brake link.
7. Disconnect the parking brake cable from the parking brake lever.

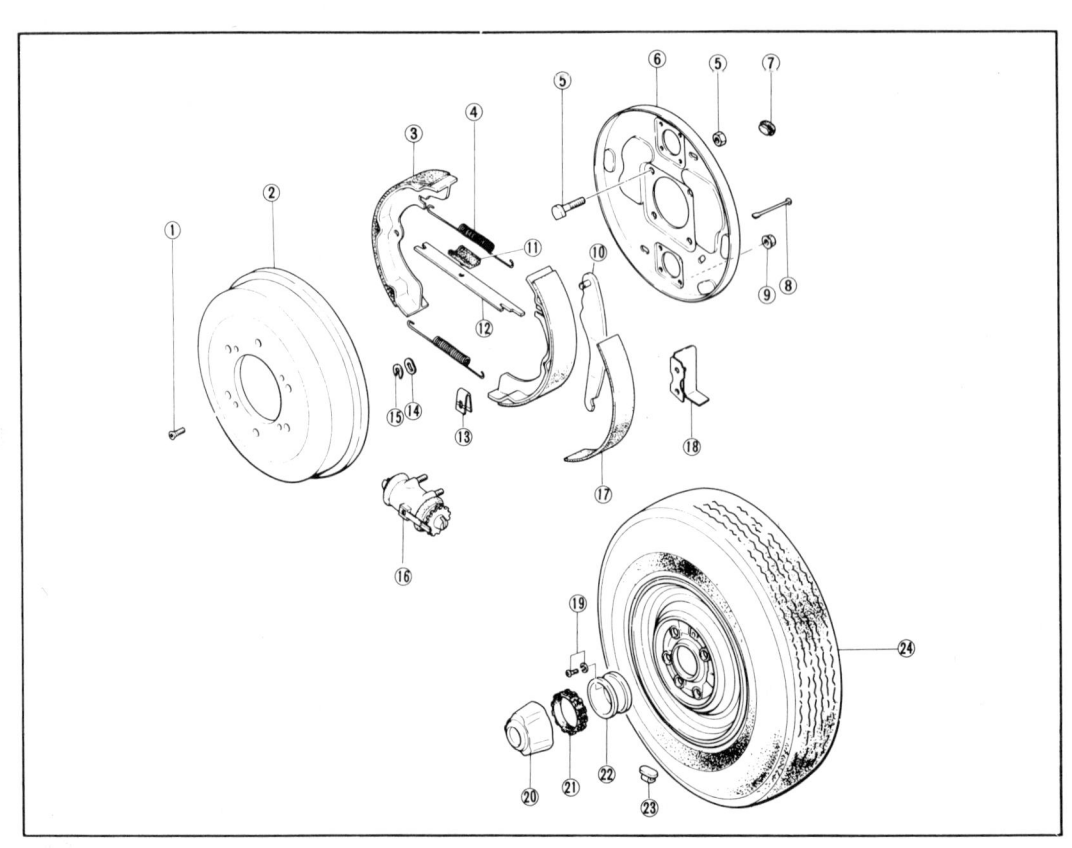

Remove the hold-down clips arrows from the brake shoes (© Toyo Kogyo Co., Ltd.)

Exploded view of rear brakes (© Toyo Kogyo Co., Ltd.)

1. Drum attaching bolt
2. Drum
3. Brake shoe
4. Shoe return spring
5. Bolt and nut
6. Backing plate
7. Plug
8. Shoe hold-down spring pin
9. Wheel cylinder nut
10. Parking brake opening lever
11. Operating strut
12. Pushrod
13. Clip spring
14. Wave washer
15. Brake shoe retaining clip
16. Wheel cylinder
17. Brake lining
18. Brake pipe guard
19. Screw and washer
20. Wheel center cap
21. Set rubber
22. Wheel center cap adaptor
23. Balance weight
24. Rear wheel

BRAKES

To install the brake shoes:

8. Lubricate the threads of the adjusting screws, mating surfaces of the shoe webs and brake backing plate with a small amount of brake paste or Lubriplate®.

9. Install the parking brake lever on the rear shoe and install the retaining clip. Hold the rear brake shoe near the brake backing plate and connect the eye of the parking brake cable to the parking brake operating lever.

Connect the parking brake lever to the rear shoe (© Toyo Kogyo Co., Ltd.)

10. Position both brake shoes on the backing plate and connect the parking brake link between both shoes. Engage the brake shoes with the slots in the wheel cylinder pistons and adjusting screws.

11. Install the shoe retaining guide pins. Depress the retaining springs and turn them 90° to lock them in place.

12. Install the brake shoe retracting springs. Be careful not to bend the hooks or stretch the springs too far.

13. Install the brake drum.

14. Install the wheel.

15. Adjust the brakes.

16. Lower the truck and check the operation of the brakes.

WHEEL CYLINDER

Removal and Installation

1. Raise and support the truck.
2. Remove the wheel, brake drum, and brake shoes.
3. Disconnect the brake line at the wheel cylinder and plug the line.
4. Remove the four nuts attaching the wheel cylinder to the backing plate and remove the wheel cylinder.

To install the wheel cylinder:

5. Wipe the end of the hydraulic line to clean it of any foreign material.

6. Install the wheel cylinder on the backing plate.

7. Connect the brake line to the wheel cylinder and tighten the tube fitting.

8. Install the links in the end of the wheel cylinder. Install the brake shoes and adjusters.

9. Install the brake drum and wheel.

10. Adjust the brakes.

11. Bleed the brakes.

12. Centralize the pressure differential valve.

13. Lower the truck and test the operation of the brakes.

Overhaul

1. Perform Steps 1, 2, and 3 of the "Wheel Cylinder Removal" procedure.

2. Remove the piston and adjusting screw with the boot attached to the adjuster.

3. Separate the adjuster screw and boot from the adjuster.

4. Remove the other piston and boot and separate the boot from the piston.

5. Press in on either piston cup and force the piston cups, cup expanders, and return spring from the cylinder.

6. Wash all parts (except the boots) in clean isopropyl alcohol. Examine the cylinder bore for roughness or scoring.

7. Check the piston-to-cylinder bore clearance. If it exceeds 0.006 in., replace with new parts.

To assemble the wheel cylinder:

8. Lubricate the cylinder bore, adjuster and new piston cups with clean brake fluid, before assembly. Always use new piston cups.

9. Install the piston return spring in a piston cup expander. Place the other piston cup expander and new piston cup on the return spring. Install the return spring, piston cup expanders and piston cups into the cylinder.

10. Install the piston boot to the piston adjuster with the smaller lip of the boot on the groove of the piston adjuster.

11. Insert the piston adjuster into the cylinder assembly and install the larger

BRAKES

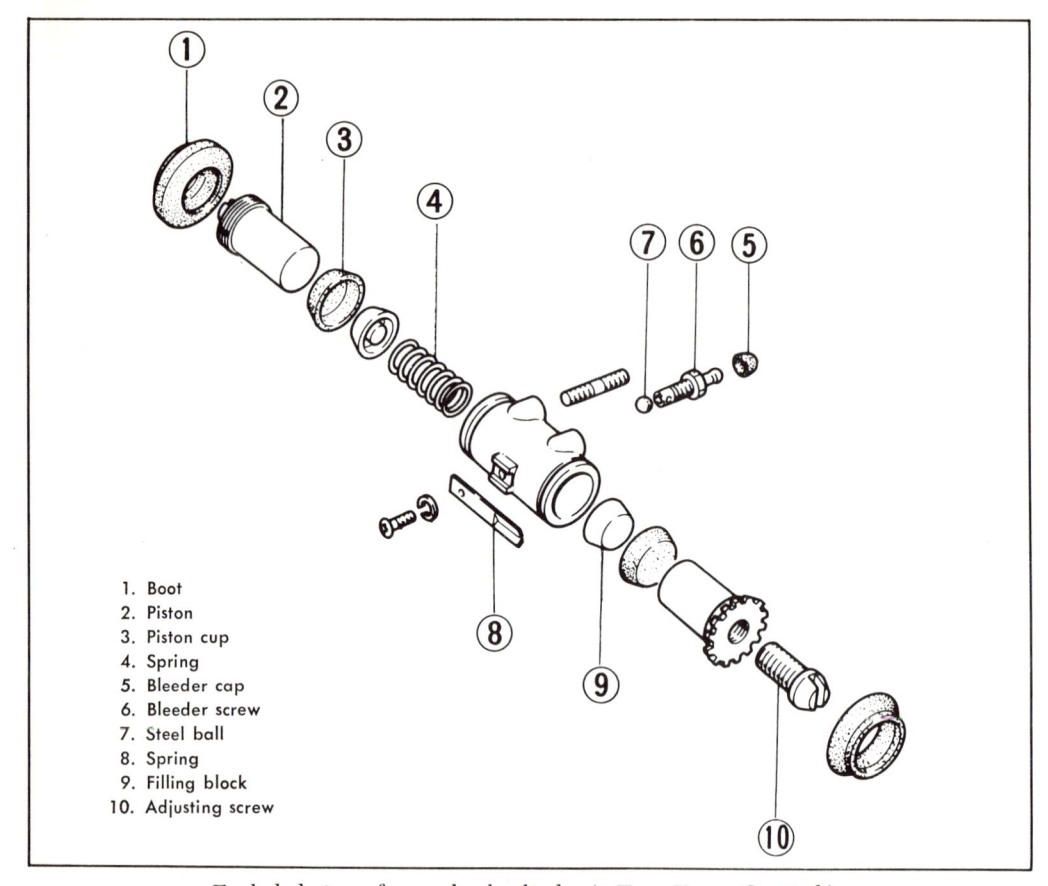

1. Boot
2. Piston
3. Piston cup
4. Spring
5. Bleeder cap
6. Bleeder screw
7. Steel ball
8. Spring
9. Filling block
10. Adjusting screw

Exploded view of rear wheel cylinder (© Toyo Kogyo Co., Ltd.)

lip of the boot in the groove of the cylinder.

12. Install the adjusting screw in the piston adjuster.

13. Perform Steps 5 and 6–13 of the "Wheel Cylinder Removal and Installation" procedure.

Parking Brake

ADJUSTMENT

1. Adjust the service brakes before attempting to adjust the parking brake.

2. Use the adjusting nut to adjust the length of the front cable so that the rear brakes are locked when the parking brake lever is pulled out 5–10 notches.

3. After adjustment, apply the parking brake several times. Release the parking brake and make sure that the rear wheels rotate without dragging. If they drag, repeat the adjustment.

FRONT PARKING BRAKE CABLE

Removal and Installation

1. Raise and support the truck.

2. Remove the serrated adjusting nut.

3. Separate the front brake cable from the equalizer and remove the jam nut.

4. Remove the cable return spring and pull the protective boot from the lower end of the front cable housing.

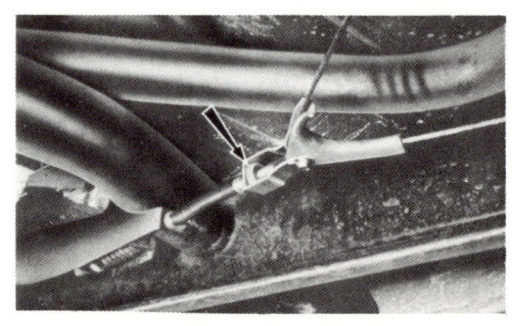

Parking brake adjustment at the adjusting nut (arrow) (© Toyo Kogyo Co., Ltd.)

5. Pull the lower cable housing forward out of the slotted frame bracket and slip the cable shaft sideways through the slot until the cable and housing is free of the bracket.

6. Disengage the upper cable connector from the brake lever by removing the clevis pin and retainer.

7. Remove the upper cable housing retaining clip and pull the upper cable and housing from out of the slotted bracket on the firewall.

8. Push the upper cable, cable housing, and dust shield grommet through the firewall opening and into the engine compartment.

9. Remove the cable and housing.

To install the front cable:

10. From the engine compartment, route the upper cable, dust shield and grommet through the opening in the firewall.

11. Connect the cable to the parking brake lever shaft with the clevis pin and retainer.

12. Install the upper cable retaining clip.

13. Route the cable and housing rearward through the slotted frame bracket.

14. Install the cable boot on the lower end of the cable housing.

15. Install the cable return spring.

16. Thread the jam nut onto the lower cable shaft and insert the shaft into the equalizer connector.

17. Install the serrated cable adjusting nut and adjust the parking brake.

18. Lower the truck.

REAR PARKING BRAKE CABLE

Removal and Installation

1. Raise and support the truck.
2. Remove the equalizer clevis pin and disconnect the equalizer from the front brake clevis.

3. Disconnect the right-hand cable from the left-hand cable at the cable connector.

4. Remove the rear brake shoes.

5. Disengage the parking brake levers from the cable connectors by rotating the hooked ends of the levers out of the cable connector.

6. Remove the cable housing retainer from the brake backing plate.

7. Pull the return spring to release the retainer plate from the end of the cable housing.

8. Pull the boot from the forward end of the housing.

9. Loosen the cable housing-to-frame bracket locknut and remove the forward end of the cable housing from the frame bracket.

10. Remove the cable housing retaining clip bolts.

11. Disengage the cable housing-to-frame tension springs and pull the cable housing and cable out of the brake backing plate.

To install the rear cable:

12. Insert the cable through the brake backing plate and install the cable housing retainer plate.

13. Assemble the rear brakes.

14. Install the forward end of the cable into the cable housing-to-frame bracket and tighten the cable housing locknut.

15. Install the cable boots.

16. Install the rear cable housing retaining clips.

17. Install the rear cable boots.

18. Route the left-hand cable through the equalizer and connect the left and right-hand cable connector.

19. Install the equalizer on the front cable clevis and install the clevis pin and retainer.

20. Adjust the rear wheel brakes.

21. Adjust the parking brake.

22. Lower the truck.

Chapter Ten
Body

Doors

REMOVAL AND INSTALLATION

If the door being removed is to be reinstalled, matchmark the position of the hinges.

1. Remove the trim panel, the weathersheets and all usable moldings (if the door is to be replaced with a new one).
2. If the door is to be replaced, remove all usable window and door latch components.
3. Support the door.
4. Remove the hinge-to-body attaching bolts and remove the door.
5. If the door is to be replaced, and the hinges are in good shape, transfer these to a new door.

To install the door:

6. Position the door and hinges on the body and tighten the attaching bolts.
7. Align the door and tighten the attaching bolts securely.
8. Install the latch mechanism, window mechanism, glass and frame components.
9. Install the weathersheets and trim panel.
10. Adjust the striker on the door.

ALIGNMENT

The holes of the hinge and/or the hinge attaching points are enlarged or elongated to provide for hinge and door alignment; but, as a matter of good workmanship, don't try to cover up poor door alignment with a latch adjustment.

Door Hinges

1. Determine which hinge bolts must be loosened to move the door in the desired direction.
2. Loosen the hinge bolt(s) just enough to allow the door to be moved with a padded pry bar.
3. Move the door a small amount and check the fit, after tightening the bolts.

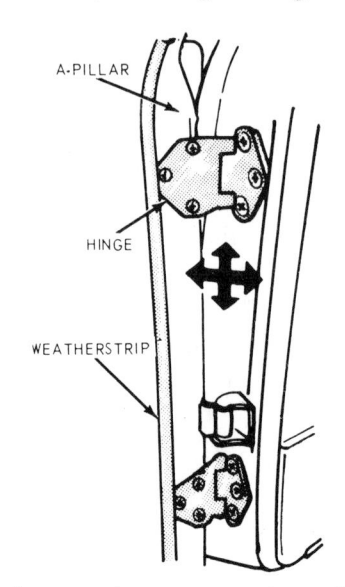

Door adjustment (© Toyo Kogyo Co., Ltd.)

176

BODY

Be sure that there is no bind or interference with adjacent panels.

4. Repeat this until the door is properly positioned, and tighten all the bolts securely.

Striker Plate

The striker plate assembly is attached to the pillar post through oversized holes, permitting movement of the striker up-and-down, as well as in-and-out.

Fore-and-aft adjustment is made by adding or subtracting shims behind the striker and B pillar post. The striker should be adjusted so that the door lock enters freely and the door closes solidly and remains closed.

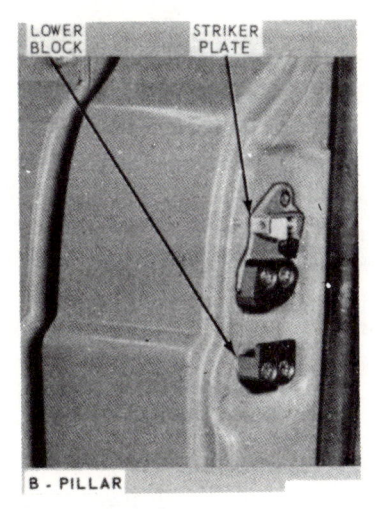

Door striker plate (© Toyo Kogyo Co., Ltd.)

DOOR PANELS

Removal and Installation

1. Invert the door and window regulator handles for easy access to the retaining pins.
2. Drive the tapered pin out of the window regulator handle and remove the handle crown washer and trim plate. Drive the tapered pin out from the bottom side.
3. Remove the tapered pin from the door handle in the same manner.
4. Remove the plastic molding from the arm rest.
5. Remove the arm rest. The screws are accessible after removing the plastic molding.
6. Carefully pry the door panel and clips (eight of them) away from the door and remove the panel from the bottom channel.

To install the panel:

7. Position the trim panel on the door, in the bottom channel.
8. Push the trim panel and retaining clips into the inner door panel holes (eight of them).
9. Install the arm rest and the plastic molding on the armrest.
10. Install the trim plates, crown washers and the window and door han-

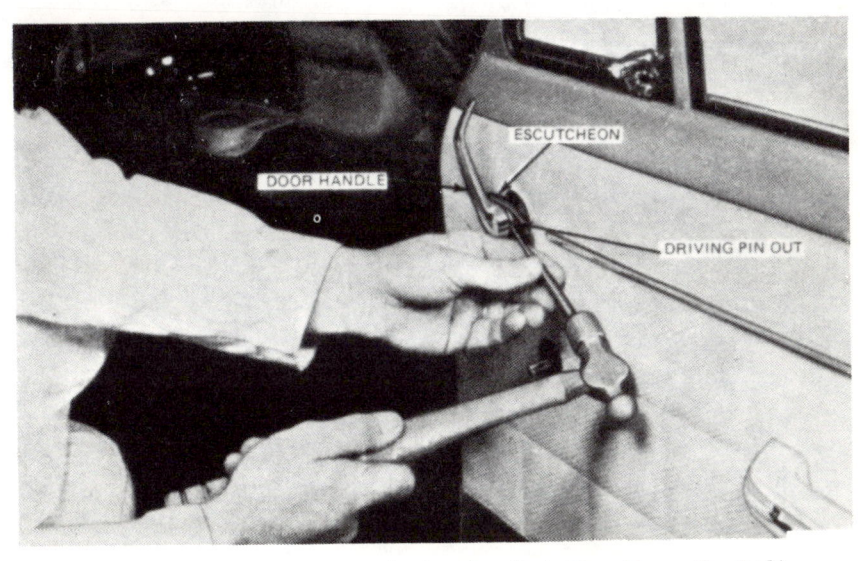

Driving out the pin to remove the door handle (© Toyo Kogyo Co., Ltd.)

178 BODY

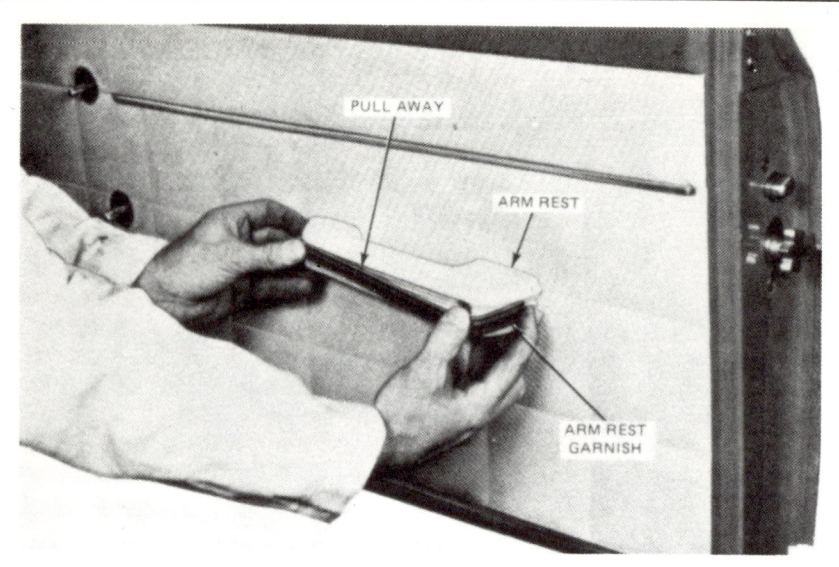

Removing the arm rest (© Toyo Kogyo Co., Ltd.)

dles. Insert the tapered retaining pins from the top and drive them into place.

DOOR GLASS

Removal and Installation

1. Remove the trim panel from the door.
2. Remove the window frame assembly from the door by removing seven screws.
3. Lower the door glass.
4. Disengage the regulator roller and arm from the door glass channel.
5. Tilt the glass and slide the glass up and out of the door.
6. Remove the tape from the door glass channel and discard the tape.

To install the door glass:

7. Install sealing tape on the door glass and install the glass and tape in the channel.
8. Position the door glass in the door and connect the regulator roller to the door glass channel.
9. Install the window frame assembly. Apply sealer to the screws and install the screws.
10. Install the weathersheets.
11. Install the door trim panel.

DOOR LOCKS

A key code is stamped on the lock cylinder to aid in replacing lost keys.

Whenever a lock cylinder is replaced, both door lock cylinders and the ignition switch lock cylinder should be replaced as a set. This will avoid carrying an extra key to fit only one lock.

Removal and Installation

1. Remove the trim panel from the door.
2. Position the weathersheet away from the access holes.
3. Using a screwdriver, push the lock cylinder retaining clip upward. Note the position of the lock cylinder before removing it.

Removing the door glass (© Toyo Kogyo Co., Ltd.)

BODY 179

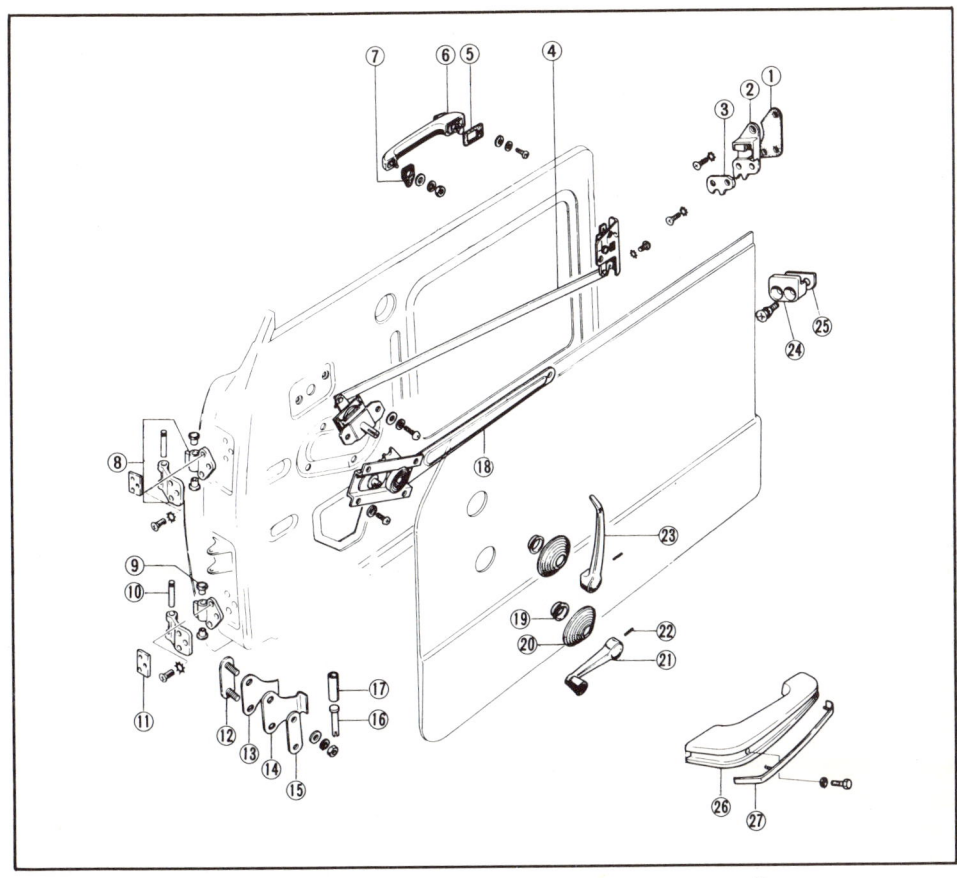

Exploded view of the front door (© Toyo Kogyo Co., Ltd.)

1. Striker seat
2. Door lock striker
3. Door lock rack
4. Door lock
5. Seat No. 1
6. Outer handle
7. Seat No. 2
8. Door hinge
9. Bush
10. Hinge pin
11. Spacer
12. Door checker set plate
13. Check sub spring
14. Check spring
15. Checker washer
16. Checker pin
17. Checker roller
18. Window regulator
19. Escutcheon crown
20. Handle escutcheon
21. Regulator handle
22. Tapered pin
23. Inner handle
24. Anti-burst block
25. Anti-burst block shim
26. Arm rest
27. Garnish

Remove the clip (arrow) to remove the lock (© Toyo Kogyo Co., Ltd.)

4. Remove the lock cylinder from the door.

5. Position the lock cylinder in the door and install the retaining clip. It should be positioned as the old one was.

6. Check the operation of the lock cylinder. It is a good idea to roll the window down in case it doesn't work.

7. Install the weathersheet and the door trim panel.

8. Lubricate the new lock with door lock lubricant or graphite.

Engine Hood

Removal and Installation

1. Open the hood and scribe marks around the locations of the hinges, where they attach to the body.

BODY

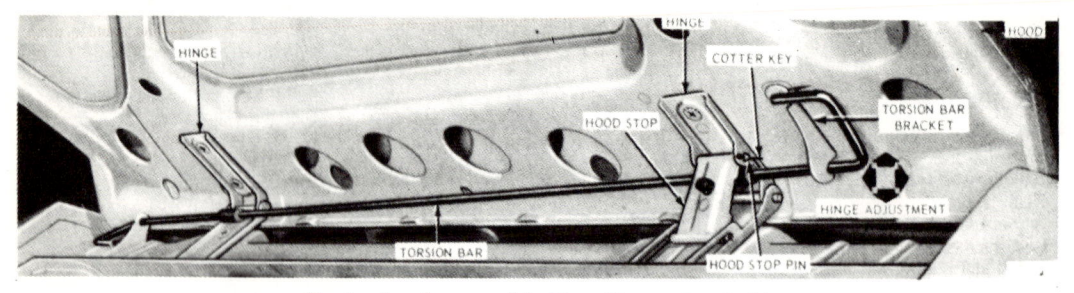

Engine hood removal (© Toyo Kogyo Co., Ltd.)

2. While an assistant holds the hood, remove the cotter pin from the right-hand hood stop retaining pin.
3. Remove the pin and hood stop from the hinge.
4. Tilt the hood forward and position the torsion bar to one side.
5. Remove the four hood hinge-to-body retaining screws and remove the hood and hinges.

To install the hood:

6. Position the hood hinges, aligning the marks made previously and install the attaching screws.
7. Insert the torsion bar into the bracket.
8. Install the hood stop, retaining pin and cotter pin into the right-hand hood hinge.
9. Close the hood and adjust if necessary.

Adjustment

The hood can be adjusted front-to-rear and side-to-side by loosening the hood-to-hinge and/or the hinge-to-body attaching screws. The front edge of the hood can also be raised by adding shims to the body under the hinges. The rear edge of the hood can be adjusted by raising or lowering the rear hood bumpers.

Tailgate

Removal and Installation

1. Open and support the tailgate.
2. Remove the hinge pins by removing the cotter pins and washers and driving the hinge pins out.
3. Installation is the reverse of removal.

Fuel Tank

Removal and Installation

1. Raise and support the rear of the truck.
2. Remove the fuel tank drain plug and drain the fuel.
3. Reinstall the drain plug.
4. Disconnect and plug the fuel pump line at the tank.
5. Disconnect the line from the condenser tank at the fuel tank.
6. If so equipped, disconnect the fuel return line.
7. Disconnect the fuel sending unit lead at the quick disconnect.
8. Remove the fuel tank attaching bolts at the mounting bracket and lower the fuel tank.

To install the fuel tank:

9. Raise the fuel tank into position and install the attaching bolts securely.
10. Connect the fuel sending unit lead.
11. Connect the fuel return line if equipped.
12. Connect the condenser tank fuel line.
13. Connect the fuel pump line.
14. Lower the truck and fill the tank.

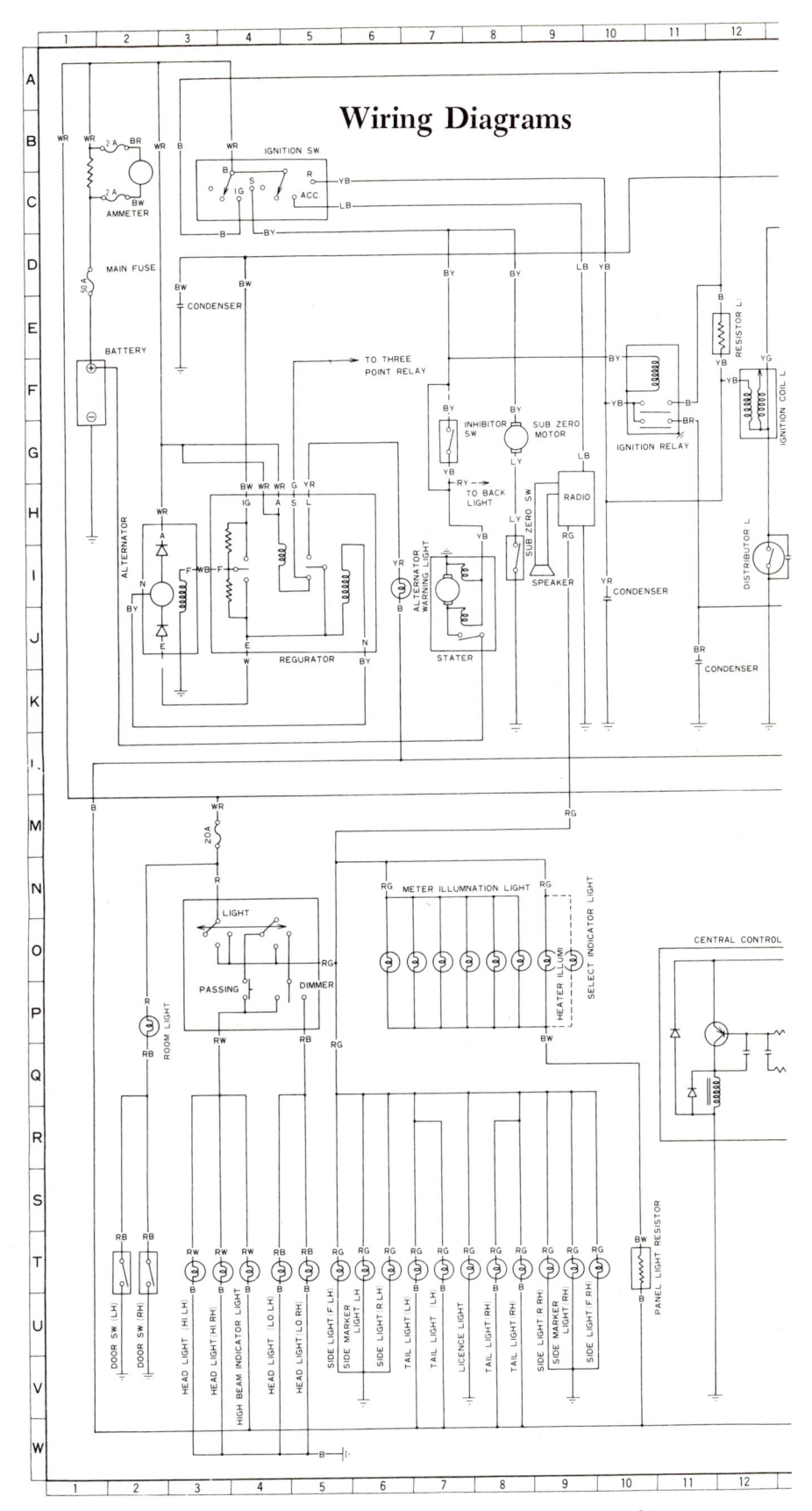

Rotary Pick-Up wiring diagram (© Toyo Kogyo Co., Ltd.)

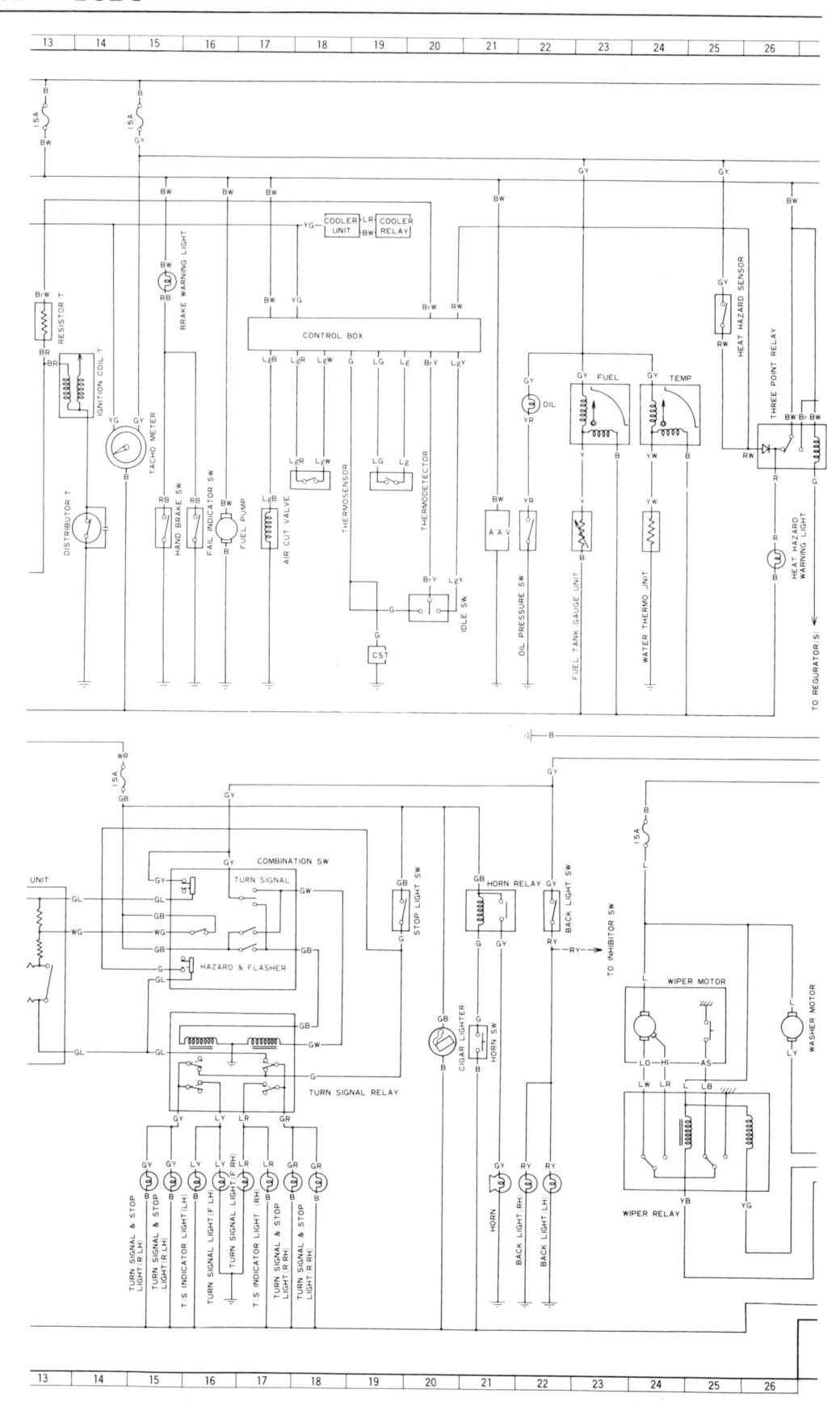

BODY

Rotary Pick-Up wiring diagram (© Toyo Kogyo Co., Ltd.)

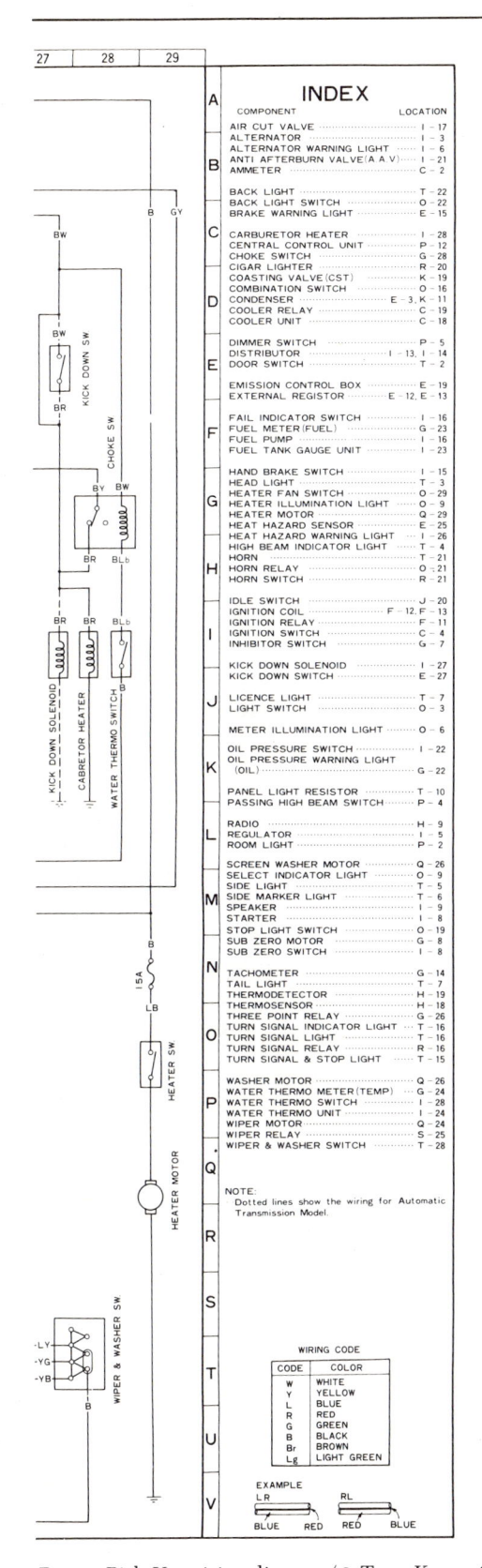

BODY 183

INDEX

COMPONENT	LOCATION
AIR CUT VALVE	I – 17
ALTERNATOR	I – 3
ALTERNATOR WARNING LIGHT	I – 6
ANTI AFTERBURN VALVE (A A V)	I – 21
AMMETER	C – 2
BACK LIGHT	T – 22
BACK LIGHT SWITCH	O – 22
BRAKE WARNING LIGHT	E – 15
CARBURETOR HEATER	I – 28
CENTRAL CONTROL UNIT	P – 12
CHOKE SWITCH	G – 28
CIGAR LIGHTER	R – 20
COASTING VALVE (CST)	K – 19
COMBINATION SWITCH	O – 16
CONDENSER	E – 3, K – 11
COOLER RELAY	C – 19
COOLER UNIT	C – 18
DIMMER SWITCH	P – 5
DISTRIBUTOR	I – 13, I – 14
DOOR SWITCH	T – 2
EMISSION CONTROL BOX	E – 19
EXTERNAL REGISTER	E – 12, E – 13
FAIL INDICATOR SWITCH	I – 16
FUEL METER (FUEL)	G – 23
FUEL PUMP	I – 16
FUEL TANK GAUGE UNIT	I – 23
HAND BRAKE SWITCH	I – 15
HEAD LIGHT	T – 3
HEATER FAN SWITCH	O – 29
HEATER ILLUMINATION LIGHT	O – 9
HEATER MOTOR	Q – 29
HEAT HAZARD SENSOR	E – 25
HEAT HAZARD WARNING LIGHT	I – 26
HIGH BEAM INDICATOR LIGHT	T – 4
HORN	T – 21
HORN RELAY	O – 21
HORN SWITCH	R – 21
IDLE SWITCH	J – 20
IGNITION COIL	F – 12, F – 13
IGNITION RELAY	F – 11
IGNITION SWITCH	C – 4
INHIBITOR SWITCH	G – 7
KICK DOWN SOLENOID	I – 27
KICK DOWN SWITCH	E – 27
LICENCE LIGHT	T – 7
LIGHT SWITCH	O – 3
METER ILLUMINATION LIGHT	O – 6
OIL PRESSURE SWITCH	I – 22
OIL PRESSURE WARNING LIGHT (OIL)	G – 22
PANEL LIGHT RESISTOR	T – 10
PASSING HIGH BEAM SWITCH	P – 4
RADIO	H – 9
REGULATOR	I – 5
ROOM LIGHT	P – 2
SCREEN WASHER MOTOR	Q – 26
SELECT INDICATOR LIGHT	O – 9
SIDE LIGHT	T – 5
SIDE MARKER LIGHT	T – 6
SPEAKER	I – 9
STARTER	I – 8
STOP LIGHT SWITCH	O – 19
SUB ZERO MOTOR	G – 8
SUB ZERO SWITCH	I – 8
TACHOMETER	G – 14
TAIL LIGHT	T – 7
THERMODETECTOR	H – 19
THERMOSENSOR	H – 18
THREE POINT RELAY	G – 26
TURN SIGNAL INDICATOR LIGHT	T – 16
TURN SIGNAL LIGHT	T – 16
TURN SIGNAL RELAY	R – 16
TURN SIGNAL & STOP LIGHT	T – 15
WASHER MOTOR	Q – 26
WATER THERMO METER (TEMP)	G – 24
WATER THERMO SWITCH	I – 28
WATER THERMO UNIT	I – 24
WIPER MOTOR	Q – 24
WIPER RELAY	S – 25
WIPER & WASHER SWITCH	T – 28

NOTE:
Dotted lines show the wiring for Automatic Transmission Model.

WIRING CODE

CODE	COLOR
W	WHITE
Y	YELLOW
L	BLUE
R	RED
G	GREEN
B	BLACK
Br	BROWN
Lg	LIGHT GREEN

EXAMPLE
LR — BLUE RED
RL — RED BLUE

Rotary Pick-Up wiring diagram (© Toyo Kogyo Co., Ltd.)

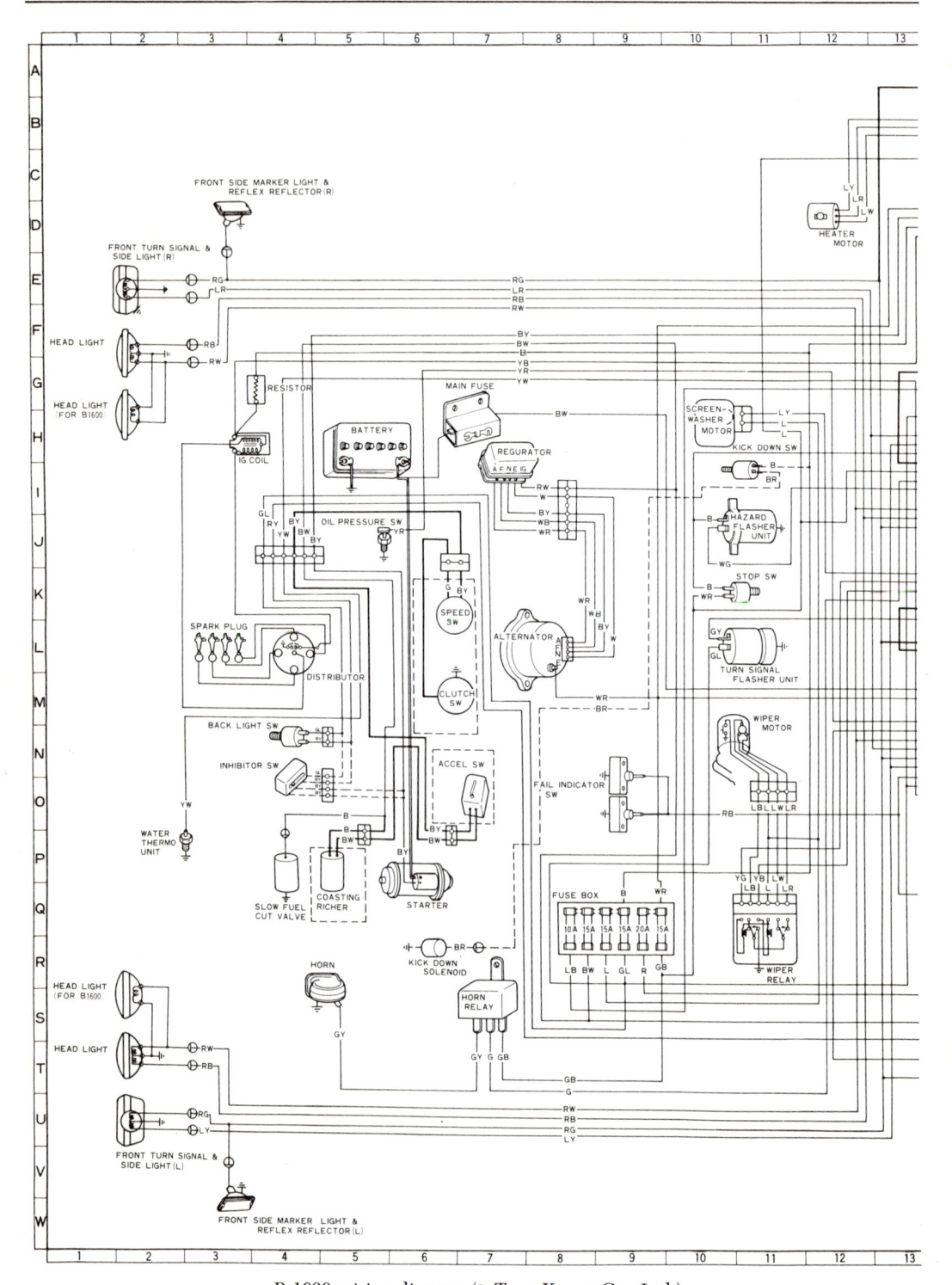

184 BODY

B-1600 wiring diagram (© Toyo Kogyo Co., Ltd.)

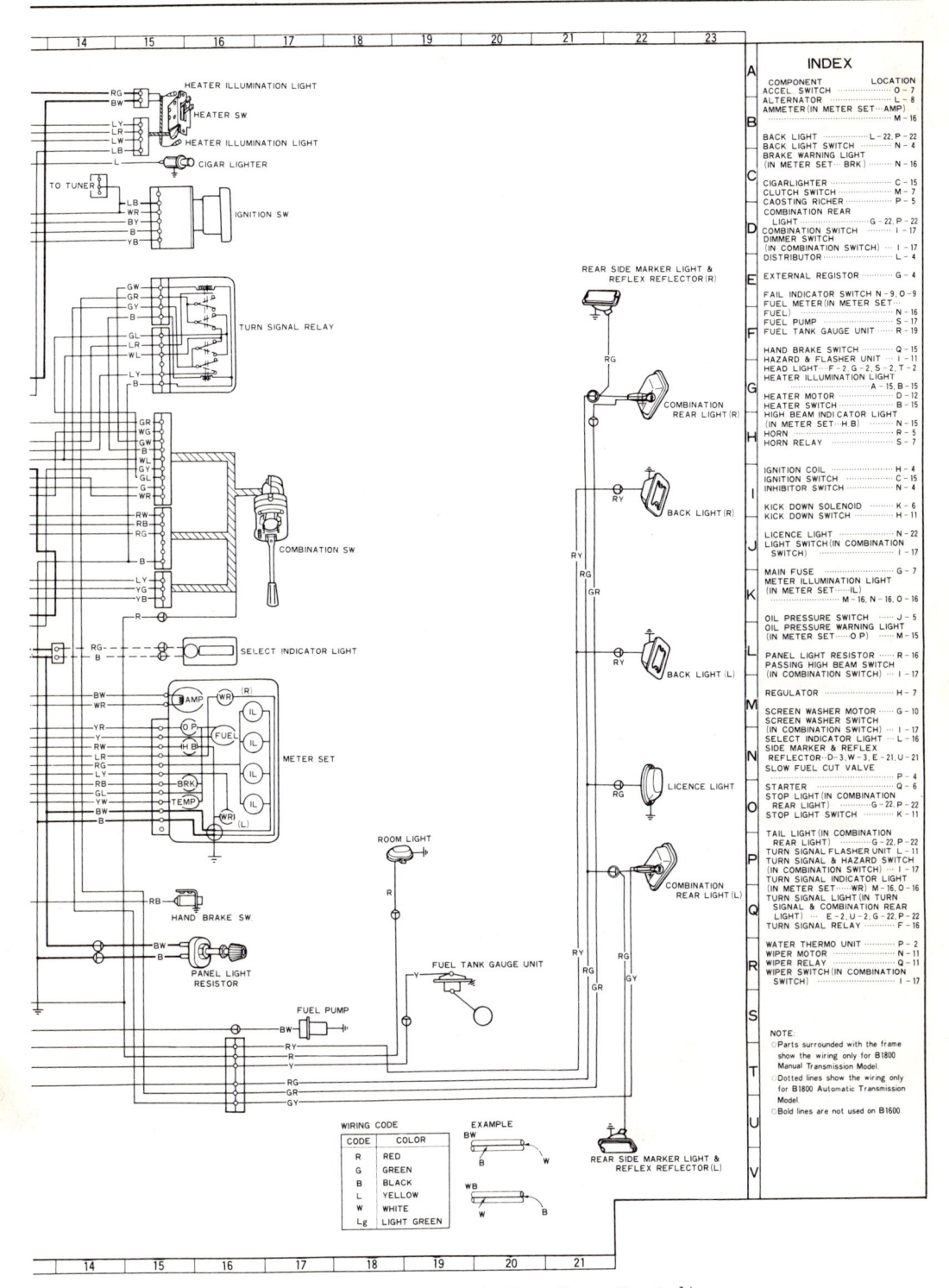

Body 185

INDEX

COMPONENT	LOCATION
ACCEL SWITCH	O - 7
ALTERNATOR	L - 8
AMMETER (IN METER SET - AMP)	M - 16
BACK LIGHT	L - 22, P - 22
BACK LIGHT SWITCH	N - 4
BRAKE WARNING LIGHT (IN METER SET - BRK)	N - 16
CIGARLIGHTER	C - 15
CLUTCH SWITCH	M - 7
CAOSTING RICHER	P - 5
COMBINATION REAR LIGHT	G - 22, P - 22
COMBINATION SWITCH	I - 17
DIMMER SWITCH (IN COMBINATION SWITCH)	I - 17
DISTRIBUTOR	L - 4
EXTERNAL REGISTER	G - 4
FAIL INDICATOR SWITCH	N - 9, O - 9
FUEL METER (IN METER SET - FUEL)	N - 16
FUEL PUMP	S - 17
FUEL TANK GAUGE UNIT	R - 19
HAND BRAKE SWITCH	Q - 15
HAZARD & FLASHER UNIT	I - 11
HEAD LIGHT	F - 2, S - 2, T - 2
HEATER ILLUMINATION LIGHT	A - 15, B - 15
HEATER MOTOR	D - 12
HEATER SWITCH	B - 15
HIGH BEAM INDICATOR LIGHT (IN METER SET - H B)	N - 15
HORN	R - 5
HORN RELAY	S - 7
IGNITION COIL	H - 4
IGNITION SWITCH	C - 15
INHIBITOR SWITCH	P - 11
KICK DOWN SOLENOID	K - 6
KICK DOWN SWITCH	H - 11
LICENCE LIGHT	N - 22
LIGHT SWITCH (IN COMBINATION SWITCH)	I - 17
MAIN FUSE	G - 7
METER ILLUMINATION LIGHT (IN METER SET - IL)	M - 16, N - 16, O - 16
OIL PRESSURE SWITCH	J - 5
OIL PRESSURE WARNING LIGHT (IN METER SET - O.P)	M - 15
PANEL LIGHT RESISTOR	R - 16
PASSING HIGH BEAM SWITCH (IN COMBINATION SWITCH)	I - 17
REGULATOR	H - 7
SCREEN WASHER MOTOR	Q - 10
SCREEN WASHER SWITCH (IN COMBINATION SWITCH)	I - 17
SELECT INDICATOR LIGHT	L - 16
SIDE MARKER & REFLEX REFLECTOR	D - 3, W - 3, E - 21, U - 21
SLOW FUEL CUT VALVE	P - 4
STARTER	Q - 6
STOP LIGHT (IN COMBINATION REAR LIGHT)	G - 22, P - 22
STOP LIGHT SWITCH	K - 11
TAIL LIGHT (IN COMBINATION REAR LIGHT)	G - 22, P - 22
TURN SIGNAL FLASHER UNIT	L - 11
TURN SIGNAL & HAZARD SWITCH (IN COMBINATION SWITCH)	I - 17
TURN SIGNAL INDICATOR LIGHT (IN METER SET - WR)	M - 16, O - 16
TURN SIGNAL LIGHT (IN TURN SIGNAL & COMBINATION REAR LIGHT)	E - 2, U - 2, G - 22, P - 22
TURN SIGNAL RELAY	F - 16
WATER THERMO UNIT	P - 2
WIPER MOTOR	N - 11
WIPER RELAY	Q - 11
WIPER SWITCH (IN COMBINATION SWITCH)	I - 17

NOTE:
○ Parts surrounded with the frame show the wiring only for B1800 Manual Transmission Model.
○ Dotted lines show the wiring only for B1800 Automatic Transmission Model.
○ Bold lines are not used on B1600

WIRING CODE

CODE	COLOR
R	RED
G	GREEN
B	BLACK
L	YELLOW
W	WHITE
Lg	LIGHT GREEN

B-1600 wiring diagram (© Toyo Kogyo Co., Ltd.)

Appendix

General Conversion Table

Multiply by	To convert	To	
2.54	Inches	Centimeters	.3937
30.48	Feet	Centimeters	.0328
.914	Yards	Meters	1.094
1.609	Miles	Kilometers	.621
.645	Square inches	Square cm.	.155
.836	Square yards	Square meters	1.196
16.39	Cubic inches	Cubic cm.	.061
28.3	Cubic feet	Liters	.0353
.4536	Pounds	Kilograms	2.2045
4.546	Gallons	Liters	.22
.068	Lbs./sq. in. (psi)	Atmospheres	14.7
.138	Foot pounds	Kg. m.	7.23
1.014	H.P. (DIN)	H.P. (SAE)	.9861
——	To obtain	From	Multiply by

Note: 1 cm. equals 10 mm.; 1 mm. equals .0394".

Conversion—Common Fractions to Decimals and Millimeters

Inches Common Fractions	Decimal Fractions	Millimeters (approx.)	Inches Common Fractions	Decimal Fractions	Millimeters (approx.)	Inches Common Fractions	Decimal Fractions	Millimeters (approx.)
1/128	.008	0.20	11/32	.344	8.73	43/64	.672	17.07
1/64	.016	0.40	23/64	.359	9.13	11/16	.688	17.46
1/32	.031	0.79	3/8	.375	9.53	45/64	.703	17.86
3/64	.047	1.19	25/64	.391	9.92	23/32	.719	18.26
1/16	.063	1.59	13/32	.406	10.32	47/64	.734	18.65
5/64	.078	1.98	27/64	.422	10.72	3/4	.750	19.05
3/32	.094	2.38	7/16	.438	11.11	49/64	.766	19.45
7/64	.109	2.78	29/64	.453	11.51	25/32	.781	19.84
1/8	.125	3.18	15/32	.469	11.91	51/64	.797	20.24
9/64	.141	3.57	31/64	.484	12.30	13/16	.813	20.64
5/32	.156	3.97	1/2	.500	12.70	53/64	.828	21.03
11/64	.172	4.37	33/64	.516	13.10	27/32	.844	21.43
3/16	.188	4.76	17/32	.531	13.49	55/64	.859	21.83
13/64	.203	5.16	35/64	.547	13.89	7/8	.875	22.23
7/32	.219	5.56	9/16	.563	14.29	57/64	.891	22.62
15/64	.234	5.95	37/64	.578	14.68	29/32	.906	23.02
1/4	.250	6.35	19/32	.594	15.08	59/64	.922	23.42
17/64	.266	6.75	39/64	.609	15.48	15/16	.938	23.81
9/32	.281	7.14	5/8	.625	15.88	61/64	.953	24.21
19/64	.297	7.54	41/64	.641	16.27	31/32	.969	24.61
5/16	.313	7.94	21/32	.656	16.67	63/64	.984	25.00
21/64	.328	8.33						

APPENDIX 187

Conversion—Millimeters to Decimal Inches

mm	inches	mm	inches	mm	inches	mm	inches	mm	inches
1	.039 370	31	1.220 470	61	2.401 570	91	3.582 670	210	8.267 700
2	.078 740	32	1.259 840	62	2.440 940	92	3.622 040	220	8.661 400
3	.118 110	33	1.299 210	63	2.480 310	93	3.661 410	230	9.055 100
4	.157 480	34	1.338 580	64	2.519 680	94	3.700 780	240	9.448 800
5	.196 850	35	1.377 949	65	2.559 050	95	3.740 150	250	9.842 500
6	.236 220	36	1.417 319	66	2.598 420	96	3.779 520	260	10.236 200
7	.275 590	37	1.456 689	67	2.637 790	97	3.818 890	270	10.629 900
8	.314 960	38	1.496 050	68	2.677 160	98	3.858 260	280	11.032 600
9	.354 330	39	1.535 430	69	2.716 530	99	3.897 630	290	11.417 300
10	.393 700	40	1.574 800	70	2.755 900	100	3.937 000	300	11.811 000
11	.433 070	41	1.614 170	71	2.795 270	105	4.133 848	310	12.204 700
12	.472 440	42	1.653 540	72	2.834 640	110	4.330 700	320	12.598 400
13	.511 810	43	1.692 910	73	2.874 010	115	4.527 550	330	12.992 100
14	.551 180	44	1.732 280	74	2.913 380	120	4.724 400	340	13.385 800
15	.590 550	45	1.771 650	75	2.952 750	125	4.921 250	350	13.779 500
16	.629 920	46	1.811 020	76	2.992 120	130	5.118 100	360	14.173 200
17	.669 290	47	1.850 390	77	3.031 490	135	5.314 950	370	14.566 900
18	.708 660	48	1.889 760	78	3.070 860	140	5.511 800	380	14.960 600
19	.748 030	49	1.929 130	79	3.110 230	145	5.708 650	390	15.354 300
20	.787 400	50	1.968 500	80	3.149 600	150	5.905 500	400	15.748 000
21	.826 770	51	2.007 870	81	3.188 970	155	6.102 350	500	19.685 000
22	.866 140	52	2.047 240	82	3.228 340	160	6.299 200	600	23.622 000
23	.905 510	53	2.086 610	83	3.267 710	165	6.496 050	700	27.559 000
24	.944 880	54	2.125 980	84	3.307 080	170	6.692 900	800	31.496 000
25	.984 250	55	2.165 350	85	3.346 450	175	6.889 750	900	35.433 000
26	1.023 620	56	2.204 720	86	3.385 820	180	7.086 600	1000	39.370 000
27	1.062 990	57	2.244 090	87	3.425 190	185	7.283 450	2000	78.740 000
28	1.102 360	58	2.283 460	88	3.464 560	190	7.480 300	3000	118.110 000
29	1.141 730	59	2.322 830	89	3.503 903	195	7.677 150	4000	157.480 000
30	1.181 100	60	2.362 200	90	3.543 300	200	7.874 000	5000	196.850 000

To change decimal millimeters to decimal inches, position the decimal point where desired on either side of the millimeter measurement shown and reset the inches decimal by the same number of digits in the same direction. For example, to convert .001 mm into decimal inches, reset the decimal behind the 1 mm (shown on the chart) to .001; change the decimal inch equivalent (.039" shown to .000039").

Tap Drill Sizes

National Fine or S.A.E.

Screw & Tap Size	Threads Per Inch	Use Drill Number
No. 5	44	37
No. 6	40	33
No. 8	36	29
No. 10	32	21
No. 12	28	15
1/4	28	3
5/16	24	1
3/8	24	Q
7/16	20	W
1/2	20	29/64
9/16	18	33/64
5/8	18	37/64
3/4	16	11/16
7/8	14	13/16
1 1/8	12	1 3/64
1 1/4	12	1 11/64
1 1/2	12	1 27/64

National Coarse or U.S.S.

Screw & Tap Size	Threads Per Inch	Use Drill Number
No. 5	40	39
No. 6	32	36
No. 8	32	29
No. 10	24	25
No. 12	24	17
1/4	20	8
5/16	18	F
3/8	16	5/16
7/16	14	U
1/2	13	27/64
9/16	12	31/64
5/8	11	17/32
3/4	10	21/32
7/8	9	49/64
1	8	7/8
1 1/8	7	63/64
1 1/4	7	1 7/64
1 1/2	6	1 11/32

APPENDIX

Decimal Equivalent Size of the Number Drills

Drill No.	Decimal Equivalent	Drill No.	Decimal Equivalent	Drill No.	Decimal Equivalent
80	.0135	53	.0595	26	.1470
79	.0145	52	.0635	25	.1495
78	.0160	51	.0670	24	.1520
77	.0180	50	.0700	23	.1540
76	.0200	49	.0730	22	.1570
75	.0210	48	.0760	21	.1590
74	.0225	47	.0785	20	.1610
73	.0240	46	.0810	19	.1660
72	.0250	45	.0820	18	.1695
71	.0260	44	.0860	17	.1730
70	.0280	43	.0890	16	.1770
69	.0292	42	.0935	15	.1800
68	.0310	41	.0960	14	.1820
67	.0320	40	.0980	13	.1850
66	.0330	39	.0995	12	.1890
65	.0350	38	.1015	11	.1910
64	.0360	37	.1040	10	.1935
63	.0370	36	.1065	9	.1960
62	.0380	35	.1100	8	.1990
61	.0390	34	.1110	7	.2010
60	.0400	33	.1130	6	.2040
59	.0410	32	.1160	5	.2055
58	.0420	31	.1200	4	.2090
57	.0430	30	.1285	3	.2130
56	.0465	29	.1360	2	.2210
55	.0520	28	.1405	1	.2280
54	.0550	27	.1440		

Decimal Equivalent Size of the Letter Drills

Letter Drill	Decimal Equivalent	Letter Drill	Decimal Equivalent	Letter Drill	Decimal Equivalent
A	.234	J	.277	S	.348
B	.238	K	.281	T	.358
C	.242	L	.290	U	.368
D	.246	M	.295	V	.377
E	.250	N	.302	W	.386
F	.257	O	.316	X	.397
G	.261	P	.323	Y	.404
H	.266	Q	.332	Z	.413
I	.272	R	.339		

ANTI-FREEZE INFORMATION

Freezing and Boiling Points of Solutions According to Percentage of Alcohol or Ethylene Glycol

Freezing Point of Solution	Alcohol Volume %	Alcohol Solution Boils at	Ethylene Glycol Volume %	Ethylene Glycol Solution Boils at
20°F.	12	196°F.	16	216°F.
10°F.	20	189°F.	25	218°F.
0°F.	27	184°F.	33	220°F.
−10°F.	32	181°F.	39	222°F.
−20°F.	38	178°F.	44	224°F.
−30°F.	42	176°F.	48	225°F.

Note: above boiling points are at sea level. For every 1,000 feet of altitude, boiling points are approximately 2°F. lower than those shown. For every pound of pressure exerted by the pressure cap, the boiling points are approximately 3°F. higher than those shown.

ANTI-FREEZE CHART

Temperatures Shown in Degrees Fahrenheit
+32 is Freezing

Cooling System Capacity Quarts	Quarts of ETHYLENE GLYCOL Needed for Protection to Temperatures Shown Below													
	1	2	3	4	5	6	7	8	9	10	11	12	13	14
10	+24°	+16°	+ 4°	−12°	−34°	−62°								
11	+25	+18	+ 8	− 6	−23	−47								
12	+26	+19	+10	0	−15	−34	−57°							
13	+27	+21	+13	+ 3	− 9	−25	−45							
14			+15	+ 6	− 5	−18	−34							
15			+16	+ 8	0	−12	−26							
16			+17	+10	+ 2	− 8	−19	−34	−52°					
17			+18	+12	+ 5	− 4	−14	−27	−42					
18			+19	+14	+ 7	0	−10	−21	−34	−50°				
19			+20	+15	+ 9	+ 2	− 7	−16	−28	−42				
20				+16	+10	+ 4	− 3	−12	−22	−34	−48°			
21				+17	+12	+ 6	0	− 9	−17	−28	−41			
22				+18	+13	+ 8	+ 2	− 6	−14	−23	−34	−47°		
23				+19	+14	+ 9	+ 4	− 3	−10	−19	−29	−40		
24				+19	+15	+10	+ 5	0	− 8	−15	−23	−34	−46°	
25				+20	+16	+12	+ 7	+ 1	− 5	−12	−20	−29	−40	−50°
26					+17	+13	+ 8	+ 3	− 3	− 9	−16	−25	−34	−44
27					+18	+14	+ 9	+ 5	− 1	− 7	−13	−21	−29	−39
28					+18	+15	+10	+ 6	+ 1	− 5	−11	−18	−25	−34
29					+19	+16	+12	+ 7	+ 2	− 3	− 8	−15	−22	−29
30					+20	+17	+13	+ 8	+ 4	− 1	− 6	−12	−18	−25

For capacities over 30 quarts divide true capacity by 3. Find quarts Anti-Freeze for the ⅓ and multiply by 3 for quarts to add.

For capacities under 10 quarts multiply true capacity by 3. Find quarts Anti-Freeze for the tripled volume and divide by 3 for quarts to add.

To Increase the Freezing Protection of Anti-Freeze Solutions Already Installed

Cooling System Capacity Quarts	Number of Quarts of ETHYLENE GLYCOL Anti-Freeze Required to Increase Protection													
	From +20°F. to					From +10°F. to					From 0°F. to			
	0°	−10°	−20°	−30°	−40°	0°	−10°	−20°	−30°	−40°	−10°	−20°	−30°	−40°
10	1¾	2¼	3	3½	3¾	¾	1½	2¼	2¾	3¼	¾	1½	2	2½
12	2	2¾	3½	4	4½	1	1¾	2½	3¼	3¾	1	1¾	2½	3¼
14	2¼	3¼	4	4¾	5½	1¼	2	3	3¾	4½	1	2	3	3½
16	2½	3½	4½	5¼	6	1¼	2½	3½	4¼	5¼	1¼	2¼	3¼	4
18	3	4	5	6	7	1½	2¾	4	5	5¾	1½	2½	3¾	4¾
20	3¼	4½	5¾	6¾	7½	1¾	3	4¼	5½	6½	1½	2¾	4¼	5¼
22	3½	5	6¼	7¼	8¼	1¾	3¼	4¾	6	7¼	1¾	3¼	4½	5½
24	4	5½	7	8	9	2	3½	5	6½	7½	1¾	3½	5	6
26	4¼	6	7½	8¾	10	2	4	5½	7	8¼	2	3¾	5½	6¾
28	4½	6¼	8	9½	10½	2¼	4¼	6	7½	9	2	4	5¾	7¼
30	5	6¾	8½	10	11½	2½	4½	6½	8	9½	2¼	4¼	6¼	7¾

Test radiator solution with proper hydrometer. Determine from the table the number of quarts of solution to be drawn off from a full cooling system and replace with undiluted anti-freeze, to give the desired increased protection. For example, to increase protection of a 22-quart cooling system containing Ethylene Glycol (permanent type) anti-freeze, from +20°F. to −20°F. will require the replacement of 6¼ quarts of solution with undiluted anti-freeze.

WHEN A PROBLEM DRINKER DRIVES, IT'S YOUR PROBLEM.

Problem drinkers were responsible for 19,000 highway deaths last year. That is your problem.

Because they didn't kill only themselves. They killed people they loved, people they'd never met, people like you.

And they didn't only kill. They crippled and maimed and destroyed lives without actually taking them.

If your friend has a drinking problem, there are many ways you can help him. But first you must help him stay alive. So others may live.

If you are really his friend, don't help him drink. Admittedly, you alone probably can't stop a problem drinker from drinking. But you can discourage it.

If he has been drinking, don't let him drive. Drive him yourself. Call a cab. Take his car keys.

It won't be easy. After all, he is your friend. You don't want to hurt him or insult him. But the alternative is perhaps losing him.

Everything you think you can't do, you must do.

Write Drunk Driver, Box 2345, Rockville, Maryland 20852.

U.S. DEPARTMENT OF TRANSPORTATION
NATIONAL HIGHWAY TRAFFIC SAFETY ADMINISTRATION

Space for this public service message contributed by CHILTON BOOK COMPANY